THE FOUNDATIONS OF
NEW TESTAMENT CHRISTOLOGY

THE FOUNDATIONS
OF NEW TESTAMENT
CHRISTOLOGY

by
REGINALD H. FULLER

CHARLES SCRIBNER'S SONS

New York

7 9 11 13 15 17 19 MV/C 20 18 16 14 12 10 86

PRINTED IN THE UNITED STATES OF AMERICA
SBN 684-31039-2
LIBRARY OF CONGRESS CATALOG CARD NUMBER 65-27240

IN PIAM MEMORIAM ALFREDI EDUARDI
IOANNIS RAWLINSON
EPISCOPI DOCTORIS
NECNON IN DISCIPLINA NEOTESTAMENTICA
EXPERTIS

Contents

7

9

*Most of the biblical quotations are taken
from the Revised Standard Version of
the Bible*

Preface

WHEN IN 1954 I published my first little essay in New Testament study, *The Mission and Achievement of Jesus*, my long term purpose was to follow it up with an extended treatment of the Christology of the New Testament, for which the proclamation and self-understanding of Jesus there elaborated should provide the "raw materials".

Since 1954 a great deal of water has flowed under the bridge. In particular, we have seen the emergence of the so-called "post-Bultmann school", one of whose major concerns is the same as mine was in 1954, to establish a continuity between the historical Jesus and the christological kerygma of the post-resurrection church. These scholars feel, as I felt, that this real continuity had been obscured, if not actually denied, by some aspects of Bultmann's own work. At the same time, in their attempt to reconstruct the historical proclamation of Jesus they continue to apply most rigorously Bultmann's methods of traditio-historical criticism, with its resultant methodological scepticism, in the belief that in the long run these methods may yield significantly positive results for the church's proclamation. In this work I have endeavoured to follow the same methods, and I hope with equally positive results.

A fellowship awarded by the American Association of Theological Schools in 1961 enabled me to spend a period of study in Germany. I was particularly fortunate to have the opportunity to consult with Professor Günther Bornkamm, who also put me in touch with his Assistant, Dr. Ferdinand Hahn. Dr. Hahn kindly allowed me to read his doctoral thesis, since published under the title of *Christologische Hoheitstitel* (1963) and, most generously, to avail myself of his bibliography. The text and footnotes will show how much I am indebted to him, even if at certain points I have come to rather different conclusions.

11

This work was to have been dedicated to Bishop Rawlinson. It must now, alas, be dedicated to his memory. It is my humble hope that perhaps this work may do something for this generation of what his Bampton Lectures did in 1926.

REGINALD H. FULLER

Seabury-Western Theological Seminary
Evanston, Illinois.

Abbreviations

13

LXX	Septuagint.
NEB	New English Bible.
NF	Neue Folge.
NTD	Neues Testament Deutsch (Göttingen: Vandenhoeck u. Ruprecht).
NTS	New Testament Studies.
MT	Massoretic Text (Hebrew Bible).
PEAKE	Peake's Commentary on the Bible (Revised edition, ed. M. Black and H. H. Rowley, 1962).
RB	Revue Biblique.
RGG	Religion in Geschichte und Gegenwart.
SB	H. L. Strack—P. Billerbeck, Kommentar zum NT aus Talmud und Midrash (Munich: Beck, 1922ff.).
SBA	Sitzungsbericht der Berliner Akademie der Wissenschaften.
SBT	Studies in Biblical Theology.
SHA	Sitzungsbericht der Heidelberger Akademie der Wissenschaften.
TWNT	Theologisches Wörterbuch zum Neuen Testament (Founded by G. Kittel and ed. G. Friedrich, Stuttgart. W. Kohlhammer, 1933ff.)
ThLZ	Theologische Literaturzeitung.
ThZ	Theologische Zeitschrift.
VIG. CHR.	Vigiliae Christianae.
WMANT	Wissenschaftliche Monographien zum Alten und Neuen Testament.
ZNW	Zeitschrift für die neutestamentliche Wissenschaft.
ZThK	Zeitschrift für Theologie und Kirche.

Chapter I

INTRODUCTION: THE APPROACH TO NEW TESTAMENT CHRISTOLOGY

1. *Theological Presuppositions*

CHRISTOLOGY is the doctrine of the person of Jesus Christ. In traditional dogmatics, Christology (the doctrine of Christ's person) precedes soteriology (the doctrine of Christ's work). Logically this is the true order. It was because he was who he was that Jesus Christ did what he did. But for the New Testament it is the other way round. In the New Testament men are first confronted by the history of Jesus of Nazareth—by what he said and did—and they respond to it in terms of a Christology, a confession of faith. Through what he does they come to see who he is.

Thus Christology is essentially a response to a particular history. It is a confessional response. For men confess their faith in what God has done in Jesus Christ in terms of a Christology. It is a kerygmatic response. For the disciples of Jesus proclaim Jesus by means of Christology as the one in whom God has acted redemptively.

Since it is men's response to Jesus, it follows that Christology is not itself a part of the original revelation or action of God in Christ. Jesus does not hand out a ready-made Christology on a plate. As we shall see, he had his own self-understanding. But the church's Christology never consisted in simply repeating that self-understanding—although, as we shall seek to show, there is a direct line of continuity between Jesus' self-understanding and the church's christological interpretation of him. The church's Christology was a response to its total encounter with Jesus, not only in his earthly history but also in its (the church's) continuing life.

2. The Plan of this Book

Since Christology is men's response to Jesus of Nazareth, it follows that the church made its response in terms of whatever tools lay to hand. Hence the next three chapters of this work deal with the tools of Christology, with the terms, images, concepts and patterns which the church picked up and used for its christological response. These tools were derived from the three successive environments in which the early church was operating—Palestinian Judaism (chap. II), Hellenistic Judaism (chap. III), and the Graeco-Roman world (chap. IV).

Since Christology includes men's response to the earthly history of Jesus of Nazareth, chapter V will deal with that history. We are not concerned here to write a "life of Jesus" —for such an enterprise is now generally acknowledged to be impossible. But we are concerned with what can be known of the words and works of Jesus, and with what these words and works disclose about his own self-understanding.

The church's christological response to Jesus of Nazareth begins with the disciples' belief in resurrection. Chapter VI will therefore consider the effect of the resurrection faith on the disciples' assessment of Jesus' work and mission, and from that will go on to examine the christological responses of the earliest Palestinian church, as it took up and used the tools investigated in chapter II.

Chapter VII proceeds to trace the christological response of the Christian mission in its preaching to Greek-speaking Jews, who were nourished in the Judaism of the LXX. In this mission the Greek speaking missionaries used the tools investigated in chapter III.

Chapter VIII then traces the christological formulations of the Gentile Mission, which picked up and used the tools examined in chapter IV.

3. Critical Presuppositions and Methods

Since we are dealing with the "Foundations of NT Christology" we shall not take the story as far as the Christology of NT writers themselves. We are concerned rather with the christological foundations of their theology. Nevertheless, much of what is commonly treated under the Christology of the NT theologians will come up for treatment, or at least be briefly indicated.

Our New Testament documents, as they have come down to us, are not only written in Greek but are almost without exception the products of the gentile mission, either of the missionaries themselves or of the churches they founded. What can be known of the historical Jesus (chap. V), of earliest Palestinian Christianity (chap. VI), and of the early Hellenistic Jewish mission (chap. VII), has to be extracted by applying critical methods to documents which emanate from the gentile mission. Even in chapter VIII we are concerned not so much with the finished products of the NT theologians (i.e. the evangelists and the authors of the epistles), as with the christological presuppositions which underlie their theology. Consequently we are dependent in chapters V through VIII upon critical analysis and reconstruction in order to differentiate between the theology of the writers themselves and the traditions which they incorporate into their writing.

In principle, then, all of the NT material may provide evidence for any of the chapters V through VIII. In practice however, only the gospels (and almost exclusively the synoptics) provide the materials for chapter V, since only they include the words of and (with a few exceptions) authentic memories of the deeds of the historical Jesus. For chapter V through VIII the gospels again provide materials, and for chapters VI through VIII the Acts and the Epistles, including to a slight degree (for chapter VI) the Revelation.

The critical presuppositions and methods which enable us to distinguish between the various strata of tradition in this document must now be briefly indicated.

We assume[1] that Mark is our earliest gospel, and that it was written between 65 and 70, later rather than earlier in that five-year period, but certainly not later than 70. Matthew and Luke were written after 70, and probably not later than 100, Luke (together with Acts) almost certainly towards the end of the first century. Matthew and Luke are essentially expansions of Mark, and both use a common non-Marcan tradition conveniently (though misleadingly in so far as it tends to suggest a single written document) known as Q. Both Matthew and Luke also incorporate special traditions of their own, designated "special Matthew" and "special Luke" respectively. It is a fallacy to suppose that Mark and Q, because they are ostensibly earlier than the attestation of the two other layers (special Matthew and special Luke) necessarily represent a more primitive tradition. The traditions in Mark and Q have passed successively through the Palestinian and Hellenistic stages. All four traditions in the synoptics have therefore been tested by methods other than purely literary analysis. The available methods for testing these traditions are those of traditio-historical criticism. These methods include form-criticism, but comprise other tests as well. Form-criticism proper enables a distinction to be drawn between the tradition and the redaction of the pericopes. Since our concern in chapter V is with the words of Jesus and with his deeds only in a very general way, it is only with the parables that the form-critical method in the strictest sense comes into play. Here we can distinguish between the parables as Jesus spoke them and the re-interpretation they have undergone in the church.[2]

As regards the sayings of Jesus, traditio-historical criticism eliminates from the authentic sayings of Jesus those which are paralleled in the Jewish tradition on the one hand (apocalyptic and Rabbinic) and those which reflect the faith, practice and situations of the post-Easter church as we know them from outside the gospels.[3] When this is done, it is still necessary that authentic sayings of Jesus should be conceivable as developments within Palestinian Judaism. They should use its categories, and if possible reflect the language and style of Aramaic. Such features as *parallelismus membrorum* offer valuable additional confirmation. On the other hand, these later features are not sufficient by themselves to establish the authenticity of dominical sayings. If sayings do not pass the other tests, they must be accounted creations of the earliest Palestinian church. Form-criticism has made it fairly certain that the passion narrative took shape very early in the Palestinian church as a continuous story. This does not mean to say that it is to be taken as it stands as straightforward history. From the very first it was shaped in accordance with the doctrinal and apologetic concerns and with the liturgical practices of the earliest church. Among these are the christological elements, and the fulfilment of scripture. Such elements become important in chapter VI, where we are concerned with the earliest Palestinian church. But they must be kept out of chapter V, where we are concerned with the historical Jesus.

We assume that the fourth gospel was written not by John the son of Zebedee but by an unknown Hellenistic Christian of the second generation, perhaps in Ephesus. Its date is highly uncertain, but we would place it towards the end of the first century. It appears to have been written entirely independently of the synoptists, including Mark. Its narrative pericopes are apparently based on oral traditions which originally existed in similar form to those of the synoptics. Its discourses as they stand are the compositions of the evangelist, but enshrine logia which go back in some cases to the earliest Palestinian, and in many cases to the Hellenistic Jewish stratum.

The use of LXX in OT quotations affords a highly important clue for the identification of the Jewish Hellenistic stratum of the gospels. This must be applied with some care, for it is always possible that an earlier Hebrew quotation from the Palestinian stratum has been deliberately altered to conform with the LXX. But there are passages where the use of the LXX is pivotal to a narrative or an argument (e.g. Mark 12:35–37). Here the material in question must be assigned to the creativity of the Hellenistic Jewish Christian community. A second helpful criterion in identifying the Hellenistic Jewish stratum in the gospels is linguistic. Where a term or phrase is demonstrably impossible in Aramaic or Hebrew, the tradition concerned must be assigned to the Hellenistic Jewish stratum. Lastly, where traditions manifest the theological perspective of what we know elsewhere about Hellenistic Jewish Christianity from the sources outside the gospels, this too must be assigned to that stratum. These criteria are applied to the gospels in chapter VII.

The materials we wish to use from the Book of Acts in chapters VI and VII occur almost entirely in the speeches. These pose an unsolved problem in tradition history. At one extreme there are those who hold[4] that Luke took the missionary speeches in his early chapters from an Aramaic source, and that they represent, not indeed what Peter actually said on these specific occasions, but a fair example of the kerygma. At the other extreme there are those[5] who regard the speeches in Acts as free compositions of the author and reflections of the kerygma current at the time when it was written. An intermediate position is represented by E. Schweizer,[6] who argues that while the bulk of the speeches as they stand are compositions of the author, they nevertheless enshrine traditional formulae, particularly in the christological parts. This is the view adopted here. Where it can be shown (as in Acts 3:20–21a and Acts 2:36) that the formulae in question exhibit a substantially different Christology from that of the author of Luke-Acts elsewhere (e.g., in the redactional elements in his gospel) it is certainly safe to conclude that the Christology in question is pre-Lucan. An auxiliary criterion is the occurrence of non-Lucan terms and phraseology. We have then the further task of assigning this pre-Lucan Christology to an earlier stratum of the tradition, and this is done by comparing it with what we know otherwise of the earlier Christologies.

In chapters VI through VIII, and especially in chapter VIII, substantial use is made of the epistolary literature of the New Testament. The epistles normally ascribed to St. Paul are accepted as genuine, including 2 Thessalonians and Colossians. Ephesians and the pastorals are assumed to be deutero-Pauline. Hebrews and the Catholic epistles without exception (including James and I Peter) are taken to be sub-apostolic.

Since we are not concerned in this work with the theology of the epistolary writers themselves, but the christological traditions which provide the foundations for their theology, it is necessary to identify the points at which they make use of traditional material. E. Norden did some valuable pioneering work in detecting traditional formulae,[7] and E. Stauffer has furnished additional criteria in a valuable appendix to his *New Testament Theology*.[8] Use has been made of the following criteria, especially in chapter VIII:

1. Contextual dislocations.
2. The continuance of the formula after its content has ceased to be relevant to its immediate context.
3. Formulae frequently use terms and phrases not characteristic of the author.
4. Formulae frequently begin with the relative pronoun ("who").
5. Formulae often show a preference for participles rather than finite verbs.
6. Formulae frequently exhibit a rhythmic style and can be arranged in lines or strophes.
7. Formulae are concerned with basic christological assertions.

Once the presence of a formula has been established, it then becomes necessary to locate it in the tradition. This is done chiefly by identifying the christological terms and patterns it employs, and linking them up with the tools and patterns investigated in chapters II–IV.

Where previous writers, working with traditio-historical methods, have already assigned traditions to particular strata and where their assignation is accepted, reference is given to the earlier work, and the location in the tradition merely stated. Where a particular author has proposed a new assignation which has not won general acceptance and that assignation is accepted here, his arguments are summarized. Where new assignations are proposed in this book, or where the present writer disagrees with a previous assignation, the arguments are presented in full.

NOTES ON CHAPTER I

1. For the reasons behind these critical assumptions see my *New Testament in Current Study*, London: S.C.M. Press, 1963, pp. 86–91, and New York: Scribners, 1962, pp. 72ff.

2. Cf. J. Jeremias, *The Parables of Jesus*, London: S.C.M. Press, 1954, pp. 20–88, esp. p. 88, on "the laws of transformation".

3. For these criteria of authenticity cf. H. Conzelmann in *RGG*[3], art. "Jesus Christus", vol. III, col. 623. Cf. *NT in Current Study*, pp. 40f. (American ed., pp. 32f.) on the limitations of this method, which however remains the only relatively certain method available to distinguish between authentic sayings and church formations. The criteria offered

by J. Jeremias *ET* 59, 1958, pp. 333–334 are auxiliary ones. Used alone they can only establish Palestinian origin.

4. So J. de Zwaan in *The Beginnings of Christianity*, ed. F. Jackson and K. Lake, London: Macmillan, 1922, vol. II, pp. 30–65. De Zwaan is followed by C. H. Dodd, *The Apostolic Preaching and Its Developments*, London: Hodder and Stoughton, 1949⁷, pp. 19f.

5. So M. Dibelius, *Studies in the Acts of the Apostles*, London: S.C.M. Press, 1956, pp. 165–174; D. E. Nineham in *Studies in the Gospels* (R. H. Lightfoot memorial), ed. D. E. Nineham, Oxford: Blackwell, 1955, pp. 228f.; the literature mentioned in J. M. Robinson, *A New Quest of the Historical Jesus* (*SBT* 25) 1959, pp. 58f., n. 1; U. Wilckens, *Die Missionsreden der Apostelgeschichte* (*WMANT* 5), 1961, pp. 32–71.

6. E. Schweizer, *ThZ* 13, 1957, pp. 1-11, cf. H. Grass, *Ostergeschehen und Osterberichte*, Göttingen: Vandenhoeck u. Ruprecht, 1962¹, p. 100.

7. E. Norden, *Agnostos Theos*, Leipzig: Teubner, 1929, pp. 380–387.

8. E. Stauffer, *New Testament Theology*, London: S.C.M. Press, 1955, pp. 338f.

Chapter II

THE TOOLS: (1) PALESTINIAN JUDAISM

1. *Messiah*

THE New Testament term χριστός (Christ), as is well known, is derived from the Hebrew term *mašiaḥ* = Anointed One, from the Hebrew verb *mašaḥ* = to anoint. Surprisingly, the term is never found in the Old Testament in its specific New Testament sense of the regent of God's eschatological kingdom. It is there used primarily of the historical kings. Beginning with Saul's anointing by Samuel (1 Sam. 10:1), the kings of Judah were customarily consecrated to their office by anointing. It is generally recognized today that the actual practice of anointing, like the institution of monarchy itself, was taken over from the surrounding Canaanite nations. With it too was taken over much of the ideology of kingship. This ideology finds expression in the royal psalms (Ps. 2; 20; 21; 45; 72; 89; 110; 132), which are now widely believed to date from the age of the monarchy. The king is hailed as the son of God (2 Sam. 7:14; Ps. 2:7). He is promised rule over the whole earth as the vice-gerent of Yahweh himself (Ps. 2:8), and his reign will be one of supernatural peace, justice, and prosperity (Ps. 72). These ideas are general in the ancient east.

Yet the concept of kingship is, like so much else that came from outside, baptized into the Yahwist religion. The monarchy is established under the covenant made by Yahweh with his people. The king remains responsible to Yahweh for the exercise of his power. If he fails to live up to his responsibilities, he incurs the outspoken censure of the prophets, who speak in the name of Yahweh himself (cf. Nathan and David, 2 Sam. 12:1–15). The Hebrew monarchy seems to have been the only truly limited and "constitutional" monarchy of ancient times. Also, despite the

23

appellation son of God (shared with the Assyrian kings) there is hardly a trace of the divinization of the king as in Egypt. The king is not ontologically divine as in Egypt: he is predestined, elected, and adopted into sonship with Yahweh which involved responsibilities as much as privileges.[1]

It is not necessary to accept all the far-reaching theories of the Uppsala school about the myth and ritual pattern of sacral kingship in order to recognize this limited influence of Assyrian and Egyptian ideas of kingship upon the royal theology of Israel.[2] The term, "The Lord's Anointed" (*meṣiaḥ YHWH*) became almost a summary of this whole theology of kingship. Thus, "messiah" throughout the Old Testament means only an empirical figure, never an eschatological one; always one reigning in the present, never one to come in the future. Two passages (Gen. 49:10 and Num. 24:17) which later at Qumran[3] and in Christian interpretation were taken messianically, were probably originally related to David and his reign.

The beginnings of what we call the Messianic hope appear to be found in the pre-exilic prophets, Proto-Isaiah and Micah (date: from *ca.* 740). Neither of these prophets, of course, uses the title Messiah = Anointed One in reference to the future deliverer. But they are beginning to speak of that deliverer in terms which suggest that he will be an ideal king like David. What gave rise to this future hope was the obvious failure of such later kings as Ahaz to live up to the Davidic ideal. The relevant passages in Isaiah are: 7:10–16; 9:1–7; and 11:1–9.

Isaiah 7:10–16 is of uncertain interpretation. But it seems reasonable to assume with J. Barr[3] that "Immanuel" (v. 14) refers to an ideal king of the Davidic line. This King will be born in the near future and will reign as the true embodiment of God's presence with his people, restoring to them peace and prosperity (indicated by "curds and honey").[4]

Isaiah 9:1–7, almost certainly a genuine prophecy of Isaiah,[5] belongs to the year 733, when Tiglath Pileser III incorporated parts of the northern kingdom into the Assyrian empire (2 Kings 16:5ff.). The prophet hopes for a new king of the Davidic line (v. 7) who will recover the lost territory and restore the peace, prosperity, and justice of

David's reign. As in the Immanuel prophecy, the perfect relation between the king and Yahweh is stressed (v. 6).

Isaiah 11:1–9 is less certainly Isaianic. Again, the ideal king is "a shoot from the stump of Jesse", a true scion of David's line. Again, too, the king's enjoyment of the divine favour (vv. 2–3a), his victory over Israel's enemies and the restoration of peace, prosperity and justice (vv. 3b–5), are stressed.

Micah 5:2–4 is a passage whose authenticity is often judged more favourably today than it used to be, and which, if genuine, is contemporary with the Isaianic prophecies which we have just examined.[6] Here the affinity of the ideal king with Yahweh is expressed in terms of ancient origin (v. 2: "whose origin is from of old, from ancient days"). This means no more than that he will come of the ancient Davidic family. Once more, as in the case of the historical king, he is promised dominion extending to the ends of the earth, with peace and security (v. 4), obviously after a successful war of liberation (v. 3). But despite the highly coloured charismatic endowments of the ideal king, the Messiah (who is not yet so called) is still an earthly figure in all of these pre-exilic prophecies.

A century later, Jeremiah was still looking for the coming of an ideal king, the righteous Branch whom Yahweh will raise up "for David" (Jer. 23:5f.). His reign again will be characterized by justice and peace, and there is a hint of charismatic endowment in the prediction that he will "deal wisely". Difficult to reconcile with this obviously traditional picture is Jer. 22:30, where it is stated roundly of Coniah (=Jehoiachin), the next-to-last Davidic king, that

> none of his offspring shall succeed
> in sitting on the throne of David,
> and ruling again in Judah.

This inconsistency has led some scholars[7] to conclude that the Branch prophecy is not a genuine oracle of Jeremiah. But perhaps the inconsistency is apparent rather than real.[8] What the prophet is saying is that the future ideal king, though descended from David, will not be descended from him through the line of Jehoiachin, but *via* another line.

A little later Ezekiel still retains something of the traditional hope of an ideal king of the Davidic line (Ezek. 34:23f.), while in 21:25-27, after referring to the deposition of the reigning king (Zedekiah?), he speaks of the restoration of the monarchy when "he comes whose right it is" (v. 27). Here there is no direct reference to one of the Davidic line. Does this mean that he—if Jeremiah had not already done so —has begun to detach the Messianic hope from the Davidic line? This is possible.[9] In any case, it would be true to say that Ezekiel (assuming that chapters 40-48 are genuine) is much more interested in the restoration of the temple than of the monarchy. The overall impression is that if Ezekiel did retain the traditional Davidic hope, he was growing cool towards it. Thus he paved the way for the emergence of a different form of the Messianic hope, that of a priest rather than a king. It is perhaps consonant with this development that it is in the P tradition that the rite for the consecration of a priest by anointing first appears (Exod. 29:7; 40:13-15; Lev. 8:1-12), thus preparing the way for the transference of the term mašiaḥ (anointed one) to the priest.

It is also in accord with this development that in Deutero-Isaiah (ca. 540) there is a vivid prophecy of the return as an eschatological event. But the hope of the restoration of an ideal king—whether Davidic, or unspecified as in Ezek. 21:27—has completely disappeared. Instead, the term mašiaḥ is used of Cyrus II of Persia (Isa. 45:1) as the agent appointed by Yahweh to faciliate the return. More important however in the thought of Deutero-Isaiah is the concept of the Servant of Yahweh. Some scholars maintain that this is a Messianic figure—a question which will be discussed below.

We may say therefore that the exile marks the emergence of varying streams of Messianic hope: in addition to the traditional Davidic hope, which for the time being seems to be falling into disfavour, there is emerging the priestly hope (Ezek. 40-48) and an eschatological hope detached from any specifically Messianic connections (Dt.-Isaiah).

For a brief period after the return the traditional Davidic Messianic hope was revived when Zerubbabel, a descendant of the Davidic dynasty, was restored to power in Jerusalem. The relevant passages are: Hag. 2:23; Zech. 3:8-10; 4:7;

6:9–14. In this case it is not a merely future Messianic hope: the Davidic ideal is itself being realized in an actual historical figure. In Zech. 6:11 it is generally agreed by commentators that the name of Zerubbabel has been removed from the text, owing to the subsequent failure of that king to fit the role of the ideal Davidic king and that in the original text Zerubbabel was actually hailed as the future ideal Davidic king in the words: "Behold, the man whose name is the Branch" (cf. Jer. 23:5; 33:15). As the text now stands, it refers less appropriately to the priest Joshua. This emendation is almost clinched by the play on words which would then follow: Zerubbabel/*zerbabili* = sprout of Babylon:[10] A notable feature of this passage is that here for the first time we find the quasi-Messianic figure of Joshua the priest side by side with the king—a combination which is to be very important later on, especially at Qumran (see below). Here is a synthesis between the older, traditional Davidic hope of Isaiah and Micah, and the newer type of hope which had been born during the exile under Ezekiel and in the growing P tradition.

After this the Davidic Messianic hope, even in its more generalized form of the expectation of an ideal king, continued for long only as an occasional flicker. It is absent from the P tradition (for which, as we have seen, the designation of the priest, rather than of the king, as *mašiah* is characteristic[11]), from 1, 2 Chron. (although in his history of the kings of Israel and Judah the Chronicler had plenty of opportunities to speak of the hope), and even from much of post-exilic prophecy. Nehemiah and Ezra are preoccupied with the organization of the restored community under the law. The eschatological passages of the later prophets (Trito-Isaiah, Malachi, Zechariah 9–14) often contain no reference to the Messianic figure, thus continuing a tradition begun by the second Isaiah. One of the few specifically Messianic passages from this period is Zech. 9:9f., where the term "king" (*melekh*) is used. There is nothing about his Davidic descent, though other features of the traditional hope reappear: victory followed by peace and world-wide dominion. A new element appears in the description of the king as "humble and riding on an ass". According to the Uppsala school and their followers this feature is another aspect of the ancient oriental royal ideology: the humiliation of the king prior to his subsequent vindication, a theme which they believe is also found in the royal psalms (e.g. Ps. 89:38–45).[12] Zechariah 9:9f. would appear, however, to speak not of humiliation followed by triumph, but of humility *in* victory. The king himself who in the earlier tradition was the helper of the poor (e.g. Ps. 72) is now one of them himself.[13] The concept seems to arise from the identification of the shepherd king with his people.

It is perhaps not surprising that the specifically Davidic form of the Messianic hope was not rekindled at the time of the Maccabean revolt (168–165). After all the Maccabees were not of the Davidic line. The predominant form of the eschatological hope in that era was apocalyptic, whose redemptive agent was a supra-historical figure, the Son of man (see below). It does not seem, however, that the Maccabees themselves were directly affected by apocalyptic. Only very occasionally does the term *mašiaḥ* figure in the apocalyptic literature. In Dan 9:25f. two figures are mentioned, each called an "anointed one". Most commentators agree that this refers not to future-eschatological, but to past-historical figures. The first is either Zerubbabel or Joshua the high priest (see above) and the second the Onias of 2 Mac. 4:7f., 23–38. The Similitudes of Enoch (Enoch 37–71) are unique among the apocalyptic writings. Here the figure of the *mašiaḥ* or anointed one has completely coalesced with the supra-historical Son of man. The problems raised by this book will be discussed later in this chapter under "Son of man".

The Testament of the Twelve Patriarchs (Test. XII Pat.) in its present form includes Christian interpolations.[14] But the discovery of parts of the work in Cave IV[15] at Qumran has put it beyond doubt that the original nucleus of the Testaments is pre-Christian. In them we find for the first time the expectation of two Messiahs, a priestly Messiah of the tribe of Levi, and a king-Messiah of the tribe of Judah:[16]

I say unto you, ye will be jealous against the sons of Levi, and will seek to be exalted over them; but ye shall not be able. For God will avenge them, and ye shall die by an evil death. For to Levi God gave the sovereignty (and to Judah with him and to me also, and to Dan and Joseph, that we should be for rulers). Therefore, I command you to hearken to Levi, because he shall know the law of the Lord, and shall give ordinances for judgment and shall sacrifice for all Israel until the consummation of the times, as the anointed High Priest, of whom the Lord spake. . . . And draw ye near to Levi in humbleness of heart, that ye may receive a blessing from his mouth. For he shall bless Israel and Judah, because him hath the Lord chosen to be king over all the nation. And bow down before his seed, for on our behalf it will die in wars visible and invisible, and will be among you an eternal king.

Here is a re-emergence of that synthesis between the earlier (Davidic) tradition of the pre-exilic prophets and the Ezekiel-priestly re-interpretation of eschatology which we first found in Zech. 6:11f. (see above), but with two significant differences. First, in Test. XII Pat. the anointed ones are not already-existing historical personages, as in Zech., but future-eschatological figures; and second, whereas in Zech. the two Messiahs are of equal rank, in Test. XII Pat. the priestly Messiah is exalted above the kingly Messiah.

Exactly the same picture reappears in the Qumran writings themselves.[17] Here are the clearest texts:

And they [the members of the sect] shall be ruled by the first laws with which the men of the community began to be disciplined, until there come a prophet and the Messiahs (*mešîḥê*) of Aaron and Israel (1 QS 9: 1of.).

[The Messiah of Aaron is obviously the priestly Messiah and the Messiah of Israel the Davidic one.]

In the description of the Messianic banquet in 1 QSa 12–17 we read:

And the Priest, the Anointed one, shall come with them, for he is the head of the entire congregation of Israel; and before him shall sit the sons of Aaron, the priests; and the conveners of the assembly (?), the honoured men, they shall sit before him, each according to his place of rank.

And then shall come the Messiah of Israel, and before him shall sit the heads of the tribes, each according to his place of honour . . . and all the heads of the congregation, together with the wise men of Israel, shall sit before them, each according to his proper place of rank.

29

To the first passage from 1 QS this passage adds the further point that, as in Text. XII Pat., the kingly Messiah was subordinate to the priestly.

For some time it was thought that the phrase "the Messiah [sic] of Aaron and Israel", which occurs three times in the Damascus Document (CD)[18] should be emended to "the *Messiahs* of Aaron and Israel" in conformity with 1 QS and 1 QSa. However, J. Milik has reported[19] further fragments of CD from Qumran in which the phrase already occurs with Messiah in the singular. It would therefore seem that the community's Messianic expectations varied at different periods of its existence, though the exact evolution is at present difficult to trace.

Perhaps too much should not be made of the precedence of the priestly over the kingly Messiah in 1 QSa. Partly it is due to the priestly interests of the community, and partly to the fact that the passage occurs in a description of a ritual meal, in which the priest quite naturally presided in order to say the blessing in the daily meal at Qumran. It is noticeable that where the term Messiah occurs alone (e.g. CDC 6: 2) it refers quite naturally to the Davidic Messiah. For the rest, the picture of the Davidic Messiah corresponds faithfully to the Old Testament picture. He is the Son of David, adopted as the Son of God, and given the eschatological dominion over the earth. He has charismatic endowments, and his reign is to last for ever and ever.[20]

Undoubtedly, the Qumran texts witness to the first significant revival since the exile of the strictly "Messianic" hope—in the sense of a Davidic king—in the century or so preceding and following the beginning of the Christian era.

This revival was not, however, confined to one stream within Judaism. The disappointment with the Hasmonean rulers, the renewed foreign conquest by the Romans in 63 B.C., the Hellenizing policy of the Herods, all combined to foster a renewal of Davidic Messianism. Nowhere is the prevalent mood just after the Roman conquest so clearly expressed as in the well-known Ps. Sol. 17. The Psalms of Solomon, according to most scholars, are an expression of Pharisaic piety.[21] Here again the term "Messiah" is used. He is son of David. He triumphs over the enemies of Israel and rules over God's people in peace, justice and prosperity. He is charismatically endowed with the Holy Spirit. A reading of Ps. Sol. 17 should dispel completely from our minds that this type, the only type of "Messiah" in the strict sense of the word, was merely political: "God will make him mighty by means of his holy spirit and wise by means of the spirit of understanding with strength and righteousness. And, the blessing of the Lord will be with him; his hope will be the Lord." Yet the Messiah is still a human figure. There is nothing here of the apocalyptic Son of man. Nor is there any suggestion of any miraculous activity on the part of the Davidic Messiah—a fact whose importance will become apparent later on.[22]

2. Son of God

As we have already seen (above, p. 23), the adoption of the empirical king as the son of God was a firmly embedded feature of the early royal ideology of Israel. The important passages are 2 Sam. 7:14 (the prophecy of Nathan in respect of David's successor) and the royal psalm 2:7 (cf. Ps. 89:26f.). The concept has its roots in the Assyrian royal mythology which differs importantly in this respect from the Egyptian.[23] In the Egyptian royal ideology the pharaoh was actually a god or divine being. In the Assyrian ideology the king was adopted as the son of God. The Assyrian form was taken up into the Yahwistic theology of Israel, and was more easily assimilated to the emphasis on the covenantal election of the king as the representative of Yahweh's kingly rule on earth, and its attendant responsibilities of obedience to Yahweh's laws. Moreover, in the Israelite tradition Israel itself is spoken of as the son of Yahweh (Exod. 4:22b–23a; Hos. 11:1), constituted as such by the exodus, and the sonship of the king is thus brought into the context of the general sonship of Israel. The king is the representative of the covenant people.

Until recently it was very uncertain whether this concept of the divine sonship was taken up into the Messianology of pre-Christian Judaism. While there is plenty of evidence in early Rabbinic tradition for the Messianic interpretation of most of the verses of Ps. 2, v. 7 is conspicuously lacking.[24]

The evidence from Enoch 105:2 and 4 Ezra 7:28f.; 13:32, 37, 52; 14:9 must be discounted. The Enoch passage is missing from the recently discovered Greek version, which is thought to be nearer the Semitic original.[25] And, as B. Violet has shown,[26] *"filius meus"* in 4 Ezra represents an original *'abhdî* ("my servant", not "my son"), and is a mistranslation of the Greek παῖς. It is not surprising therefore that those who nevertheless believe that son of God was a pre-Christian Jewish Messianic title can only consider it probable.[27] Others such as Dalman, Bousset, and more recently Kümmel, have roundly denied that it was so used.[28] Now, however, we are in a position to carry the somewhat hesitant conclusions of Bultmann and others to positive certainty. For the Dead Sea Scrolls have provided evidence that "son of God" was indeed used as a Messianic title in pre-Christian Judaism. In 4Q Flor. (Florilegium) 10-14 we read:

> [And] the Lord [tell]s you that he will build a house for you, and I will set up your seed after you, and I will establish his royal throne [for eve]r. I will be his father, and he shall be my son. This is the sprout of David.

Lövestam describes this as a succinct summary of Nathan's prophecy[29] in 2 Sam. 7:10b–14.

We may therefore conclude that, like son of David, son of God *was just coming into use* as a Messianic title in pre-Christian Judaism, and was ready to hand as a tool for the early Christians to use in interpreting Jesus of Nazareth. It meant not a metaphysical relationship, but adoption as God's vice-gerent in his kingdom.

There are two other uses of son of God in Judaism which call for brief mention. One was as a designation for angels in Gen. 6:2, where we read of the sons of God who had intercourse with human women, and in Job 38:7, where we read that at the creation "all the sons of God shouted for joy". That this usage had any influence either on Jewish Messianology or the Christian assessment of Jesus is out of the question.

The other usage is in application to the high priest. The writer is indebted to Gerhard Friedrich for having sent him an offprint of his article "Messianische Hohepriestererwartung in den Synoptikern".[30] Friedrich quotes Mal. 1:6 to show that the empirical priests were called "sons of God" in a special sense. An examination of this passage shows, however, that this is not so: all it means is that the priests should (though they do not) honour God as a son honours his father. In Test. Lev. 4:2 Levi at his consecration is called υἱὸς τοῦ θεοῦ. In Test. Lev. 18:6 God speaks to the Messianic high priest with a "fatherly voice", and this, according to Friedrich, implies that God regards him as his son. But, as Friedrich himself admits, the evidence is meagre. In any case, the term high priest was not applied to Jesus until Hebrews, while Son of God was applied, as we shall see, at a much earlier stage of christological reflection. It is therefore most unlikely that this usage should be considered as a source for the Christian use of Son of God as a title for Jesus.

3. Son of David

It is not necessary to devote much space to this term, for most of the material has already been covered in our consideration of the Messiah or Anointed One. As we have already seen, the expected Messiah from Isaiah down to the Rabbinic literature was almost invariably a scion of the house of David. The only possible exceptions are in certain passages of Jeremiah (see above). Until Ps. Sol. 17 the actual term "son of David" does not occur in a Messianic context, the usual term being ṣemaḥ Dawîdh, shoot or sprout of David (Jer. 23:5; 33:15; cf. Zech 3:8; 6:12). It would seem therefore that son of David was not crystallized as a Messianic title in Judaism until the first century B.C. There is, however, no reason to infer, as some have done, that the term was a Christian coinage, or that it was interpolated by a Christian hand at Ps. Sol. 17:20, for it occurs with relative frequency in post-Christian Judaism,[31] and it is hardly likely that the Rabbis would have adopted it after it had become current in the Christian Church. The New Testament itself provides evidence for its currency in first-century Judaism. In Mark 12:35 Jesus is made to ask: "How can the scribes say that the Christ is the son of David?". That the expectation of a Davidic Messiah was very much alive in popular Jewish piety at the time of Jesus is indicated by the Benedictus (Luke 1:69): "and has raised up a horn of salvation in the house of his servant David". There are good grounds for supposing that the Benedictus is a pre-Christian Jewish hymn.[32] Also, in the Lucan annunciation story we read (Luke 1:32f.):

> He will be great, and will be called the Son of the Most High; and the Lord God will give to him the throne of his father David, and he will reign over the house of Jacob for ever; and of his kingdom there will be no end.

There is nothing specifically Christian about this passage, except for the context in which Luke has inserted it, and it may well be a pre-Christian Jewish fragment.[33]

4. *Son of Man*

The terms we have been considering thus far are Messianic in the strictest sense of the term. They all arise from the basic concept of Israel's anointed king. Originally applied to the empirical, historical king, they are later transferred to the agent of eschatological redemption. This eschatological redemption is conceived in strictly historical terms, however. The kingdom thus inaugurated is entirely a this-worldly affair. The eschatological regent is an entirely human figure, however much his intimate relation with God and his charismatic endowment may be emphasized. The term, Son of man, to which we now turn, is also commonly called "Messianic", though it is not so in the strict sense of the word. It does not spring from any of the earlier uses of the word *mašiaḥ*. Only occasionally and exceptionally is the complex of ideas clustering around the earlier concept *mašiaḥ*, or indeed the term itself, applied to the Son of man. Its creative milieu is late Jewish apocalyptic.

Apocalyptic[34] is generally recognized as having arisen out of the earlier prophetic eschatology, but to have been extensively influenced by the dualistic eschatology of Iranian religion. Its basic difference from prophecy is its sharp distinction between the present age and the age to come. The present age is this-worldly, and historical. The age to come transcends history; it entails a new heaven and a new earth. Apocalyptic depicts the end of this age and the inauguration of the age to come in a series of mysterious and bizarre images with a cosmic dimension far surpassing anything in the future predictions of earlier prophecy. Early fragments of apocalyptic material are found in Isa. 24–27; Zech. 9–14; and in the Book of Joel. But the golden age of apocalyptic was in late Judaism, from the second century B.C. through the first century A.D., thus overlapping the beginnings of Christianity. The first full-blooded apocalypse is the canonical Book of Daniel, which was inspired by the Maccabean revolt and was written between 168 and 164 B.C. The Book of Daniel set the pattern for a whole spate of apocalyptic works during the next two and a half centuries. They include the Books of Enoch, Test. XII Pat., the Jewish Sibylline oracles, the Assumption of Moses, the Apocalypse of Ezra (4 Ezra or 2 Esdras) the Apocalypse of Baruch, etc.[35]

The term Son of man occurs as an eschatological figure for the first time in Jewish literature in Dan. 7:13f.:

> I saw in the night visions,
> and behold, with the clouds of heaven
> there came one like a son of man (Aramaic: *kᵉbhar 'enoš*)
> and he came to the Ancient of Days
> and was presented before him.
> And to him was given dominion
> and glory and kingdom,
> that all peoples, nations, and languages
> should serve him;
> his dominion is an everlasting dominion,
> which shall not pass away,
> and his kingdom one
> that shall not be destroyed.

Later, in verse 18, we read that "the saints of the Most High shall receive the kingdom, and possess the kingdom for ever, for ever and ever" (cf. also v. 27). This verse has led many, especially British scholars, to infer that Daniel's term "one like a son of man" is not a title for an individual eschatological figure, but a collective symbol for the elect.[36] In favour of this corporate interpretation is the further fact that the passage in question is preceded by a vision of four world empires, symbolized respectively by a lion with eagles' wings, a bear, a leopard with four wings of a bird, and a beast with ten horns. Thus, it is argued, the kingdom of the elect is correspondingly symbolized by a man-like figure. It has, however, been suggested[37] that the interpretation in 7:15f., 27 is secondary. The writer of Daniel has certainly given the term a corporate interpretation. But behind Daniel, it is held, there lies an earlier tradition of the Son of man as an individual eschatological agent of redemption, which re-appears independently in Enoch and 4 Ezra (see below). The complex history of the tradition or traditions behind Dan. 7: 13 has not yet been solved. The present writer is now inclined to think that the poem in Dan. 7:13f. is from an earlier source in which the term was used of an individual eschatological figure, that the writer of Daniel has combined it with the four earlier visions and added the interpretations vv. 15–18 and the poem of v. 27. But in doing so that writer does not intend to abandon the original individual under-standing of the man-like figure. He is expanding it to be, like earthly kingship in Israel, the representative of the saints of the Most High over whom he rules. Similarly, the four beasts of the preceding verses are both individual kings and representatives of their empires.

If the foregoing view be correct, it raises already here the problem which has been raised by many scholars over the origin of the term "Son of man" in Ethiopian Enoch and 4 Ezra. The History of Religions school has sought its origin in an oriental gnostic myth of the Heavenly Man.[38] Alter-natively, the Uppsala school has sought to derive it from the same root as the *mašiah* concept, namely from the oriental myth and ritual pattern of sacral kingship.[39] Others again have sought the origin of Son of man within the Old Testa-ment Jewish tradition itself, notably A. Feuillet, who thinks it is a combination of (*a*) the prophetic Messiah, (*b*) the Ezekielic Son of man as a title for the prophet, (*c*) the hypostatization of Wisdom in the sapiential literature.[40] It must be concluded that the problem is at present unsolved. Without going into it more deeply, it would seem that since apocalyptic generally emerged out of prophecy, the roots of the Son of man concept are *prima facie* to be sought within prophecy, and therefore in the expectation of the king—a Messiah. But just as under foreign (Persian) influence the prophetic eschatology was transcendentalized in apocalyptic, so too it is reasonable to suppose that it was under the same foreign influence that the agent of redemption was transcendentalized into the Son of man. But once the process has been accomplished, the two redemptive figures remain on the whole as sharply distinguished from one another as the eschatologies of prophecy and apocalyptic. Whatever its origin, there seems to be good reason for assuming that the Son of man had firmly established itself as the title for the transcendental agent of redemption in Jewish apocalyptic. If our interpretation of Daniel is correct, this had happened already before 168–164, in the pre-Danielic development of apocalyptic. If this interpretation be rejected, then the crystallization of the term must have taken place much later.

That crystallization had certainly taken place by the time Eth. Enoch 37–71 (the Similitudes of Enoch) were written. But here again, we face another much controverted problem. Continental European scholars of all schools of thought never seem to have any difficulty in taking the Similitudes as an authentic part of the Book of Enoch, which is dated anywhere between 175 and 63 B.C.[41] British scholars[42] have well-founded doubts about the pre-Christian origin of the Similitudes. The present writer first heard these doubts expressed in the late thirties in lectures by Professor C. H. Dodd at Cambridge. He pointed out that in the not inconsiderable Greek fragments of Enoch which had then turned up, the Similitudes had been conspicuously lacking. Since then, these doubts have apparently been confirmed by the same state of affairs at Qumran: there too among the Semitic fragments of Enoch which have turned up, the Similitudes are again notably absent.[43] Outside of continental Europe, therefore, it is frequently concluded that the Similitudes are Christian interpolations[44] and that the Son of man was not a pre-Christian Jewish apocalyptic title[45] for the eschatological redeemer.

Nevertheless, it seems that certain considerations of a general character may be advanced on the other side, without necessarily deciding in favour of a pre-Christian Jewish origin for the Similitudes themselves. First, as the present writer pointed out,[46] the Son of man in the Similitudes lacks the distinctively Christian differentia, viz., the identification with Jesus of Nazareth in his ministry (which, as we shall see, is a very early Christian use of the Son of man) and in his passion (which, as again we shall see, is, though not quite the earliest, at least a Palestinian feature). Second, the logia of Jesus, as again we shall see, seem to presuppose a reduced apocalyptic in which the future coming Son of man as eschatological judge was part of the traditional imagery. Third, although 4 Ezra is admittedly later than Jesus and dates from about the time of the destruction of Jerusalem, and although in its present form it has certainly undergone Christian interpolation, the sections which speak of the Son of man again lack the same Christian differentia as the Similitudes. Thus it may again be reasonably inferred that 4 Ezra, like the Similitudes, is drawing upon a pre-Christian Jewish apocalyptic tradition. So we may conclude that despite the well-founded doubts of British scholars about the Similitudes, there is good reason to believe with the majority of scholars outside Britain, both in continental Europe and in America, that the figure of the Son of man was established in pre-Christian Jewish apocalyptic as the eschatological agent of redemption.

While, therefore, we cannot be sure that the Similitudes themselves antedate the Christian era, we may treat them with some degree of confidence as evidence for a tradition in Jewish apocalyptic which is pre-Christian.[47]

First, we note that as compared with Daniel, the term is an actual title. In ten occurrences it is prefixed with a demonstrative: "this son of man". According to Charles[48] "that" and "this" are usually renderings of the Greek article. Hence "that Son of man" is the equivalent of ὁ υἱὸς τοῦ ἀνθρώπου. ("*the* Son of man"). There is thus no doubt that, whatever the case may be with Dan. 7:13f., we have here a title for an eschatological figure. Here are the important passages which elucidate the person and the work of the Son of man:

> and this Son of Man whom thou hast seen
> shall (put down) the kings and the mighty from their seats...
>
> Eth. En. 46:4

And at that hour the Son of Man was named
In the presence of the Lord of Spirits,
And his name before the Head of Days.

Yea, before the sun and the signs were created,
Before the stars of the heaven were made,
His name was named before the Lord of Spirits.

48:2f.

For from the beginning the Son of Man was hidden.
And the Most High preserved him in the presence of His might,
And revealed him to the elect.
. . . . . .
And all the elect shall stand before him on that day.
And all the kings and the mighty and the exalted ones and
    those that rule the earth
Shall fall before him on their faces,
And worship and set their hope upon that Son of Man
And petition him and supplicate for mercy at his hands.
. . . . . .
And (He will deliver them) to the angels for punishment,
To execute vengeance on them because they have oppressed
His children and His elect.

62:7–11

And with that Son of Man shall they (viz. the elect) eat
And lie down and rise up for ever and ever.

62:14

And the sum of judgment was given unto the Son of Man,
And he caused the sinners to pass away and be destroyed
    from off the face of the earth,
And those who have led the world astray.
. . . . . .
For that Son of Man has appeared,
And has seated himself on the throne of his glory,
And all evil shall pass away before his face,
And the word of that Son of Man shall go forth. . . .

69:27–29

Here emerges the most complete picture of the Son of man
in the Jewish apocalyptic tradition. He is a pre-existent
divine being (48:2f.; 62:7). He is hidden in the presence of
God from before all creation (48:2). He is revealed "on that
day", i.e. at the End. He appears in order to deliver the elect

from persecution (62:7ff.). He judges the kings and rulers who have persecuted the elect (46:4; 62:11; 69:27). He presides as a ruler in glory over the elect as a redeemed community in eternity. Note especially the allusion to the Messianic banquet (69:29; 62:14).

Two further problems call for discussion. In other passages the Son of man is given additional titles, notably "the Elect One" (chaps. 49, 51) or "the Righteous and Elect One" (53:6). He is "the Lord's Anointed One" (48:10; 52:4). He is to be the "Light of the Gentiles", (48:4),[49] like the Servant of Yahweh in Deutero-Isaiah (Isa. 42:6; 49:6). Clearly, the Son of man in Ethiopic Enoch is a composite figure, in which motifs from the Davidic Messianology and from the Isaianic Servant of Yahweh have been combined with apocalyptic features. This circumstance lends colour to the thesis of Bentzen and Riesenfeld that the whole Son of man concept sprang from the myth and ritual pattern of the royal mythology. Since, however, the apocalyptic traits (pre-existent redeemer, transcendental origin, supernatural appearance, suprahistorical reign) are absent from the royal ideology, while the features from that ideology which are combined in Enoch with the transcendental apocalyptic tradition are absent from our other two sources (Dan. 7 and 4 Ezra), we must conclude that Enoch represents an exceptional syncretistic combination. How far this combination influenced Christian Christology will be discussed later.

Second, in Eth. Enoch 71 Enoch is himself exalted to heaven and, apparently in answer to his own question (though this part of the text is defective), is told "Thou art the Son of man who art born to righteousness." Charles proposed to avoid the identification of the Son of man with Enoch by emending the text to: "This is . . . who is", but without warrant. On this identification Sjöberg[50] has based his thesis of a Son of man who becomes incarnate in the person of Enoch and who is subsequently exalted to heaven. Thus he finds in the Similitudes a pre-Christian foreshadowing of the pre-existence, incarnation, and exaltation of the Son of man. It could also support the Uppsala school's theory that this in turn was part of the pattern of royal ideology: every king at his enthronement thus becomes an incarnation of the Son of man—archetypal man.[50a] All this however is pure construction. Hahn's suggestion is worth quoting:

> Enoch however is not "identified with the pre-existent Son of man", but as the only righteous one among the first of mankind he is the representative of man created in the image of God, and is taken up as (Son of) man. It seems as though we have here a specifically Jewish attempt to elucidate the concept of the archetypal man (which was hovering in the background) in the light of the biblical doctrine of creation.[51]

Attractive as this way out of the difficulty is, it has the disadvantage of postulating the use of Son of man in two entirely different senses in juxtaposed contexts. The problem of Eth. Enoch 71 remains unsolved, and this final denouement of the Son of man's identity had better be regarded as a peculiarity of the Similitudes, not as representative of the general apocalyptic tradition. Nothing therefore should be based upon it for the understanding of New Testament usage.

The fourth and last possible source for apocalyptic use of the term, Son of man, is 4 Ezra, in the sixth of a series of visions.[52] The seer sees "something like the figure of a man" (*quasi similitudinem hominis* 13:2). This language is closer to the Danielic *kᵉbhar 'enosh* (one like to a Son of man), and would seem to indicate a less developed tradition than the full title used in the Similitudes—despite its ostensibly later date. This "man" arises out of the sea and flies on the cloud of heaven (v. 3a cf. Dan. 7:13) as the terrifying judge of the world (vv. 3b–4). Then follow two judgment scenes (vv. 5–7 and 8–11) in which the wicked are gathered together to fight against the judge, but are consumed by a stream of fire issuing from his mouth. Then follows a third scene in which the elect are gathered to the man-like figure. The ensuing interpretation of these scenes is not part of the tradition, but the author's own addition.[53] It is in this interpretation that the man-like figure is addressed by Yahweh as "my son", which, as we have seen, is now generally accepted as representing an original *'abhdî*, "my servant" (vv. 32, 37, 52). This identification is another instance of the combination of

41

the original apocalyptic tradition of the Son of man with other elements from the Old Testament, similar to what has happened in the Similitudes.

To summarize, therefore, there is a body of evidence which, on a plausible interpretation, indicates that the figure of the Son of man as the pre-existent divine agent of judgment and salvation was embedded in the pre-Christian Jewish apocalyptic tradition. This tradition provides the most likely source for the concept of the Son of man as used by Jesus and the early church.

Before we leave this subject, we must take a brief look at two other usages of the term in the Hebrew Old Testament. One is in the Psalms, where it occurs in synonymous parallelism with "man" (Ps. 8:4, *ben 'adham*; Ps. 80:17, *ben 'adham*; Ps. 144:3, *ben 'enos*). In the first and third of these passages the context shows that the reference is to man as such,[54] mankind, humanity. Ps. 8 plays a role in the interpretation of Jesus only in the later strata of the New Testament. By this time the apocalyptic Son of man had fully established itself in the sayings of Jesus (1 Cor. 15:27, Heb. 2:6) and in connection with the *humiliated and exalted* Christ. The latter notion, as we shall see, is certainly early, but somewhat later than the identification of Jesus with the coming Son of man. Psalm 8:4 does not therefore come into question as a possible source for the New Testament usage. Psalm 144:3 is never quoted in the New Testament. Psalm 80:17 poses a different problem, for here "son of man" refers most probably to the king.[55] It thus adds colour to the Uppsala theory that the term Son of man has its roots in the royal ideology.[56] This theory, however, we have already rejected on other grounds. And in any case, while it has a possible bearing on the origin of the Son of man within Judaism, it is again irrelevant to the New Testament usage of the term Son of man. For this particular psalm is never quoted in the New Testament.

The second Old Testament usage which has played some part in the quest for the origin of the Son of man concept, particularly in British[57] scholarship, is its use in Ezekiel. Repeatedly (nearly a hundred times) the prophet is addressed in his visions as Son of man (*ben 'adham*). No explanation is offered in the text as to the meaning of the term.

A. Richardson[58] suggests that "it seems to indicate the dignity of the otherwise insignificant person whom God has condescended to address".

The present writer has submitted a critique of the Ezekielic theory elsewhere,[59] and the argument need not be repeated here. Since then A. J. B. Higgins has written: "It is questionable whether the apocalyptic Son of Man can be relegated to the periphery in this way, and if Jesus borrowed from Ezekiel his scant references to the Spirit are in surprising contrast to the frequent association in Ezekiel of the 'Son of Man' in the Spirit."[60] Hahn simply dismisses the theory with the words "it requires no serious refutation."[61] We may agree.

Finally, there is the view[62] that Jesus' use of Son of man has no biblical origin at all, but simply reflects current conversational usage in Aramaic, in which it is alleged that *bar 'enoš* simply meant "man", or "one" (*on dit, man sagt*). As an explanation of Jesus' usage it could be taken in two ways: either as a self-effacing substitute for the first person singular: "The Son of man has nowhere to lay his head" = "*I* have nowhere to lay *my* head"; or "*one* has no where to lay *one's* head"—i.e. having nowhere to lay one's head is part of our general human lot. As late as 1948 Bultmann[63] still explained the "present" usage in the synoptic gospels (Mark 2:10, 28; Matt. 8:20 par., 11:19 par., 12:32 par.) in one or other of these two ways. The present writer has endeavoured to refute this interpretation of the passages in question,[64] and is glad to find that more recent writers in the Bultmann school agree that in all of these passages Son of man is a title of majesty.[65]

Therefore, when we come to examine the Son of man in the sayings of Jesus and in the development of his sayings in the early church, we shall assume that the term is throughout derived from the pre-Christian Jewish apocalyptic tradition.

5. *The Servant of the Lord*

The Hebrew word for servant is *'ebhedh*, from the verb *'abhadh* meaning "to work". It is used in an ordinary secular sense for a slave or for one in the service of a king. What concerns us here is religious use. Here it generally occurs in the possessive case followed by "Yahweh"; or with the first person singular suffix (with Yahweh as the speaker) "my servant"; or with the second person suffix, "thy servant", in address to Yahweh. At the back of this usage would seem to be a common oriental notion that the deity is like an oriental despot before whom his subjects should grovel.[66] Thus it is found in many of the psalms on the lips of the devout: "Behold, I am thy servant." From here it is but a small step to apply it to the religious men in Israel *par excellence*, the patriarchs, to kings (especially David)[67] and to prophets,— (especially to Moses, the prophet *par excellence*).[68] The servant is thus an individual member of Israel who is called by God to a special task in the execution of his purposes in history. As we shall seek to show, it is probably this Mosaic usage which is behind the use of παῖς in Acts, with overtones of the Davidic usage.

It is in the Servant Songs of Deutero-Isaiah (42:1–4; 49:1–6; 50:4–9; 52:13—53:12) that the concept of the Servant of the Lord acquires for the first time the possibility of being used in an eschatological context. We need not here concern ourselves with the much debated question as to the original meaning of the "servant" in the Songs.[69] In relation to our present subject, what concerns us is its interpretation in Judaism at the time of Christian origins. Were the Songs interpreted messianically? If so, was the suffering of the servant incorporated into the concept of Messiahship? Lastly, and most important, was this suffering then accorded atoning significance?

Our first question is, were the Songs interpreted messianically in pre-Christian Palestinian Judaism? One of the first impressions from Jeremias' analysis[70] is of atomistic interpretation. There was no one interpretation of the servant throughout the Songs, and any one interpretation of the 19 occurrences of the term servant must on no account be applied by inference to any of the other passages. From the Targums Jeremias produces evidence to show that some passages were interpreted collectively of Israel (i.e. places where the text itself demanded this interpretation). The other ten passages, including Isa. 53, are, however, never interpreted to mean Israel collectively. Some passages are applied to various groups within the Jewish community.

Some passages are applied to specific individuals in the Old Testament (Jacob, David, etc.). These interpretations are generally based on explicit or inferred allusions in the text.

Jeremias then goes on to discover various Messianic interpretations, not of the Songs in general, but of specific passages, viz. Isa. 42:1; 43:10; 49:6; 52:13; 53:11. He has little difficulty in showing that there is a fairly widespread tendency to call the Messiah the Servant of the Lord. In itself that could come either from the Old Testament ascription of the title to David, thus referring strictly to the Davidic Messiah or anointed one, or from the prophet—second Moses complex of ideas, which will be discussed later. It is not in itself to be taken as evidence of the influence of the Servant Songs, e.g. 4 Ezra 13. There is also a tendency to fill out the picture of the eschatological redeemer with traits from the Songs. For example the Son of man in the Similitudes is not only combined with the anointed one but is also called the light to lighten the gentiles, the Elect One, the Righteous One, etc. In such cases, however, the distinctive feature of suffering, to say nothing of atoning suffering "for many", is lacking. The main evidence which Jeremias cites for the Messianic interpretation of Isa. 53 is in the Greek translations (LXX, Aquila, Theodotion) and the Peshitta. Miss Hooker[71] is quite right in rejecting this evidence partly because it is too scanty, and partly because some of it is open to the suspicion of Christian influence. The remarkable interpretation of Isa. 53 in the Targum,[72] in which all the references to suffering are transferred from the servant (whom it does interpret messianically) either to Israel or to the nations is taken by Jeremias as anti-Christian polemic, and he contends that in earlier Jewish interpretation the suffering had been recognized as that of the Messiah himself.[73] But this is a hazardous *argumentum e silentio*. Another consideration has been brought forward by E. Lohse.[74] The concept of the atoning power of vicarious suffering was very widespread in first-century Judaism, yet Isa. 53 was never adduced in support of it. This consideration will be important later on when we come to investigate the place of Isa. 53 in New Testament Christology.[74a]

The results of our investigation are somewhat disappointing

"Servant of Yahweh" was a subsidiary title both of the Davidic Messiah and of the Mosaic prophet. In Eth. Enoch traits of the Isaianic servant have been absorbed into the Son of man. Yet Jewish precedent for the messianic interpretation of the atoning power of the vicarious suffering of the Messiah is patently lacking. This means that unless we can find in the New Testament specific allusions to atoning suffering *for many* (for which there is no Jewish precedent) we cannot postulate the influence of the characteristic feature of Isa. 53. And wherever we find the title "Servant" or other allusions to the Servant Songs, we must avoid reading into these passages the concept of the atoning power of vicarious suffering. More light on the Isaianic servant will come from the ensuing discussion of the eschatological prophet.

6. *The Eschatological Prophet*

Yet another form of the late Jewish eschatological expectation, and one which provided some of the tools for the primitive Christian assessment of Jesus, was the concept of the eschatological prophet.[75] Every reader of the New Testament is familiar with the idea that the (Davidic) Messiah is to be preceded by Elijah. But it is not commonly realized that this represents a fusion of two originally different traditions, the Davidic Messiah, and the eschatological prophet. The latter figure was originally quite distinct and existed in its own right.

The hope of an eschatological prophet took two forms. First, there was the hope of a return of Moses, or of a prophet like him. This was based upon Deut. 18:15–19. The original meaning of this passage[76] was that a series of prophets would arise after Moses—not eschatological prophets, but historical figures. The passage continued to be interpreted historically even in the Rabbis, who sometimes referred it to one of the Old Testament prophets such as Jeremiah, sometimes to some future prophet as yet unknown.[77] But there is also evidence for the application of Deut. 18:15ff. to an eschatological prophet. That there was such an interpretation was first contended by Gfrörer, but on inadequate evidence.[78] For long Gfrörer's theory was a matter of controversy since Deut. 18:15ff. is never so interpreted in the Rabbinic literature.[79] Recently, however, A. Bentzen[80] has put forward good grounds for supposing that the suffering servant in Deutero-Isaiah was intended by the original author of the Songs to be the eschatological prophet like unto Moses, a view which commends itself to both Cullmann and Hahn.[81] More certain than this theory of Bentzen's, however, is the appearance of an eschatological prophet as one of three eschatological figures alongside of the kingly and priestly Messiahs at Qumran.[82] Again, in the Dead Sea Scrolls Deut. 18:18f. is explicitly applied to the eschatological prophet.[83]

Since our surviving evidence takes us no further, it is difficult to say with certainty what the functions of this eschatological prophet were expected to be. But certain Mosaic functions are later ascribed to the Davidic Messiah, a figure which originally had nothing to do with Moses. This is the case with the Samaritan Ta'eb, who "performs miracles, restores the law and true worship among the people, and brings knowledge to other nations",[84] and with the Rabbinic Moses/Messiah[85] typology.

Having been originally an independent eschatological figure, the Mosaic prophet loses his independent identity. Either he sinks, as at Qumran, to the status of forerunner (like Elijah, see below). Or he contributes his essential functions to the Davidic Messiah, as in the Rabbis and, in a different way, in the New Testament Christology. Yet there are still clear traces of its independent existence as an eschatological figure in the popular Palestinian expectation at the time of Jesus (cf. John 1:21, 25; 6:14). Moreover, as we shall see, this concept has contributed materially to the interpretation of Jesus in the earliest church.

Several further terms may be mentioned which are associated with the concept of the eschatological prophet. One is the term ὁ δίκαιος, the Righteous One. This term has a wide use. It is applied to the devout in Israel, notably in Hab. 2:4. It is also used as an attributive adjective for the Davidic Messiah, e.g. Jer. 23:5 cf. Ps. Sol. 17:35. (Wisd. 2:18 is not Davidic-Messianic, but refers to the devout).[86] But in Acts 3:14 and 7:52 it is applied to Jesus in a context which clearly enshrines pre-Lucan and probably quite early material. Here Jesus is presented not as Davidic Messiah, but as an eschatological figure of the Mosaic prophet-servant type (see below). Moses was the "Righteous One" *par excellence* in Israel, and the eschatological prophet-servant is already accorded this title in Isa. 53:11.

The second title is ὁ ἅγιος τοῦ θεοῦ, the Holy One of God. The oldest material in the New Testament in which the attributive adjective ἅγιος ("holy") is applied to Jesus is in connection with the Mosaic prophet-servant concept (Acts 3:14 with δίκαιος, "righteous"; 4:27, 30). It would seem to be from this line of thought rather than from the concept of the priestly Messiah[87] that the term is derived. Elisha in 2 Kings 4:9 is called a "holy man of God", while ἅγιος in the New Testament is commonly used as an attributive adjective for the OT prophets (cf. Wisd. 11:1, in reference to Moses). Isaiah 61:1f, where the servant is endowed with the πνεῦμα ("spirit"), again suggests the application of ἅγιος to the prophet-servant. Both ἀρχηγός ("leader", "prince", Acts 3:15) in a Mosaic context again, and 5:13 and σωτήρ ("Saviour"))—although this, as we shall see, was predominantly a Hellenistic title with other roots—may well have been originally derived from the same Mosaic-prophet-servant complex. The analogous term λυτρωτής ("redeemer") is used for Moses himself in Acts 7:35. The primary notion of σωτήρ ("Saviour") is similar. Jesus as the Mosaic servant-prophet—the Redeemer and Saviour—leads the eschatological people of God into the promised land of the kingdom of God. Jeremias[88] gives six or seven instances in the Rabbinic literature where the principle is stated: "Like the first redeemer (Moses), so the last redeemer (Messiah)."

The second prophetic figure who acquired eschatological significance was Elijah. The starting point for this expectation is Mal. 4:5f. (MT 3:23f.). In this passage, an editorial note commenting on Mal. 3:1,[89] Elijah appears as the fore-runner not of the Messiah[90] but of Yahweh himself (cf. "my —Yahweh's—messenger", 3:1, followed by the coming of Yahweh to his temple for the eschatological judgment; and 4:5, "before the great and terrible day *of the Lord* comes").

In Ecclus. 48:10 the same expectation appears in relative purity: Elijah is still the last emissary of Yahweh before he comes in his wrath, though there the Elijah figure has been combined, as we have seen, with traits from the servant of Deutero-Isaiah. In the later literature however Elijah has lost his independence. In Eth. Enoch 90:31 he appears together with Enoch as the forerunner of the Son of man, and in the Rabbinic literature as the forerunner of the Davidic Messiah. Unfortunately, this Rabbinic evidence is all later than the origins of Christianity. But the New Testament itself gives us clear evidence that Elijah had already been relegated to the position of forerunner of the Davidic Messiah (Mark 9:11) by the time of Jesus. Perhaps, too, the relegation of the Mosaic prophet to the same status at Qumran (see above) is due to the influence of the Elijah-prophet. Finally, the transfiguration narrative (Mark 9:4f.) witnesses to a similar combination of Moses and Elijah as forerunners of the final agent of redemption. The eschatological functions of the Elijah-prophet differ from those of the Moses-prophet. Whereas the Moses-prophet is a redeemer who works miracles and gives the definitive exposition of the Torah (or a new Torah), the Elijah-prophet is a preacher who announces the imminent coming of the end, and urges repentance in preparation for it.[90a]

7. Rabbi

We come finally to two terms which have no pre-history in Jewish eschatology. Both of them were used in a non-eschatological sense in Palestinian Judaism and were applied to Jesus by his followers.

Rabbi[91] is the possessive of the adjective rabh, meaning "great". Rabh was used already in the OT for one in a high position (e.g. 2 Kings 25:8, translated RSV "the captain of the bodyguard"). In the possessive, rabbi = "my great one" is used in post-biblical Hebrew and Aramaic by an inferior in addressing his superior. In Aramaic a strengthened caritative form, Rabbun,[92] was also used, giving the possessive form Rabbouni, "my dear master", familiar to us from Mark 10:51 (AV) and John 20:16. Rabh and Rabbi came to be used most frequently for a teacher of the Torah. The earliest evidence for this is ca. 110 B.C. where it is used absolutely: rabh = teacher.[93] The disciple addressed his teacher as Rabbi, "my great one", as a title of respect and submission. So frequent was this address that Rabbi gradually lost its possessive force, and became the title applied exclusively to a teacher of the Torah. This process was already happening in Palestine in NT times, as has been shown by an ossuary discovered in 1931 and dating from a generation or so before A.D. 70.[94] Gradually too, both as an address and as a title, Rabbi became restricted to a properly trained and educated Rabbi. But this restrictive process had not yet prevailed in the time of Jesus, for Jesus, though appearing as a teacher, had neither formal Rabbinic training nor ordination.

8. *Mari*

As an address the Aramaic term *mari*[95] = "my Lord" was also used. While Rabbi was coming to be used exclusively for teachers of the Torah, *mari* had a wider use, as Rabbi had originally, though it could be used also of a teacher. The important thing to notice about it is that *mari* does not connote divinity: it is simply a recognition of human authority.[96] Even when used of equals, it is always a term of politeness.

Another equally important negative consideration to bear in mind is that the term *'adhon* = "Lord" and *'adhonai* = "my Lord". In the OT these terms had been used more indiscriminately, but by the time of the NT they were becoming increasingly reserved for Yahweh. It would not therefore have been natural for Palestinian Jewish Christians to use *'adhon* or *'adhonai* in application to Jesus. Hence their use of *mar, mari,* or *maran* (our Lord),—cf. *marana tha*.

Appendix: THE ESCHATOLOGICAL PROPHET AT QUMRAN[97]

From 1 QS 9:11 it appears that the Qumraners looked for a Prophet in addition to their two Messiahs:

> . . . and they shall not deviate from the whole counsel of the Torah to walk in the stubbornness of their [own] heart but shall be judged by the first decisions [laws] by which the men of the Community commenced to be disciplined, *until a Prophet comes and the Messiahs of Aaron and Israel.*

Despite Dupont-Sommer's attempt to identify the Prophet here mentioned with the sect's founder, the *môreh ha-ṣedek* (Teacher of Righteousness), it is clear from the context that the Prophet is still expected to come in the future, together with the two Messiahs.[98] This interpretation is clinched by 4 Q Test., where OT *testimonia* are given in turn for the three eschatological figures, the *testimonium* for the Prophet being Deut. 18:18. Clearly all three figures belong together.

But this is not the whole story. In CD 19:34 we read:

> All the men who entered into the New Covenant in the "Land of Damascus", but have again acted faithlessly and turned aside from the well of living water, shall not be reckoned in the council of the people, nor be inscribed in their book, from the day the Teacher of the Community died until the Messiah of Aaron and Israel arises.[99]

It is clear that this represents a changed Messianic hope. The two Messiahs have been reduced to one, and the Prophet has disappeared. Or does the text identify the Teacher with the Prophet? Such is the view, not only of Dupont-Sommer, who naturally interprets this passage in the light of his own interpretation of 1 QS 9:11, but also of others who do not follow Dupont-Sommer at that point.[100] In favour of this interpretation of CD 19:34 it may be argued that there are other places in the scrolls where prophetic functions are clearly ascribed to the Teacher, notably 1 Qp Hab 7:3–5, which reads:

> . . . the Teacher of Righteousness to whom God made known all the mysteries of the words of his servants the Prophets. (Tr. G. Vermés)

W. H. Brownlee, in an article entitled "Messianic Motives of Qumran and the New Testament"[101] has carried this case much further. He considers it certain that the sect identified the Teacher with the Prophet like unto Moses. There are, it is true, no passages in which the identification is explicitly made. But there are passages which by verbal allusions seem to ascribe to the Teacher the functions of the second Moses and which describe his fate in terms of the suffering servant of Deutero-Isaiah.

CD calls the Teacher a "lawgiver". In 1 QH 4:5f. the teacher's function is described in terms of Isa. 42:6 as one whose mission is associated with the Covenant to bring light to men:

> I will praise thee, O lord, for thou hast enlightened me for thy covenant's sake. . . . And as the sun thou hast dawned upon me to be a light to them.

Here, however, it would seem that the "I" who speaks is the collective of the community, rather than the Teacher.[102] The same objections apply to other passages which Brownlee cites from the *Hodayoth*.

There is another passage in CD (6:11) in which the phrase occurs: "until the Righteous Teacher arises in the end of the days". This has led J. M. Allegro[103] and others to propound the theory that the Teacher is expected to return at the End. Some hold that he was to return as Prophet, others as Priest. In a later article[104] Allegro produced further evidence for the view that the Teacher was to return, as the priestly Messiah. This he infers from 4Q Flor. 2, which reads:

> He is the shoot of David who will arise with the Interpreter of the law. . . .

In the first of these two passages the meaning is highly uncertain. In the immediately preceding passage there is a reference to a historical figure called the Staff, who is the expositor of the law. If this is the Teacher-Founder of the sect, then the Righteous Teacher may be the same figure returning at the end.[105] On the other hand, he may be a different figure.[106] Or again, the Staff may be a yet earlier historical figure who preceded the Teacher-Founder.[107] The passage is so uncertain that it is hazardous to draw any definite conclusions from it.

As for Allegro's second passage, he is probably right in identifying the expositor of the law in this context with the priestly Messiah. But his further identification of the Expositor with the returning historical Teacher-Founder is highly uncertain. Nowhere else is the Teacher-Founder explicitly identified with the future priestly Messiah.[108] Hahn, following SB and van der Woude, suggests that the priestly Messiah is here identified with Elijah, not indeed as the forerunner, but as the Messianic high priest whose function was the true exposition of the Torah.

From all this we may deduce that there is some evidence to show that at least in a more developed stage the Qumran community identified its historical founder with the Prophet like unto Moses. But it is very important to note the limits of this identification. He is the second Moses as the true interpreter of the Mosaic law. He is not the giver of the *new* law, like Jesus in Matthew's gospel. He is the Prophet in the sense that he heralds the coming of the End time. But he is not the agent of its coming. He is not a soteriological figure. He performs no miracles. Even if Brownlee is right in finding allusions which suggest the Teacher's identification with the Deutero-Isaianic servant, nowhere are his alleged sufferings ascribed an atoning value for the many. Brownlee quotes allusions to Isa. 53:3f. in 1 QH 8:26f. ("I was a man forsaken and despised") and to Isa. 40:5 in 1 QH 8:35f. ("All my lip was dumb"—should this not rather allude to Isa. 53:7?) but never to Isa. 53:11f. It has sometimes been suggested that the Teacher suffered a martyr's death (Dupont-Sommer) and even (Allegro) that he was crucified. But even if this were established, there is nowhere any suggestion that his death was ever interpreted in accordance with Isa. 53:11f. as an atonement for "the many".

The only value which the Dead Sea Scrolls have in this connection is that they provide additional evidence that the concept of the eschatological Prophet was alive in Palestinian Judaism in the first centuries B.C. and A.D. They may also suggest that the concept could be applied to a figure of the past. But the use they make of the concept is strikingly different from the Christian application of it, even where, as in the case of the Prophet as lawgiver, they overlap. Under no circumstances can we say that Qumran usage here provided a ready made christological concept which could be transferred directly to Jesus of Nazareth. The later Christian concept of the eschatological prophet was controlled by what Jesus himself had said and done.

NOTES ON CHAPTER II

1. Cf. *TWNT* I, pp. 563ff. (Kuhn s.v. βασιλεύς.)

2. See I. Engnell, *Studies in Divine Kingship in the Ancient Near East*, Uppsala, 1943; A. R. Johnson, *Sacral Kingship in Ancient Israel*, Cardiff: University of Wales Press, 1955; S. H. Hooke (ed.), *Myth, Ritual and Kingship*, Oxford: Clarendon Press, 1958. A more moderate statement of these theories will be found in H. Ringgren, *The Messiah in the Old Testament*, London: S.C.M. Press (*SBT* 18), 1956. The Uppsala thesis is that (*a*) the empirical monarchy in Israel was already impregnated with eschatological ideas; (*b*) these ideas found expression in the enthronement festival held each new year's day. (*a*) is extremely doubtful and (*b*) speculative. We are prepared to accept first, that the royal ideology of Israel borrowed extensively from the royal ideologies of the surrounding nations; and second, that this ideology found expression in the cultus.

3. So J. Barr in *HDB*, p. 652 s.v. "Messiah"; more cautiously H. Ringgren *op. cit.* (note 2) pp. 26f.

4. So Barr, *ibid.* But see G. von Rad, *Theologie des Alten Testaments II* (only vol. I has thus far been translated), Munich: Chr. Kaiser Verlag, 1960, pp. 183f. Von Rad is less certain of this interpretation.

5. On this passage see the exhaustive study by A. Alt, *Kleine Schriften zur Geschichte des Volkes Israel*, Munich: C. H. Beck, 1953, I, pp. 206–225. Alt strongly inclines to its authenticity to Isaiah (pp. 223–225).

6. So Barr, *art. cit.* (note 3); contrast D. W. Thomas in Peake *ad. loc.*, who thinks that the passage presupposes the exile and return.

7. E.g. S. Mowinckel, *He that Cometh*, New York and Nashville: Abingdon Press (n.d.), pp. 19f.

8. Cf. J. Barr, *art. cit.* p. 650: "It would seem more reasonable to take 23:1–8 as being in substance his thought, and to suppose that like Isaiah he looked for one who should be more truly a representative of anointed kingship than the present rulers were." Those who reject 23:1–8 naturally dismiss 17:19–27 and 33:14–16 as well (so e.g. Mowinckel (note 7) pp. 19f.; 165; 456).

9. So Barr, *loc. cit.* Contrast F. Hahn, *Christologische Hoheitstitel*, Göttingen: Vandenhoeck u. Ruprecht (*FRLANT* 83), 1963, p. 138: "In other prophets of the Exilic period the hope for a new Davidic king palpably fades, for instance in Ezekiel."

10. See the complete reconstruction of this passage in Peake *ad. loc.*

11. Cf. Hahn, *Hoheitstitel*, p. 140, n. 1.

12. A. R. Johnson (see above, note 2) pp. 102f.

13. Cf. Hahn, *Hoheitstitel*, p. 140.

14. R. H. Charles, *Apocrypha and Pseudepigrapha*, Oxford: Clarendon Press, 1913, vol. II, p. 291.

15. F. M. Cross, Jr., *The Ancient Library of Qumran*, Garden City, N.Y.: Anchor Books, 1961 (Revised), p. 44. A part of Test. Levi in Aramaic and of Test. Naph. in Hebrew are reported there.

16. Test. Reub. 6:5–12. Cf. Test. Lev. 8:11–15 and Test. Jud. 24. For the interpretation see G. R. Beasley-Murray in *JTS* 48 (1947), pp. 1–13 (written prior to the publication of any of the Qumran material). For a complete list of Messianic references in Test. XII Pat. see Kuhn in *The Scrolls and the New Testament*, Ed. K. Standahl, New York: Harper & Brothers, 1957, p. 58.

17. The relation between Test. XII Pat. and the Qumran sect and writings is unsolved. J. Barr (note 3) appears to regard Test. XII Pat. as earlier than the Qumran literature, a view we have followed here. F. M. Cross (note 15) pp. 198f. thinks that at least Test. Lev. and Test. Naph. were actually Qumran products. His reasons: the resemblance in Messianic doctrine and the use of the same calendar. F. Hahn (note 9) p. 149 deals with Test. XII Pat. separately from and after the Qumran literature, and regards the Test. as influenced by the theology of the Qumran sect.

18. CD was first discovered in a Cairo genizah in 1896 and published by S. Schechter in 1910. The relevant passages are: 12:23; 14:9; 19:10. Cf. CD 20:1. The emendation was proposed by both Kuhn and Milik, and was for a long time widely accepted.

19. J. T. Milik, *Ten Years of Discovery in the Wilderness of Judea*, London: S.C.M. Press (*SBT* 26), pp. 125f. Milik supposes that in this document the priestly Messiah has taken over the functions of the Messiah of Israel.

20. Relevant passages about the Davidic Messiah are:

4Q Patr. Bless 3f.: "Until the Messiah of righteousness comes, the branch of David."

4Q p Isa. 1: "He is the Branch of David who will arise . . . in the latter days."

Commentary on Genesis 29 (10): ". . . until the coming of the Messiah of righteousness, the branch of David; for to him and to his seed is given the covenant of kingship of his people until the generations of eternity."

4Q Flor. 10: "This is the branch of David who will arise with the seekers of the law and who will sit on the throne of Zion at the end of the days" [quotation from Amos 9:11 follows].

1QSb 20–29: [A passage too long to quote, the blessing of the "Prince of the congregation". His eschatological reign will be characterized by justice for the poor, victory over enemies, charismatic endowments as in Isa. 11, with allusion also to Num. 24:17–19.]

21. Charles, *Pseudepigrapha* (note 14), pp. 627–630.

22. For the messianology of the Rabbinic literature see J. Klausner, *The Messianic Idea in Israel*, New York: Macmillan, 1955, Part III, pp. 388–517, "The Messianic Idea in the Period of the Tannaim".

23. See G. Dalman, *The Words of Jesus*, Edinburgh: T. & T. Clark, 1909, pp. 272f.

24. See E. Lövestam, *Son and Saviour* (*Coniectanea Neotestamentica* XVIII) Lund: C. W. K. Gleerup, 1961, pp. 11ff. Only in later Rabbinic literature do specific references to Ps. 2:7 occur (*op. cit.*, p. 21, n. 2). Even

Hahn, *Hoheitstitel* p. 285, can only find a reference dating from 2nd century A.D.

25. Cf. my *Mission and Achievement of Jesus*, London: S.C.M. Press (*SBT* 12), 1954, p. 81, n. 2.

26. B. Violet, *Die Apokalypsen des Esra and des Baruch in deutscher Gestalt*, Leipzig: J. C. Hinrichs, 1924. Violet's thesis has been widely accepted e.g. by Jeremias in W. Zimmerli and J. Jeremias, *The Servant of God*, London: S.C.M. Press (*SBT* 20), 1957 (Eng. Tr. of art. παῖς θεοῦ in *TWNT* V); O. Cullmann, *The Christology of the New Testament*, London: S.C.M. Press, 1959, p. 274; F. Hahn, *Hoheitstitel*, p. 285 (with the qualification (n. 1) that "my servant" has nothing to do with Deutero-Isaiah, but like Ezek. 34:23f.; 37:24f. ("my servant David") and Zech. 3:8 ("my servant the Branch") is a designation of the kingly Messiah, so that to that extent the rendering "*filius meus*" is after all not so wide of the mark).

27. P. Volz, *Die Eschatologie der jüdischen Gemeinde*, Tübingen: J. C. B. Mohr (P. Siebeck), 1934, p. 174: "we must be cautious in asserting that it was not used or that it was impossible"; R. Bultmann, *Theology of the New Testament*, vol. I, London: S.C.M. Press, 1952, p. 50: "uncertain and debated . . . but perfectly possible"; O. Cullmann, *Christology*, p. 274: "difficult not to assume that this royal attribute should not occasionally have been transferred to the Messiah"; Lövestam, *Son and Saviour*, p. 21, n. 7: "may be assumed to have been in the back of the mind" (*sc.* wherever Ps. 2 is quoted messianically).

28. See Cullmann, *ibid.*; W. G. Kümmel, in *Aux Sources de la Tradition Chrétienne* (Mélanges M. Goguel), Paris: Delachaux et Niestlé, 1950, p. 130.

29. *Son and Saviour*, p. 12.

30. In *ZThK* 53 (1951) 3, pp. 265–311.

31. Cf. Dalman, *Words*, p. 317.

32. So above all H. Gunkel in *Festgabe . . . A von Harnack dargebracht*, Tübingen: J. C. B. Mohr, 1921, pp. 43–60; cf. M. Dibelius, *Botschaft und Geschichte* I, Tübingen: J. C. B. Mohr (P. Siebeck) 1953, p. 3, also art. "Magnificat" by the present writer in *HDB*, p. 611.

33. So Hahn, *Hoheitstitel*, pp. 247f.

34. On the whole subject cf. H. H. Rowley, *The Relevance of Apocalyptic*, London: Lutterworth Press, 1947 (revised ed. 1963); Mowinckel (note 7) pp. 261–279. For a spirited discussion of the difference between prophecy and apocalyptic see J. A. T. Robinson, *In the End God*, London: James Clarke, 1950, pp. 36–43. See also Cross, *Qumran*, pp. 76f., n. 35a.

35. Most of the available literature will be found in English translation in Charles (note 14), vol. II. 4 Ezra = 2 Esdras will be found in the Apocrypha.

36. See above all T. W. Manson, *The Teaching of Jesus*, Cambridge: University Press, 1935², pp. 211ff., a view which Manson consistently maintained in his later writings.

37. The argument is accessible to English speaking readers in Mowinckel (note 7), pp. 348–353, following Reitzenstein, Volz, and Kraeling. E. Stauffer, *Jerusalem und Rom*, Berne: Francke Verlag, 1957, p. 139,

n. 7, regards Dan. 7:27 as secondary. Cullmann (note 26), p. 139, decides "One cannot be certain whether it (*sc.* Son of man) originally concerned the figure of an *individual* redeemer."

38. The elaboration of this theory was the work of Reitzenstein, Bousset, and Gressmann. It was later taken up and clarified by C. H. Kraeling, *Anthropos and Son of Man*, New York: Columbia University Press, 1927. An account of it with (incomplete) bibliography to date will be found in W. Manson, *Jesus the Messiah*, London: Hodder and Stoughton, 1945[4], pp. 174–190. See also, for more recent observations, Cullmann, *Christology*, p. 143; A. J. B. Higgins in *New Testament Essays*, Manchester: University Press, 1959, pp. 121f.

39. Notably A. Bentzen, *King and Messiah*, London: Lutterworth Press, 1955, pp. 39–47; H. Riesenfeld in *The Background of the New Testament and its Eschatology*, ed. W. D. Davies and D. Daube, Cambridge: University Press, 1956, pp. 81–95. The chief supporting evidence is sought in Ps. 8:4 (this psalm is taken to be a royal psalm by the Uppsala school) and in Ps. 80:17. In both cases "Son of man", it is argued, is a title applied to the king-Messiah.

40. A. Feuillet in *RB* 60 (1953), pp. 170–202, 321–346.

41. Thus Stauffer, *Jerusalem und Rom*, p. 42. Among continental Europeans who accept the Similitudes without question are such different scholars as Mowinckel and Riesenfeld among the Scandinavians, Otto, Bultmann, Jeremias, Stauffer, Tödt, and Hahn among the Germans, and Cullmann (Swiss). Most of them do not even raise the question of their authenticity. Even Hahn, who is not unaware of the problem, decides that "despite the absence of ancient Palestinian attestation of the Similitudes it cannot be contested that in them ancient apocalyptic tradition has been taken up, just as in the case of 4 Ezra at the end of the 1st century A.D." (p. 19, n. 3).

42. E.g. most emphatically J. Y. Campbell in *JTS* 48 (1947), pp. 145–155; Cf. C. H. Dodd, *According to the Scriptures*, New York: Scribners, 1952, p. 116f., and *The Interpretation of the Fourth Gospel*, Cambridge: University Press, 1953, pp. 242f., and most recently J. Barr in *HDB art. cit.* Contrast B. M. Metzger, *ibid.* s.v. *Pseudepigrapha*, p. 821.

43. See F. M. Cross, *Qumran*, pp. 202f., n. 7. Cross concludes that the Son of man concept "either belongs to a post-Essene stage of the development of apocalyptic, or, less plausibly, to another, parallel apocalyptic tradition".

44. So most recently J. Barr (note 3), who suggests that they are a product of syncretistic Christianity.

45. So again J. Barr: "It seems unlikely that a completely independent figure entitled 'the Son of Man' ever existed." Barr interprets Dan. 7:14 (Peake *ad loc.*) as the guardian angel of Israel.

46. *Mission and Achievement*, p. 98.

47. The relevant passages in the Similitudes are: 46:4; 48:2; 62:9, 14; 63:11; 69:26f.; 70:1; 71:1.

48. R. H. Charles, *The Book of Enoch*, Oxford: Clarendon Press, 1912, pp. 86f.; also in *op. cit.* (note 14) p. 214 *ad* 46:2.

49. For other allusions to the servant of the songs see Jeremias, *Servant*, pp. 59f.

50. E. Sjöberg, *Der Menschensohn im äthiopischen Henochbuch*, Lund, 1946.

50a. For an exploitation of this theory for the understanding of the Son of man in the gospels see F. H. Borsch, *ATR* 45 (1963), pp. 174–190.

51. *Hoheitstitel*, p. 21, n. 4.

52. For English translation of the text see the Apocrypha (2 Esdras). It is translated from the Latin, itself a version of the Greek original.

53. See H. Tödt, *Der Menschensohn in der synoptischen Überlieferung*, Gütersloh: Gerd Mohn, 1959, p. 21, n. 5.

54. Despite H. Riesenfeld, *Jésus Transfiguré*, Uppsala, 1947, p. 63f., and Bentzen (note 39), who take Ps. 8 as a royal psalm.

55. So Peake *ad. loc.*

56. Cf. Bentzen, *King and Messiah*, p. 43.

57. So J. Y. Campbell in *A Theological Word Book of the Bible*, ed. A. Richardson, London: S.C.M. Press, 1950, pp. 231f.; G. S. Duncan: *Jesus, Son of Man*, London: Nisbet, 1948; and more recently, A. Richardson, *An Introduction to the Theology of the New Testament*, London: S.C.M. Press, 1958, pp. 145f. Richardson however does not exclude the influence of Dan. 7 upon Jesus (*ibid.*). Among American scholars Pierson Parker supports the Ezekielic derivation, *JBL* 60 (1941), pp. 151–157, and complains that this view has received insufficient attention from NT scholars—which is hardly true in Britain!

58. *Introduction*, p. 129.

59. *Mission and Achievement*, p. 99.

60. *NT Studies*, p. 124.

61. *Hoheitstitel*, p. 20, n. 4.

62. Stated in J. Wellhausen, *Einleitung in die drei ersten Evangelien*, Berlin: G. Reimer, 1911², pp. 123–130. Hahn (p. 14, n. 3) informs us that Wellhausen first propounded it in an essay published in 1899. Dalman traces back to Beza the theory that it was a simple *self*-designation (*Words*, p. 249).

63. In *Theology* I, p. 30. The date given above is that of the German original.

64. In *Mission and Achievement*, pp. 100, 106f. Cf. also A. Richardson, *Introduction*, p. 129.

65. G. Bornkamm, *Jesus of Nazareth* (Eng. Tr. of German of 1956), London: Hodder and Stoughton, pp. 229f.; H. Tödt, *Menschensohn*, pp. 106–124; Hahn, *Hoheitstitel*, p. 24.

66. W. Zimmerli in *Servant*, p. 14 alludes to Ashurbanipal, who calls himself the servant of Nebo.

67. In the Deuteronomic history David is the *'ebhedh YHWH par excellence*, and what this means is stated with particular clarity at 1 Kings 11:34.

68. According to Zimmerli, *op. cit.*, the title *'ebhedh* is ascribed to Moses forty times. Zimmerli calls particular attention to Num. 12:7f. (E).

69. Various views have been propounded by scholars in modern times. For a complete history of their views to date see C. R. North, *The Suffering*

Servant in Deutero-Isaiah, Oxford: University Press, 1948, pp. 23–116. The views fall into the following categories: (1) collective: (*a*) the nation; (*b*) a group within the nation, such as the elect remnant; (2) individual: (*a*) a historical figure, e.g. an OT king or prophet; (*b*) the prophet himself; (*c*) a future figure, e.g. the Messiah.

70. *Servant*, pp. 43–78.

71. M. D. Hooker, *Jesus and the Servant*, London: S.P.C.K., 1959, pp. 55f. In this argument Jeremias was following H. Hegermann, *Jesaja 53 in Hexapla, Targum und Peschitta*, Gütersloh, 1954.

72. Fifth century A.D. in its present form, but enshrining earlier traditions.

73. *Servant*, p. 76.

74. E. Lohse, *Märtyrer und Gottesknecht*, Göttingen: Vandenhoeck u. Ruprecht, (*FRLANT* NF 46) 1955, esp. pp. 66–78. Miss Hooker is mistaken in suggesting that "it seems doubtful whether the doctrine (*sc.* of the atoning power of vicarious suffering) was prevalent as early as the time of Jesus", and in thinking (*Jesus and the Servant*, pp. 56–71) that when it does appear, this is due to the influence of Isa. 53. As Lohse has shown, this doctrine arose independently of Isa. 53.

74a. For W. H. Brownlee's theory about the suffering servant at Qumran see Appendix.

75. See Jeremias in *TWNT* II, pp. 936–938 (s.v. 'Ηλ(ε)ίας) and *ibid.* IV, pp. 860–867 (s.v. Μωυσῆς); G. Friedrich, *ibid.* VI (s.v. προφήτης) pp. 826–828; H. W. Teeple, *JBL Monograph* X (1957); O. Cullmann, *Christology*, pp. 14–23; Hahn, *Hoheitstitel*, pp. 351–371.

76. See commentaries, most recently G. Henton Davies in Peake *ad loc.*: "a succession of prophets; the word 'prophet' is singular collective, and means 'many prophets'".

77. Jeremias, *TWNT* IV, p. 862.

78. In 1838.

79. Jeremias, *ibid.*; Hahn, *Hoheitstitel*, p. 359.

80. Bentzen, *King and Messiah*, pp. 65–67, following a suggestion of E. Sellin in *Mose und seine Bedeutung für die israelitisch-jüdische Religions-geschichte*, Leipzig, 1922, pp. 81–113: "It must therefore be considered very probable that the Ebed Yahweh in the scheme of Deutero-Isaiah played the role of the New Moses." Teeple, pp. 56–58, summarizes the views of Sellin and Bentzen. Sellin understood the servant as Moses come to life again. For Bentzen the Servant is a *second* Moses, not a Moses *redivivus*.

81. This view, says Cullmann, is "not impossible" (*Christology*, p. 17), and, says Hahn, p. 358, "has much to commend it, and deserves attention". Teeple is less favourably disposed to this theory, but thinks that "This servant of the Songs, nevertheless, reveals to us an early stage of the national hope which later sometimes caused belief in an eschatological leader like Moses" (p. 58).

82. 1QS 9:10f. "until the coming of the prophet and the Messiahs of Aaron and Israel". Note that the prophet is *not* called the Messiah.

83. 4Q Test. 5-8. The Testimonia are a series of OT prophecies which

in the belief of the sect were Messianic or eschatological. Deut. 18:15ff., is the first of the passages quoted; the other passages refer to the two Messiahs.

84. Cullmann, *Christology*, p. 19. The evidence for the Ta'eb is set out in Jeremias *TWNT* IV, p. 863, n. 126. The whole subject was investigated at Length by A. Marx, *Der Messias oder Ta'eb der Samaritaner*, Giessen: Töpelmann, 1909.

85. See Jeremias, *TWNT* IV, pp. 864f. The earliest evidence he offers is R. Aqiba (*ca.* A.D. 90–135). Jeremias is convinced that the Moses-eschatological-redeemer typology is earlier, that it is traceable in CD, Josephus and the NT, and that it played a role in the Messianic revolts of the first century. Cf. Friedrich, *art. cit.*, p. 827.

86. See E. Schweizer, *Lordship and Discipleship*, London: S.C.M. Press (*SBT* 28), 1960, pp. 29f. on Wisd. 2-5.

87. *Contra*, Friedrich, *art. cit.* (note 30), pp. 275ff.

88. *TWNT* IV, p. 864. The Heb. word for redeemer is הוֹשִׁיעַ. This Rabbinic principle appears to combine the Davidic Messiah with traits drawn from the Mosaic prophet, according to Hahn, *Hoheitstitel*, p. 360.

89. See the commentaries. So most recently G. Henton Davies in Peake *ad loc.*

90. Contrary to G. Henton Davies, *ibid.*, there is no reference to "Messiah" in the context.

90a. On the eschatological prophet at Qumran see Appendix to Chapter II, pp. 50–53.

91. Cf. E. Lohse, s.v. ῥαββί, *TWNT* VI, pp. 962ff.

92. W. F. Albright in W. D. Davies-D. Daube, *The Background*, p. 158.

93. "Get to yourself a teacher (*rabh*)."

94. Albright, *ibid.*

95. Cf. W. Foerster, s.v. Κύριος, *TWNT* III, pp. 1083f. The original form was מָרֵא, later abbreviated to מַר with possessive form מָרִי, which, like Rabbi, lost its possessive force in course of time.

96. There are examples in Rabbinic literature of its application to the historical high priest and to Pharaoh. But it is never used there of any eschatological figure.

97. Probably the best treatment of the subject (so Cross, *Qumran*, p. 220, n. 44) is to be found in A. S. van der Woude, *Die messianischen Vorstellungen der Gemeinde von Qumran*, Assen, 1957, which has not, however, been accessible to the present writer. Cf. also M. Burrows, *More Light on the Dead Sea Scrolls*, New York: Viking, 1958, pp. 324–341: Cross, *ibid.*, pp. 219–230. The translations in the text are from Cross, except where noted.

98. So Cross, *ibid.*, p. 224; Hahn, *Hoheitstitel*, p. 367.

99. On the singular "Messiah" in CD cf. above, p. 30 and n. 18. The text has been corrected to conform with the more recently discovered MS of the Damascus Document. In translating "Teacher of the Community" Cross evidently accepts van der Woude's emendation of היחיד (unique) to יחד or יהוד (cf. Hahn, *ibid.*, p. 367, n. 3).

100. So Hahn, *ibid.*, pp. 366f.

101. *NTS* 1956, pp. 12–30, esp., pp. 17–20.

102. See on this question M. Burrows, *More Light*, pp. 325–327.

103. J. M. Allegro, *The Dead Sea Scrolls*, London: Penguin, 1957[3], pp. 148f.

104. *JBL* 75 (1956), pp. 176f.

105. The possibility is entertained by Cross, *ibid.*, p. 228.

106. So Hahn, *ibid.*, p. 368.

107. Also considered as possible by Cross. But the title "expositor of the law" (*dôres hat-tôrah*) corresponds exactly to what we know of the Teacher of Righteousness, and it is difficult to suppose that it could refer to any other figure.

108. Cf. Cross, *ibid.*, p. 228.

109. On this question see M. Burrows, *More Light*, p. 339. The theory that the Teacher underwent crucifixion and resurrection and that he was expected to return at the End rests upon a number of questionable reconstructions of uncertain texts. and upon the false method of the older History of Religions school (see below, p. 90) in interpreting non-Christian documents in Christian categories. Is it likely that the alleged crucifixion and resurrection of the Teacher should be so peripheral to the Qumran documents if they had actually occurred, or at least had played a significant role in their faith?

Chapter III

THE TOOLS: (2) HELLENISTIC JUDAISM

1. *Preliminary Considerations*

IT was, as we have seen, the occupation of Palestine by the Romans which led to a revival both of popular religious-national eschatology and of apocalyptic during the first centuries B.C. and A.D. Here was a combination of religion and political nationalism comparable to the alliance of Roman Catholicism and nationalism in nineteenth-century Ireland or Poland. In the diaspora things were very different. The Jewish communities were flourishing in the Graeco-Roman world, and while, no doubt, sentiment would lead them to sympathize with Messianic movements in Palestine—as American Jews may sympathize with Zionism —the whole question would be for them far more academic. True, they had the Old Testament, and with it its Davidic-Messianic and apocalyptic passages. So neither prophetic nor apocalyptic eschatology were unknown to them. But their own problems were of a different order. They were the kind of problems which faced the Jewish communities of Europe after the French revolution and still more after 1848. How could they adapt the traditions of their forefathers to life in the contemporary world? How could they achieve assimilation without loss of essentials? Hence their attention was diverted from eschatology to the predominant concerns of Hellenistic thought—to cosmology and ethics, to a pre-occupation with life in this present age, rather than with the age to come.[1] Thus the tools which Hellenistic Judaism offered for the Christian interpretation of Jesus of Nazareth were not so much the vocabulary of prophetic eschatology and apocalyptic—although to some extent they could offer these terms in a Greek dress—but ethical and cosmological categories.

2. Christos

First, then, let us look at the terminology of prophetic and apocalyptic eschatology in their Greek dress. In the LXX *ha-mašiah* ("The Messiah") has already been translated ὁ χριστός ("the Christ"). Since, however, the term *mašiah* is never used in an eschatological sense in the MT, it never appears thus in the LXX either. Was the eschatological sense of χριστός ("the Christ") already familiar in Hellenistic Judaism? The only example of it in an eschatological sense is found in the Greek version of Ps. Sol. 17:36 and 18:6, 8. The exact date of this translation is uncertain. Charles can give no more precise date than "prior to A.D. 70".[2] Yet on the whole it is unlikely that a Jewish author should have adopted this term (though of course the LXX could have pulled him in that direction) for the eschatological Messiah after it has been pre-empted by the christians. It is noteworthy that in Aquila, *mašiah* is rendered ἠλειμμένος (anointed), precisely in order to avoid the now fully established Christian usage. Thus we cannot be absolutely certain that χριστός ("the Christ") was already familiar as an eschatological title in pre-Christian Judaism. Yet it was the natural word for both pre-Christian Hellenistic Jews and for Greek speaking Christians to use for *mašiah*. The very rarity of χριστός ("the Christ") in Hellenistic Judaism— just at the time when *mašiah* was becoming so common in Palestinian Judaism—simply confirms the comparative lack of interest for the Messiah in Hellenistic Judaism. More important for us is the fact that χριστός ("the Christ") was not so decidedly eschatological in its associations as was *mašiah* by this time in Palestine. This would facilitate both its de-eschatologization and its reduction to the status of a proper name in Hellenistic Jewish Christianity, processes which we shall trace later.

It would be wrong, however, to suppose that apart from the LXX Hellenistic Judaism knew nothing of eschatology. The tradition was so firmly embedded that even Hellenistic Judaism could not shake it off altogether, although its main interests lay in other directions. 2 Maccabees[3] contains eschatological ideas, though it is a mainly de-messianized individualized eschatology.[4] Only at 2:17f. do we read of the promise of the kingdom, which Klausner[5] takes to imply the restoration of the house of David. But here it is already happening in history. There is even less eschatology in the Book of Wisdom. This book combines an earlier stratum of popular Palestinian piety with a later sophisticated stratum of philosophical religion from Hellenistic Judaism.[6] While the author sometimes thinks of a universal day of judgment in which the righteous are rewarded and the ungodly punished,[7] elsewhere he is thinking of individual reward or judgment at death. There is no place for a Messiah or for the re-establishment of the Davidic kingdom.

Of the Sibylline oracles[8] only No. III provides any relevant material. Both parts contain a reference to a Messianic figure. In 46–50 we hear of a holy ruler, $\check{\alpha}\nu\alpha\xi$ ("Lord") "who shall have rule over the whole earth for all ages of the course of the sun". The term $\chi\rho\iota\sigma\tau\acute{o}s$ ("the Christ") is not used.

Philo of Alexandria (*ca.* 25 B.C.–A.D. 40) has almost completely individualized, spiritualized and allegorized Jewish eschatological teaching, as we should expect. The more surprising is it therefore to find in one of his voluminous works, *De Praemiis et Poenis*, 16:95–97,[9] a futurist national eschatology. Here Philo gives a Messianic interpretation of Num. 24:7 and speaks of a warrior king who is to defeat Israel's enemies and to "establish a sovereignty which none can contest".[10] As Volz says, this passage is a "foreign body" in Philo's teaching. Yet it testifies to the strength of the Messianic tradition, even in Alexandria.

From this hurried survey of the evidence, we may conclude that when the early Christians went to the Hellenistic Jewish world proclaiming Jesus as $\chi\rho\iota\sigma\tau\acute{o}s$ ("the Christ"), they could expect their hearers to associate this term with the eschatological prophecies in the LXX. And yet, on the other hand, the term would not have been so intimately associated with contemporary nationalistic politics as to make it dangerous to use. Further, this lack of strong Messianic associations facilitated the de-messianizing of the term, as we shall see.

7. The Eschatological Prophet

There is—and this is no surprise in the view of the absence of any marked eschatological interest—no evidence in pre-Christian Hellenistic Judaism of the eschatological interpretation of Deut. 18:15ff. Yet, as Philo's *Life of Moses* indicates, there was considerable interest in the figure of Moses. The biblical accounts, which even for Philo remain basic, are embroidered with legendary material depicting Moses as a religious hero of the Hellenistic type, θεῖος ἀνήρ ("divine man"), the very epitome of all human virtues. In all this it is clear that Philo is not merely creating a new tradition, but drawing upon a picture of Moses which was widely accepted in Hellenistic Judaism in Egypt.[16] Although eschatology does not enter into this picture, it did provide some materials for the elaboration of the Moses/redeemer typology in Hellenistic Jewish Christianity. As we shall see, this is evident from Stephen's speech in Acts 7. The popularity of this legend ensured the continuation of this typology long after the concept of Jesus as the eschatological prophet had come to seem totally inadequate for the assessment of his person.

Hellenistic Judaism would have been familiar with the eschatological role of Elijah as it appears in Mal. 3–4; Ecclus. 48. But in its lack of concern with eschatology it does not appear to have shown any lively interest in Elijah as an eschatological figure. In any case, the Elijah typology had already pre-empted for John the Baptist in Palestinian Jewish Christianity.

8. Kyrios ("Lord")

With this term we pass beyond the tools for the eschatological interpretation of Jesus. Such tools as we found in Hellenistic Judaism which had eschatological associations were either de-eschatologized, or were merely retained as part of the tradition. Hellenistic Judaism yields nothing creative for the eschatological interpretation of Jesus. Its contribution lay in the shift that was taking place from the strictly eschatological to the cosmological[17] and ethical interpretation of his person and work.

The first of these non-eschatological terms is *kyrios* (Lord).

This term connotated in classical Greek the rightful authority of a superior over an inferior. It was used by the LXX[18] translators for the tetragrammaton, YHWH. In so doing, they attached to the word *kyrios* a whole complex of associations going far beyond its sociological meaning in Greek and implying the whole Yahwistic theology of the covenant and redemptive history. Also, the title *'adhonai*, which in Greek would be more naturally rendered δεσπότης ("ruler"), is most frequently represented by *kyrios*. Kyrios had fully established itself as the title of Yahweh in the post-LXX period. But in the LXX it is not restricted to a God and can be used in places where *'adhonai* is used of an earthly superior, such as a king. The two uses appear side by side in Ps. 110:1, "The Lord said unto my Lord." In the Hebrew the first "Lord" is the tetragrammaton, the second (the king) is *'adhonai*. The LXX uses Kyrios for both words (εἶπεν ὁ κύριος τῷ κυρίῳ μου).

Here we have a number of tools for the Hellenistic Jewish Christian assessment of Jesus. To begin with, *kyrios* lay to hand as the translation of *mar* (see chapter II, p. 50).[19] This would lead to the application of Ps. 110:1 to Jesus.[20] Again, once κύριος was firmly established as a title for Jesus, this would pave the way for the transference to Jesus of certain LXX passages where in the original κύριος = Heb. YHWH. This process will be traced in detail in chapter VII. It was linguistically impossible in Hebrew and Aramaic, but quite feasible in Greek and on the basis of LXX usage. This does not mean however that the distinction between Jesus and God is blurred, or that Jesus was by now regarded as a divine being in an ontological sense. All that the LXX usage opens up at this stage is a *functional* identity between the exalted Kyrios and the Yahweh-Kyrios of the Old Testament and LXX.

9. *Son of God (Divine Man)*

It is extraordinary how widely German scholarship has accepted the theory that as a christological title in the New Testament, Son of God is derived from the Hellenistic conception of the θεῖος ἀνήρ (divine man). It would appear that this theory was first suggested by W. Bousset in the first edition of his *Kyrios Christos* in 1913.[21] It was then taken up and elaborated by G. P. Wetter[22] and further investigated by H. Windisch[23] and L. Bieler.[24] More recently it has taken on a new lease of life through Bultmann's *Theology of the New Testament*.[25]

Bultmann is not quite clear whether the influence of the Hellenistic divine man concept came into early Christianity directly from Hellenism, or *via* Hellenistic Judaism, for his study does not make a sufficiently clear distinction between Hellenistic Jewish and Hellenistic Gentile Christianity. To have done this is one of the great merits of the recent work of F. Hahn.[26] Accordingly Hahn has contended that the divine man concept had already infiltrated Hellenistic Judaism, and that the term Son of God as used by Hellenistic Jewish Christianity was already coloured by Hebraic-Jewish associations.[27]

The evidence for this penetration of Hellenistic Judaism by the Hellenistic concept of the divine man consists of the *Letter of Aristeas*, 140, Josephus, *Jewish War*, VII, 344, and above all, Philo's *Life of Moses* and other writings. The author of the *Letter of Aristeas* claims for the heroes of the Jewish OT the Hellenistic term ἄνθρωπος θεοῦ, man of God (=divine man.) Josephus similarly employs the Hellenistic adjective θεῖος, "divine", for Moses and the OT prophets. Philo elaborates his picture of Abraham, the OT prophets and above all Moses with traits drawn from the Hellenistic concept of the divine man. He avoids the actual term θεῖος (divine), preferring instead the term θεσπέσιος ἀνήρ, which significantly stresses divine inspiration rather than divine essence.

This impressive theory, which has gained so much currency in the Bultmann school,[28] suffers, even in the form propounded by Hahn—who fully recognizes the extent to which the divine man concept when taken over by Hellenistic Judaism is modified by the OT tradition[29]—from the fact that never in the available evidence is the term υἱὸς θεοῦ ("son of God") used for this concept in Hellenistic Judaism.[30] What is also surprising is that those who polemize against the theory in question have not looked any further in Hellenistic Judaism for any alternative use of the term Son of God.

Now in an article written some years ago[31] Miss Huntress called attention to the fact that the suffering righteous man in Wisd. 2 is called the son of God. She then suggested that it was this picture of the suffering righteous man which was determinative for the use of the term Son of God by the earliest Palestinian church. Unfortunately, the form in which she stated her theory was implausible. It is not impossible, of course, that the Book of Wisdom was familiar to Aramaic speaking Jerusalem Christians. But nowhere else does it appear to be constitutive for the Palestinian Aramaic stratum of the NT. And in any case, in so far as the term Son of God is used in the earliest church, it comes from Ps. 2:7 and the Davidic-Messianic motive. And it is used with reference not to the earthly life of Jesus, but first of his coming at the parousia, and then a little later in connection with his exalted state. Miss Huntress would have had a much stronger case if she had looked instead to Hellenistic Jewish Christianity.

Let us look a little closer at the usage in the Book of Wisdom. The relevant passages are 2:13, 2:16–18, and 5:5. A picture is drawn of faithful Jews who are being persecuted by their gentile neighbours. The devout Jew claims to have a knowledge of God. He is a devout observer of the law (2:12), and because of the resultant strangeness of his manner of life, excites the disapprobation of his pagan neighbours. So they persecute and torture him and put him to death. But God vindicates his righteousness. He calls himself the child ($\pi a\hat{\imath}s$) of God, (2:13) and boasts that God is his father and he himself the son of God ($v\dot{\imath}\grave{o}s\ \theta\epsilon o\hat{v}$).

This picture of the devout Jew is drawn from real life in Alexandria. But it is also partly derived from the picture of the righteous man in the Old Testament and especially the suffering servant of Deutero-Isaiah.[32] According to Bousset,[33] traits of the Hellenistic divine man are also apparent here. There is, e.g., the use of "gnosis", and the claim to be son of God and to have God as Father. In these descriptions, says Bousset, we have left the ground of the Old Testament. It represents "the influx of a new mysterious element into Greek piety"—such as is clearly seen also in 2:23.

Now Bousset may be perfectly right. But at the same time

it must be acknowledged that the author of Wisdom has selected just those elements in the picture of the Hellenistic divine man which are most readily compatible with the OT conception of the righteous man. In the MT of Isaiah 53:11 knowledge (*da'ath*) is attributed to the servant. LXX uses σύνεσις ("understanding"). And the choice of γνῶσις ("knowledge") in Wisd. 2:13 is doubtless influenced by Hellenistic religiosity. But still, the idea is not altogether alien to the OT. Again, we may admit that the individualization of the son of God is due to Hellenistic influence. After all it is an individualization of Israel's corporate sonship of God in the OT, like the concept of God as Father. Perhaps too the use of παῖς θεοῦ in Wisd. 2:13 although it probably means "*child*", was suggested by Isa. 53 LXX.

The author of Wisdom 2 has picked out what will serve his purpose and left much else unused. For instance, he has bypassed those elements in the Hellenistic portrait of the divine man which were incompatible with the OT tradition. He says nothing about the metaphysical origin, of the divine man, his "en-thusiasm" or possession by God, his ability to work miracles as an attestation of his divinity, above all the term "divinity" itself. Philo in his portrait of Moses went somewhat further in this direction, though it is arguable that he just managed to keep within the bounds of the OT tradition. We can well imagine that the author of Wisdom was deliberately and polemically opposing this picture of the righteous man to the Hellenistic concepts of ideal humanity.

Later, in Wisd. 5:5 we read further in reference to the persecuted righteous man:

> Why has he been numbered among the sons of God,
> And why is his lot among the saints?

In other words the devout Alexandrian Jew is counted among the saints and sons of God in the OT, the OT heroes. We see here under the influence of Hellenistic religious terminology the emergence of "son of God" as a title for the OT worthies, for Abraham, Moses and the prophets.[34] Now, as we have already hinted, Jesus was already identified with the Mosaic eschatological prophet in Palestinian Judaism. Moreover, he had already been identified in the same stratum with the future coming and, a little later, with the already regnant Davidic Messiah, the Son of God. What then could be more natural than that the term, Son of God, transplanted to a Hellenistic Jewish environment, should have assumed wider aspects derived from the Hellenistic Jewish concept of the son of God as the righteous man? Thus it became a tool for the understanding not only of the work of the redeemer at the parousia and as the exalted One in his church, but also of his earthly existence. That the divine man of Hellenistic religiosity has played a role in contributing to this composite picture of the son of God in Hellenistic Judaism we need not deny. But it was a contribution of form rather than content. Certainly this interest in the individual achievement of heroes of the past is Hellenistic rather than biblical. Certainly, too, the selection of certain features rather than of others for the portrait, e.g. the knowledge of God, is characteristically Hellenistic. But the dominant features of the Hellenistic Jewish son of God are biblical—faithful adherence to the law amid persecution and final vindication by God.

10. *Wisdom*

The concept of Wisdom in Judaism goes back to the Old Testament, and it may be thought more appropriate had it been included in the chapter on the christological tools provided by Hebraic Judaism. The reason for presenting it here is that all the evidence suggests that it was on Hellenistic Jewish soil that the concept of wisdom was first exploited for christological use. This is not surprising. For after an early start (Job 28:23–28; Prov. 1–9, especially 8:22–31) *ḥokhma*, wisdom, was not much further developed in Palestinian Judaism. In the Rabbinic literature all the tendencies that might have contributed to development of *ḥokhma* are syphoned off to the concept of Torah. *Ḥokhma* plays a certain role in Apocalyptic[35] and a slightly more prominent role in the Qumran literature,[36] but neither of these sources provided direct tools for NT wisdom Christology. It is in Hellenistic Christianity that we first find the influence of the σοφία (wisdom) speculation.

To understand how *sophia* was developed in Hellenistic Judaism we must first take a look at *ḥokhma* in the OT.

In Job 28:23–28 wisdom is an entity beyond the reach of man. Man cannot by searching find it out. But God found it out and used it in the creation of the world. Here wisdom is a pre-existent entity, independent of God, but scarcely as yet a hypostatized figure.

In Proverbs wisdom is often no more than a prudential ethical concept, but there are passages in which it plays a religious role and becomes a matter for theological speculation. Wisdom is something men must search after to acquire truth and the knowledge of God. She is the agent of revelation (8:1–21). In the central passage, 8:22–31, the nature of wisdom is described at length. She is a creation of God (contrast Job, where God sought her out), and was brought into being before all creation. She was present when God created the world, though as yet she played no active role in creation. The picture painted is that of a child in his father's workshop (vv. 30f.). Wisdom here is figuratively personified, but is hardly as yet a hypostatization.

In Hellenistic Judaism *sophia* is much further developed. In Ecclesiasticus there are exhortations to pursue her reminiscent of Proverbs, and still within Palestinian terms (6:18–31; 14:20–27). But in 24:3–22 she speaks for herself, declaring that she has proceeded from the mouth of God (and is thus pre-existent). She pervades the whole creation, and seeks to find a resting place among the peoples of the world. But all apparently reject her save Israel. There she becomes the mediator of revelation.

The concept of wisdom as the mediator of revelation is much more developed in the Book of Wisdom. She is now fully hypostatized. She is distinct from, yet closely related to, the being of God himself:

> She is a breath of the power of God,
> and a pure emanation from the glory of the almighty;
> . . . . . .
> For she is a reflection (ἀπαύγασμα) of eternal light,
> A spotless mirror of the working of God,
> and an image (εἰκών) of his goodness. (7:25f.)

She is the agent of creation, "the fashioner (τεχνῖτις) of all things" (7:22). She pervades the whole created universe

73

(7:24), and is the mediator of revelation and truth to men (7:21f.). As the agent of revelation she dwells with God (8:3f.) and with those who accept her she likewise comes to dwell (8:2b, 9, 16, 18a).

As we would expect, wisdom plays a prominent part in the thinking of Philo. The term occurs over two hundred times in his writings according to Wilckens.[37] The classic treatment of the subject is Philo's *De Migratione Abrahami*. For Philo, Abraham is the supreme example of the wise man, who leaves his native land (the visible world) to seek wisdom. As is commonly recognized,[38] the Philonic *sophia* is a highly syncretistic product, composed of elements derived from the earlier *ḥokhma* tradition, from Platonic and Stoic sources and even from the Isis mysteries. This makes Philo hardly typical of Hellenistic Judaism. But the general outline of the Hellenistic Jewish concept as we have found it above all in the Book of Wisdom can still be discerned in Philo, e.g. in his exposition of Prov. 8:22 (*de Ebrietate* 30f.). Here again, *sophia* is the companion of God and the agent of creation as well as of revelation.

Wilckens insists that it is inadequate simply to attribute this development to a process of increasing hypostatization within Judaism. Already in Proverbs, the concept of *ḥokhma* had been taken over from an ancient oriental myth. For long, the borrowing continued to be restrained (Job, Proverbs, and parts of Ecclesiasticus). But in the Hellenistic period the borrowing became increasingly uninhibited. This is seen above all in the idea of wisdom as the personified companion of God who also becomes the companion of the wise man. A succinct outline of the wisdom myth can be found in Eth. Enoch 42.[39]

> Wisdom found no place where she might dwell;
> Then a dwelling-place was assigned her in the heavens.
> Wisdom went forth to make her dwelling among the children of men,
> And found no dwelling-place.
> Wisdom returned to her place,
> And took her seat among the angels.

This is the myth that underlies each successive stage of the development of the wisdom concept in Judaism. It appears in various forms, sometimes more Judaized, sometimes less.

Characteristic of the myth is Wisdom's descent, her rejection, the "resignation" and return to heaven.

The concept of *sophia* was thus firmly established in Hellenistic Judaism, and lay ready to hand as a christological tool for Hellenistic Jewish Christianity. It offered the possibility of an interpretation of Christ as the pre-existent agent of creation and of the government in the world, and as the agent of revelation of religious truth (especially in the terms εἰκών ("image") and ἀπαύγασμα ("reflection") to mankind in general, in Israel's history in particular, and in the kerygma of the church. Finally, it offered the possibility of the interpretation of the historical emergence of Jesus in terms of a descent from heaven, and thus made an important contribution to the doctrine of the incarnation.

11. *Logos*

The Logos concept of Hellenistic Judaism is closely related to Wisdom. In Wisd. 9:1b–2a, the two terms appear in synonymous parallelism:

> who hast made all things by thy word (ἐν λόγῳ σου)
> and by wisdom hast formed man. . . .

The Logos plays a very prominent part in Philo, in whose writings it occurs more than 1,300 times, according to Kleinknecht.[40] It is used in many different senses and contexts. In one of them it appears as the divine logos in close association with *sophia*. The relation between *sophia* and *logos* is a very complicated question[41] and need not detain us now. In Philo the divine logos has the same highly syncretistic background as *sophia*, and his logos doctrine must not be taken as typical of Hellenistic Judaism. Philo is a highly daring thinker, given to a more adventurous syncretism than any other Hellenistic Jewish writer. Like *sophia*, the logos is distinct from, yet intimately related to, the being of God. He is the son of God[41a]—so much so that Philo can go so far as to call the logos δεύτερος θεός ("second God").[42] Like *sophia* in Wisd. 7:26, the Philonic logos is the image (εἰκών) of God, and the agent of creation[43] and revelation[44] (cf. Wisd. 7:7–14, etc.).

We have deliberately picked out those features of the

Philonic logos which are the same as those ascribed to wisdom. Both Philo and the Book of Wisdom witness to a gradual substitution within Hellenistic Judaism of the term *logos* for *sophia*. It is sufficient to explain this process from the popularity of the term in Hellenistic philosophy,[45] without postulating, with Bultmann,[46] further direct borrowing from "gnostic" mythology.

Given the sophia myth as it had already established itself within Hellenistic Judaism, and given this terminological shift from *sophia* to *logos*, we have already sufficient background to account for the use of *logos* in the Johannine prologue. To say, as Bultmann does, that the Johannine prologue is derived from "oriental gnosis" is confusing, quite apart from the question-begging term, gnosis. For in the Johannine prologue it is not a question of direct borrowing from oriental mythology, but the direct adaptation to Christology from Hellenistic Judaism of a concept which had long been firmly embedded in Judaism, but which from time to time had received enrichments from extra-Jewish mythology.

12. The "First" or "Heavenly Man"

English-speaking readers are familiar with discussion of Philo's idea of the two Adams.[47] The relevant passages are:

de Opificio Mundi 134: ". . . he who was after the divine image was an idea of type or seal, and object of thought only, incorporeal, neither male nor female, by nature incorruptible." [The passage continues to stress at great length Adam's physical beauty and moral perfection.]

Leg. All. I, 31f.: "There are two types of man: the one a heavenly, the other an earthly. The heavenly man being made in the image of God is altogether without part or lot in the corruptible or terrestrial substance . . . the heavenly man was not moulded but stamped in the image of God."

Quaest. in Gen. I, 4 (On Gen. 2-7)[48] [The passage distinguishes between the heavenly and earthly man, continuing]: "man made according to the image of God is intelligible and a likeness of the archetype so far as this is visible."

It is clear that certain features of the First or Heavenly man are the peculiarities of Philo himself—notably the

Platonizing in *de Opificio Mundi*, and probably also the differentiating exegesis of Gen. 1:27 and 2:7. Yet the perfection of Adam is a fairly common theme in pre-Christian Judaism, to some extent in its Palestinian, though more markedly in its Hellenistic, form. In Palestinian Apocalyptic we have 2 Enoch 30:5–14, where it is stated that only Eve fell. Satan proved powerless against Adam! In Hellenistic Judaism brief allusions to Adam's perfection occur in Ecclus. 49:16 and in Wisd. 10:1f. A more elaborate picture is given in the *Life of Adam and Eve*, 12–17.[49] There is much here to support the thesis of the History of Religions school[50] that this development of the Adam tradition is inexplicable from within Judaism or simply as an interpretation of Gen. 1:27. Here, it is claimed, is an enrichment of the Jewish tradition with material borrowed from outside sources, namely the oriental myth of the Heavenly Man,[51] such as appears in the Iranian figure of Gayomart.

Unfortunately much of the discussion has been bewildering because of the insistence of the History of Religions school on speaking of the Heavenly Man *redeemer* myth. It is probably true, as Cullmann has pointed out, that both the eschatological redemptive figure of the Son of man and the Heavenly man go back ultimately to the same source. But this has happened along two separate lines of development,[52] one within Palestinian and the other within Hellenistic Judaism. One line produces the wholly eschatological figure of the Son of man, who though pre-existent is inactive, and of whom nothing is said about his creation in the divine image. The other line produces the glorification of Adam, of whom nothing is said about his eschatological functions. Yet Cullmann maintains that in the NT, notably in 1 Cor. 15, the two separate lines converge again. For Paul the Heavenly man, identified with Christ, is also the eschatological Son of man.

It must however, be strongly insisted that in Hellenistic Judaism the Heavenly or First man is always a ctisiological figure. And although Paul brings the man from heaven into connection with the eschatological redeemer, he is not thereby bringing together again the Heavenly man and the Son of man, however much it looks like it at first sight in 1 Cor. 15, where the Heavenly man is brought into connection with the parousia. For this latter feature is a peculiar development in St. Paul, and occurred *after* the term Son of man had been replaced by "Christ" in the context of the parousia (1 Cor. 15:22f.).[53] What Hellenistic Judaism provided as a tool for the interpretation of Christ in its Adam doctrine was a term which could offer the possibility of a contrast between the obedience of Adam and the obedience of Jesus in his earthly life, and the respective effects of that disobedience or obedience. The Palestinian eschatological concept of the Son of man has nothing to do with the First or Heavenly man of Hellenistic Judaism, despite their probable remote common origin.

Finally, it is to be noted that there is some connection between *sophia, logos*, and the First or Heavenly man. All are equated with the image of God.[54] The identification of the logos and the Man is expressly stated in Philo, *de Conf. Ling.* 146: "And many names are his (*sc.* of the logos), for he is called . . . his Word, and the Man after his image."

From Philo we may conclude that the three terms, *sophia, logos* and heavenly or first man all have a common mythological background. Whether the underlying myth was eschatological and redemptive[55] as well as ctisiological and revelatory need not concern us here. In Hellenistic Judaism the myth appears only in its ctisiological and revelatory form. The question of the "gnostic redeemer myth" will be discussed in the following chapter.

Meanwhile, let us note that in the three concepts *sophia, logos* and heavenly or first man, Hellenistic Judaism provided for the Christian church a rich collection of tools whereby the concept of the divine sonship of Jesus could be enlarged to include creative and revelatory functions.

13. *The High Priest*

In Philo the logos is further identified with the High Priest. In one group of passages (*de Fuga et Inventione* 108; *de Spec. Leg.* I 230; *de Gigantibus* 52 and *de Migr. Abr.* 102) this identification is made in the context of an allegorization of the Levitical High Priest.

In *de Fug.* 108ff. we are told that the High Priest is not a man, but a divine word (λόγον θεῖον). In 109 his complete sinlessness is stressed; the High Priest is undefiled (ἀμιάντος) because he has God for his Father and Wisdom for his mother. In 110 the high priestly vestments are allegorized and equated with the world (κόσμος). In this paragraph the High Priest is called ὁ πρεσβύτατος τοῦ ὄντος λόγος, "the senior logos of him who is". In 112 he is called "the word of him that is the bond of all existence". In 115 the High Priest is said to be the embodiment of perfection, its highest form, undefiled by earthly things. In 116ff., Philo has to come to grips with the difficulty that scripture speaks of and makes provision for the death of the High Priest. He explains this as meaning the removal of the logos from the soul. It will be seen here that the High Priest-logos represents two different concepts. On the one hand, he is a cosmological figure (110, 112). On the other hand he is psychological, the logos in the soul of man (115).

In *de Spec. Leg.* I 230 Philo is concerned to explain away— for him the logos is the sinless High Priest—the provisions made in Lev. 4:3 for dealing with the sins of the High Priest himself.

In *de Gig.* 52, there is an allegorical interpretation of Lev. 16:2, 34 in application to the "High Priest logos".

In *de Migr. Abr.* 102 the vestments of the Levitical High Priest are allegorized and applied to the "High Priest-logos". The vestments have two types of beauty. The one is derived from "the realm of pure intellect", the other from the realm of sense perception.

The second group of passages identifies the logos-high priest, not with the Levitical High Priest, but with Melchizedek. The passages are: *Leg. All.* III 79–82; *de Congressu* 99; *de Abrahamo* 235.

In *Leg. All.* III 79–82 we have an allegorical interpretation of Melchizedek. First comes an exposition of his title, king of Salem. As in Heb. 7:2 this is explained to mean "king of peace". The bread and wine which he brought are allegorized. The wine stands for divine intoxication! The central passage is 88:

But let Melchizedek instead of water (which the Ammonites, etc. refused to bring) offer wine, and give to souls strong drink, that they may be seized by a divine intoxication, more sober than sobriety itself. For he is a priest, even Reason (Greek: λόγος).

The passage from *de Congressu* contains a casual reference to Melchizedek as the holder of the priesthood: presumably Philo has the *logos* in mind here, but he does not explicitly refer to it.

In *de Abrahamo* 235 Philo gives a "moralizing paraphrase" (the phrase is Wuttke's) of Gen. 14:17–20. Melchizedek is not mentioned by name, though it is clear from the context that he is the "High Priest" in question. Nor is he identified with the *logos*. Although this passage is usually quoted, it is not really relevant to our present consideration.

Thus both the Levitical High Priest and Melchizedek are indifferently allegorized and equated with the *logos*. Also, the *logos*, thus equated, is used in two different senses. Sometimes he is a transcendent figure, belonging to the upper world, and having cosmic functions. At other times he is psychologized, becoming the principle of reason within the soul of man. This ambivalence is clearly due to Philo's syncretism.

What is the source of Philo's speculation? H. Windisch is convinced that Philo is drawing upon the same tradition as the author of Hebrews. Both writers put this common tradition to their own different uses. Since both Philo and the author of Hebrews come from a Hellenistic Jewish background, one is tempted to suppose that the high-priest-logos-Melchizedek tradition was a pre-Philonic development within Hellenistic Judaism. Unfortunately, we have no clear evidence for such a development. The nearest we come to it is in Ecclus. 45:6–22 and Wisd. 18:24. Both passages show a tendency to glorify the Aaronic High Priest as described in Leviticus, while the second passage occurs in a context in which the whole of Israel's sacred history is interpreted as the work of the divine wisdom. Perhaps here we see the beginnings of a speculation (or a further borrowing of mythology) which ascribed to wisdom as the cosmic mediator a high-priestly role.

E. Käsemann,[58] following M. Friedlander, has gone much further and suggested that Philo was borrowing upon a gnostic redeemer myth, in which *sophia*, *logos*, and the First Man—a single figure under different names—were already identified as a high priest. This redeemer myth, Käsemann supposes, is independently the source of Philo's speculation, and of the Epistle to the Hebrews' identification of Jesus with the High Priest after the order of Melchizedek. The flaw in this theory in the form in which Käsemann has stated it is that in Philo the logos-High Priest has only cosmological and psychological, not soteriological functions. The gnostic redeemer myth will be discussed in the next chapter. But for the moment we can safely say that there is no trace of a *redeemer* myth in Hellenistic Judaism, but only of a cosmological and revelatory myth. We may suppose that Philo has taken this cosmological myth and has given it a psychological twist, while the author of Hebrews has taken the same myth and given it an eschatological-soteriological application.

NOTES ON CHAPTER III

1. Cf. R. Bultmann, *Primitive Christianity in its Contemporary Setting* London: Thames and Hudson, 1956, p. 100 (on Philo).

2. *Pseudepigrapha*, p. 628.

3. 2 Macc. is an abridgment of an earlier work by a Hellenistic Jew, Jason of Cyrene. In Charles, vol. I *Apocrypha*, the original work is dated "roughly after 130," the abridged version "later than the first half of the first century B.C." (p. 129).

4. For individual resurrection: 2 Macc. 7:14, 23; 12:43f., 14:46.

5. J. Klausner, *Messianic Idea*, p. 263.

6. P. Volz, *Eschatologie*, p. 58.

7. Corporate and historical eschatology: day of judgment: Wisd. 3:13, 18; reward of the righteous: 3:7-9, 13f; punishment of the ungodly: 1:9, 3:10. Individualized eschatology: reward of the righteous: 3:1ff., 5:5; punishment of the ungodly: 1:6; 2:24; 3:18; 4:18f.

8. An Alexandrian work, but in close touch with Palestine. The oldest part, III 97-828, dates from early Maccabean times (Volz, p. 54), from *ca.* 140 B.C. (Klausner, p. 371); III 1-92 dates from the Roman occupation, i.e. after 63 B.C.

9. Throughout this book texts from Philo are quoted from the Loeb edition, ed. F. H. Colson and G. H. Whitaker.

10. P. Volz, *Eschatologie*, p. 60.

11. Statistics from Zimmerli, *Servant*, p. 35: παῖς (παίδιον, παιδάριον) 340 times; δοῦλος 327 times; οἰκέτης 63 times; θεράπων 46 times.

12. *Ibid.*, pp. 40–42. It is curious that Miss Hooker (ch. II, note 71) pays no attention to the LXX translators of the Servant Songs in her discussion of Jewish interpretation of the Servant (pp. 53–61).

13. Zimmerli, *Servant*, p. 41 tries to link the translation of יוֹנֵק by παιδίον in Isa. 53:2 with Isa. 9:5 where παιδίον also occurs. But in view of the atomistic exegesis customary at the time (a fact to which Miss Hooker has rightly called attention) this linkage is very doubtful.

14. *Servant*, p. 51.

15. *Ibid.*, p. 53. But the examples from Wisdom are hardly collective; they are rather references to the individual righteous man. Thus παῖς θεοῦ merges with the Hellenistic υἱὸς θεοῦ for which see below, p. 66.

16. See Jeremias, *TWNT* IV, s.v. Μωυσῆς, pp. 854–856.

17. "Cosmological" is used here to include both the post-resurrection Lordship of Christ and also the function of the pre-existent agent of creation.

18. The reason for this is that the name יהוה' was never pronounced (except by the high priest once a year on the day of atonement), and the title אֲדֹנָי substituted. See C. H. Dodd, *The Bible and the Greeks*, London: Hodder and Stoughton, 1935, pp. 3–24.

19. It is highly important to note that אֲדֹנָי is never used in Hebrew of the Davidic (or Aaronic) Messiah (cf. Hahn, *Hoheitstitel*, p. 114). Thus Ps. 110:1 could only have been applied to Jesus after Κύριος had already established itself as the accepted rendering for מָר as an invocation of the coming Son of Man.

20. The designation of Jesus as Κύριος is not initially derived from the LXX. Cf. Bultmann, *Theology* I, p. 124.

21. The first edition is inaccessible to me. In the second edition see pp. 52–57.

22. G. P. Wetter, *Der Sohn Gottes (FRLANT NF 9)*, Göttingen: Vandenhoeck u. Ruprecht, 1916.

23. H. Windisch, *Paulus and Christus (UNT 24)*, Leipzig: J. C. Hinrich, 1936, pp. 24–89.

24. L. Bieler, ΘΕΙΟΣ ΑΝΗΡ, 2 vols, Vienna, 1934–35.

25. Bultmann, *Theology* I, pp. 128–133.

26. *Hoheitstitel*, p. 11. Hahn notes that the older distinction between the earliest Palestinian church and Pauline Christianity was next further divided into Palestinian, pre-Pauline Hellenistic and Pauline by Heitmüller (1912), followed by Bousset and later by Bultmann. Dibelius then paved the way for a further distinction between Jewish Hellenistic and gentile Hellenistic Christianity, in his essay *Jungfrauensohn und Krippenkind*, 1932, reprinted in *Botschaft und Geschichte* I (see ch. II, note 32), pp. 1–78. It is the great merit of Hahn that he has worked with this fourfold stratification in NT Christianity throughout his book.

27. Hahn, *Hoheitstitel*, pp. 292–294; cf. Jeremias, *TWNT* IV, pp. 852–878, esp. 854–856.

28. cf. also H. Braun, *ZThK* 54 (1957), pp. 341–377, esp. 353–360. J. M. Robinson, *JBR* 30, 3 (1962), p. 203, where he refers to an unpublished dissertation of D. Georgi, "Die Gegner des Paulus in II Kor. 2:14–7 und 10–13" (Heidelberg, 1957). (Since published, see below, ch. VIII, n. 60.)

29. *Hoheitstitel*, p. 295, n. 2, but he adds, "the material pre-suppositions for this were absent, however".

30. J. Bieneck, *Sohn Gottes also Christusbezeichnung der Synoptiker (AThANT* 21), Zurich: Zwingli-Verlag, 1951, pp. 27–34; O. Cullmann *Christology* (see ch. II, note 26), pp. 275ff. The reason for this failure is that both writers are concerned to find a home for "son of God" in its widest (not merely Davidic-Messianic) sense in Palestinian Christianity, and even in the sayings and self-consciousness of Jesus himself. But since the wider use of "son of God" (as opposed to its strictly Messianic use) belongs to the Hellenistic Jewish stratum of the NT (as will be shown later), we must—and here the Bultmann school are right—look for the tools of this extended usage within Hellenistic Judaism.

31. E. Huntress, *JBL* 54 (1935), pp. 117–126.

32. So, rightly, Miss Huntress, *ibid.*, p. 122.

33. *Kyrios Christos*, 1921, pp. 48 and 53.

34. Further references to "son of God" as a recognized type in Wisd. 12:19c, 21a; 16:26a (in 16:26 the author refers to the people of Israel as the "son of God", thus showing that the individualized use, however much it may owe to the Hellenistic environment, has its roots in the OT corporate usage); Ecclus. 4:10.

35. E.g. Eth. En. 93:8; 94:5; 98:3; 4 Ezra 5:9f.; Syr. Bar. 48:36. *Hokhma* in apocalyptic usage is the plan of God in *Heilsgeschichte*.

36. E.g. 1 QS 3:64 (the spirit of truth imparts "almighty wisdom"); 4:22 ("wisdom of the sons of heaven"); 4:24 ("they walk in wisdom and folly"); 11:5f. ("my eye has beheld wisdom"); 1 Q Hab. 9:23f. ("for all the seasons of God come to pass at the appointed time according to his decree ... in the mystery of his wisdom"); 1 QM 10:16 ("we know these things because of thy wisdom"); CD 2:3 ("wisdom and knowledge are his ministers"). Thus in the Qumran writings wisdom appears in three senses: 1. the revealed knowledge possessed by the sect; 2. the agent of divine revelation; 3. the plan of *Heilsgeschichte*. The usages reflect either OT *hokhma* or the apocalyptic usage. There is no significant developlent and no further borrowing of the extra-Jewish sophia myth at Qumran.

37. *TWNT* VII, s.v. σοφία, pp. 501f.

38. U. Wilckens, *ibid.*, Cullmann, *Christology*, p. 256.

39. This section is an interpolation of quite different origin from the text of the *Similitudes*: see U. Wilckens, *Weisheit und Torheit (BHTh* 26), Tübingen: J. C. B. Mohr (P. Siebeck), 1959, pp. 160–162. Wilckens' article in *TWNT* (note 38) is largely a summary of his book.

40. *TWNT* IV, s.v. Λόγος, p. 86.

41. On the relation between sophia and logos see E. R. Goodenough, *By Light, Light*, New Haven: Yale University Press, 1935; H. A. Wolfson,

Philo, Cambridge (Mass.): Harvard University Press, 1947, I, 253–261. In *de Fuga et Inventione* 97 it is stated that logos is the fountain of sophia, and a little later (109) that sophia is the mother of the logos. In *Leg. All.* I, 65 they are identified: ἡ δὲ (σοφία) ἐστιν ὁ θεοῦ λόγος. It is clear that as a result of his syncretism Philo uses logos in a variety of senses. But one of the basic senses is as an equivalent to sophia. In such passages what is said about logos is derived from the sophia myth.

41a. E.g. *de Agricultura* 51: τὸν ὀρθὸν αὐτοῦ λόγον καὶ πρωτόγονον υἱόν.

42. *Qu. Gen.* II, 62. In *Leg. All.* II, 86 there is a more cautious statement: δεύτερος ὁ θεοῦ λόγος—the logos is second to God.

43. *Spec. Leg.* I, 81.

44. Logos does not frequently appear in Philo as the agent of revelation. Kleinknecht (note 40) gives no references. But see *de Somniis* I, 190, where the divine logos is said to be responsible for the revelations conveyed in dreams.

45. So Kleinknecht, *art. cit.*, p. 87.

46. R. Bultmann, *Das Evangelium des Johannes* (*K-EKNT*) 1950[11], pp. 8ff. Bultmann is right in maintaining that the Philonic usage is not to be explained from the philosophical use. The borrowing is merely terminological, the term being then wedded to the sophia myth.

47. See most recently, Cullmann, *Christology*, pp. 148–150.

48. Cullmann ignores this passage in giving the Philonic evidence.

49. The passage is too long for quotation in full. See the text in Charles, *Pseudepigrapha* II, pp. 123–154, and for date and provenance *ibid.*, pp. 126ff. (Hellenistic Jewish, probably 1st century A.D.).

50. W. Bousset, *Die Religion des Judentums*, pp. 352ff.

51. For literature see ch. II, note 38.

52. In a remarkable discussion in *Christology*, pp. 144–150, Cullmann explains the "inner necessity" for this separate development.

53. On the relation of the Son of man to the Heavenly Man in early Christianity Hahn writes (*Hoheitstitel*, p. 21): "We must be cautious in assuming too hastily (with Cullmann) a relationship between other developments of the First Man doctrine, e.g. the Adam/Christ typology in Paul."

54. Cf. e.g. Wisd. 7:26 with Philo, *de Confusione Linguarum*, 147.

55. E.g. R. Bultmann, *Johannes*, pp. 8–15.

56. For discussions of the Philonic high-priest-logos and the Melchizedek speculations see the literature given in Cullmann, *Christology*, p. 85, nn. 2–8, and add H. Windisch, *Der Hebräerbrief* (*HNT*) 1931[2], excursus: "Die Melchisedekspekulation," pp. 61–63, and *TWNT* III (Schrenk, s.v. ἀρχιέρευς), pp. 271–274.

57. See note 56.

58. *Das wandernde Gottesvolk*, Göttingen: Vandenhoeck u. Ruprecht, 1939 (*FRLANT* NF 37), pp. 125–140.

Käsemann finds further traces of this First Man-High Priest redeemer myth in late Jewish speculation about Adam as High Priest and successive incarnations of the High Priest-First Man in Melchizedek, Shem,

Moses, Elijah, the archangel Michael, and the figure Metatron. Further evidence is in documents much later than the NT, but according to Käsemann they all enshrine much older traditions. Further traces of it in the NT occur also, according to Käsemann, at Rev. 1:13 (Christ as Anthropos and High Priest) and 11:3ff. (Elijah as Messianic High Priest).

Chapter IV

THE TOOLS: (3) HELLENISTIC GENTILE

1. *Preliminary Considerations*

IN our examination of the influence of the Hellenistic
concept of the divine man upon Hellenistic Judaism
we saw how Hellenistic Jews appropriated those aspects
of that concept which were compatible with their own
tradition. They used the terminology—son of God, and
sometimes even the adjective θεῖος ("divine"). They
selected for emphasis those elements in their own tradition
which found a corresponding emphasis in the concepts of the
surrounding world. They ignored or rejected those elements
which they felt to be incompatible with their own tradition,
and even polemized against them. Yet there was also an unconscious assimilation of some of the gentile ways of looking
at things. It is antecedently probable that when the early
Christians came to preach the Christian kerygma to the
purely gentile world—as in the Pauline mission—they
followed the same cautious procedure. They were not afraid
to borrow the terminology of the gentile world—especially
when the terms in question were already in use in the
Palestinian and Hellenistic Jewish Christian mission. They
were prepared to select for emphasis those elements in the
already existing Christian tradition which had counterparts
in the gentile world. And they rejected and combated those
features of the gentile tradition which were radically incompatible with the Christian kerygma. Yet at the same time
there was an unconscious adoption of some gentile points of
view.

In both the Pauline and the non-Pauline Hellenistic
mission—e.g. in the tradition underlying Johannine Christianity and I Peter—this procedure was necessary and
inevitable. In a community such as Antioch the gentile

Christians had already lived on the fringe of the synagogue prior to their conversion, and with them the Hellenistic Jewish tradition (LXX) was dominant. But in communities such as Corinth the gentile element was dominant, and it was in such churches that the Christian missionaries had to come to terms with the previous traditions of the converts. In this chapter we shall be investigating the christological tools provided by the gentile world.

It will be convenient to divide our investigation into three main areas: the imperial cultus, the mystery religions, and pagan "gnosticism".[1]

2. *The Imperial Cultus*

There is no need here to trace the spread of ruler-worship from the orient through the diadochoi (i.e. successors of Alexander the Great), who ruled the Hellenistic world from 323 until the mid-first century B.C., and how the Roman Caesars took over this cultus for themselves ready-made in the east and gradually encouraged it in the west.[2] Here we are concerned with some of the vocabulary of the imperial cultus.

First, there is the term *kyrios*.[3] As we have seen, this was originally a sociological term, used of a superior in relation to his inferior. It was not in itself a religious word, and although there are a few instances of its use for a Greek deity from the time of Pindar down to the Roman empire, this concept was not constitutive for Greek religion. Generally to address a deity as "Lord" was slavish and oriental—unworthy of the democratic Greek. It is only under the influence of the oriental cults that flooded the Greek world after Alexander's conquest that it became a constitutive religious title.

The earliest evidence for *kyrios* as applied to a ruler is from Egypt, where the term is frequently attested between 64 and 50 B.C.[4] The earliest evidence of its application to the Roman emperor is also from Egypt (Augustus in 12 B.C.),[5] and from then on the examples multiply.

Foerster[6] insists that *kyrios* as applied to the Roman emperors does not by itself connote divinity. It does so only in combination with θεός (god). When used alone, he maintains, it still retains its primary sociological sense. Cullmann, however, while recognizing that in theory this was so holds that in practice it would be very difficult to separate religion and politics in this connection.[7] In the Greek speaking, eastern part of the empire the emperor was accorded divine honours. *Kyrios* too was by this time becoming an increasingly familiar designation of the cult deities. Hence it would have surely been impossible to dissociate *kyrios*, when used alone of the emperor, from its religious associations. Cullmann is surely right. The distinction between the newer religious and the original sociological use of κύριος would be apparent only to the academic mind. By the time of Nero it had certainly been forgotten, for in a Greek inscription dating from A.D. 66 Nero is hailed as "Lord of the whole world",[8] an ascription which undoubtedly implies divinity. The imperial cultus is not of course the origin of the Christian use of *kyrios* for Jesus. Whether the title contributed any essential content to Christology will be discussed later.

In close connection with the title *kyrios*, the appellation θεός, god, was used without inhibition in the imperial cultus.[9] The early Christians were very restrained in calling Jesus God, and it is not frequent until Ignatius.[10] But in John 20:28, in one of the latest strata of the gospel material, the risen Jesus is addressed in a formula which, as Deissmann notes,[11] could have been lifted straight from the imperial cultus: "My Lord and my God." That the emperor could be called a god would undoubtedly facilitate the ascription of this appellation to Jesus. In a world which was used to the imperial cultus the kind of scruples which the Jewish mind would have against it would be less operative. What the emperor falsely claimed to be is true of Christ!

The emperor is sometimes called the son of God (υἱός [τοῦ] θεοῦ).[11a] As we have seen, this term first came into Christian usage from Davidic Messianism, and then took on associations from the Jewish Hellenistic modification of the Hellenistic divine man and from the sophia myth, so quite obviously the imperial cultic use was in no way creative or constitutive for Christian use. At the same time, however, we must suspect an influence on the popular level. It is not for nothing that of the various christological terms which the Hellenistic Jewish missionaries brought to the Hellenistic world, it was the two which were also prominent in the imperial cultus, *kyrios* and son of God, which "stuck".

In the ruler cults the term σωτήρ, saviour,[12] was first ascribed to the Ptolemeys in thankfulness for the benefits of their rule. It meant no more originally than *"Wir danken unserm Führer"*. But since as an ancient title of Zeus it already had religious associations it quickly acquired a religious significance when used for the ruler. *Kaisar soter* had become one of the regular slogans of the imperial cultus by the first century A.D. The word σωτήρ was of course also used in connection with the oriental religions. So its appearance in the later strata of the NT as a christological term cannot be derived exclusively from the imperial cultus. But in such a formula as "the epiphany of our Saviour, Jesus Christ" (2 Tim. 1:10)[13] it is obvious that this is *one* source of the term. It was borrowed in the same way as General Booth took tunes from the dance hall for his Salvation Army—"Why should the devil have all the good tunes?". Nevertheless the content of the salvation brought by Jesus is very different from the "we've never had it so good" salvation conferred by the political rulers. It is determined rather by the OT *yaša'* and the eschatological redemption associated with the Mosaic prophet.

Thus we see that the use of tools from the imperial cultus is of a marginal character: there is little or no direct introduction of vocabulary from that source. Only on the popular level may it have contributed something to christological understanding. On the official level it often determines the selection, but never intentionally the content of the vocabulary.

3. *The Mystery Religions*

The mystery cults fall into two main classes.[14] First, there are the older Greek mysteries. These include the Eleusinian mysteries, the cult of Dionysus, and the Orphic mysteries. Second, there are the Oriental mysteries. These include Cybele and Attis (Phrygia), Adonis and Atargatis (Syria), Isis-Osiris and Serapis (Egypt), and the much later and very different post-Christian Mithras cult (Persia). Originally, nearly all of these mysteries were fertility or vegetation rites.

They were also of a purely local character. Later on, they developed into more spiritual religions, offering not merely physical fertility, but a blessed immortality after death. It was in this form that they became great missionary religions and competitors with Christianity.

Fifty years or so ago, wild theories were being promulgated about the relation between the mysteries and Christianity. It was held that Christianity was essentially a plagiarization from the mystery cults. The myth of a dying and rising God, which was held to be basic to these cults, was transferred to Jesus of Nazareth. The Christian sacraments of baptism and the eucharist were held to be adaptations of the rites of these pagan cults.

But the death and resurrection of Jesus of Nazareth are vastly different. They have nothing to do with fertility cults or the seasons of the natural year. They are attached to a historical person of the recent past. Moreover, they are a central feature of the Christian kerygma from the very earliest days of the Palestinian church,[15] which was outside the range of the mystery cults. Further, it has been a constant fault of the students of the mystery religions to read back into their interpretations of the evidence, and to use in their presentations of the results, the language of Christianity. This both prevents the possibility of gaining an objective picture of the mystery religions, and creates the impression of closer parallels between these cults and Christianity than the evidence actually warrants.[16] Particularly this is the case with the oft-repeated theme of the "dying and rising God". It is true that the mystery religions almost invariably are centred on a myth in which the deity symbolizes the death of nature in winter and its rebirth in spring. But they do not appear to speak of the deities as "dying and rising" again. They may descend into the lower world, and come out of it again. But the idea of resurrection in the biblical sense appears to be foreign to antiquity. And as for the initiate, the documents prefer to speak of their sharing the "sufferings" ($\pi\acute{a}\theta\eta$) of the god, rather than of death, and of rebirth rather than of resurrection.[17]

The theory of plagiarism in its extreme form has been generally abandoned by serious scholars, though even today it is occasionally met in the publications of the Rationalist Press Association. But it still persists in the modified form elaborated by Bousset.[18] According to this, the mystery religions have affected Christianity in a more restricted way at two related points: in the designation of Jesus as *kyrios* and *soter* (saviour) and in the conception of the sacraments as the means of participation in the death and resurrection of Jesus. Certainly Bousset recognizes that the title *mar* = Lord was used in Palestinian Christianity, and that baptism and the Lord's Supper were practised there. But in Hellenistic Christianity there was a radical shift in the meaning of *Kyrios*, and in the understanding of the sacraments. *Mar* had meant Jesus as the coming Son of man: Kyrios means Jesus as a cult deity. The sacraments in Palestinian Christianity were eschatological—they offered a foretaste of life in the future kingdom of God. In Hellenistic Christianity, under the influence of the mystery religions, they became means of sacramental participation in the fate (i.e. the death and resurrection) of the cult deity. Both parts of Bousset's theory still enjoy considerable vogue in the Bultmann school.[18a] The *sacramental* aspect of this theory need not detain us here, but the question of the derivation of *kyrios* and *soter* is obviously pertinent.

To begin with, let us note an attempt which was made first by P. Wendland[19] to rule the mystery religions out of court completely in any discussion of Christian origins. In an oft-quoted sentence Wendland wrote: "The *floruit* of the mystery cults belongs to the romanticism of the second century A.D." This argument has been repeated by E. Meyer, A. Schweitzer and most recently by F. C. Grant.[20] This is an attractive short-cut to the solution of the problem, but it does not quite fit the facts. The impression that the second century was the great period of the flourishing of the mystery cults is perhaps not altogether mistaken. But to some extent it is due to the fact that the second century apologists and the Alexandrians, notably Clement of Alexandria, devoted so much attention to these mysteries and to their relations with Christianity. Undoubtedly, the mysteries represented at that time a particularly dangerous challenge to Christianity. But of course the mystery cults (with the exception of Mithraism) existed long before then in their homelands, and were certainly alive there in the first century.

Moreover, the Christian missions were active at that time in the very neighbourhood where these cults were flourishing. Antioch was in close contiguity with the Adonis cult, Ephesus with the Cybele and Attis cult, Corinth with the Eleusinian mysteries—a circumstance which is particularly important for 1 Corinthians. And some of these cults had by that time already been transplanted beyond their homeland. For instance, the Cybele and Attis cult is first attested in Rome as early as 204 B.C., while the antiquarian-minded emperor Claudius (A.D. 41–54) reorganized that cult in Rome during his reign. The Isis cult was introduced into mainland Greece in much earlier times (Athens, 333 B.C.). The Adonis cult likewise was known in both Greece and Italy long before the Christian period.[21] We cannot therefore on chronological grounds rule out the antecedent possibility of Christian adaptations, conscious or unconscious, from the mystery religions. Whether this actually occurred must be decided from case to case.

But the chronological question arises in a more restricted context in connection with the terms *kyrios* and *soter*. Were these terms current in the mystery religions in the first century A.D.? *Kyria* (feminine) is attested for Isis in Egypt in 99–90 B.C.[22] From the time of Augustus we have an inscription from Syria designating the god Kronos as *kyrios*.[23] Last but not least there is the evidence of Paul himself (1 Cor. 8:5) that there were "gods many and lords (κύριοι) many" in the pagan world at the time of the Pauline mission. The impression is that in NT times the term *kyrios* was on the increase as a designation for cult deities. The mystery cults could not have been the origin of the Christian usage of *kyrios*, for as we already saw in the foregoing chapter, that was given by Ps. 109(110):1, LXX. Yet it is not antecedently impossible that in *some* passages in the NT the mystery concept of the *kyrios* as a cult deity in whose fate the initiate participated in the sacraments should have contributed to the Christian understanding of *kyrios*. Whether it did, only exegesis of the particular passages can decide.

In his article of 1905, already mentioned, P. Wendland

found no early use of *soter* for a mystery cult deity.[24] Since then, Bousset has come up with an instance dated in the reign of Ptolemy IV where it is used of Serapis and Isis.[25] Here however it is probably merely a votive use, i.e. in thanksgiving for some particular benefit received from the god. It is not used in the theological sense of salvation from death.[26] Even later the use of the term in the mysteries does not seem to have been common. Prümm[27] notes that it is used only "here and there", to denote the god as the saviour from death, etc. There is insufficient evidence to justify Bultmann's sweeping statement,[28] "The general sense of the mysteries may be defined as the imparting of 'salvation' ($\sigma\omega\tau\eta\rho\iota\alpha$): hence the deities are called 'saviours' ($\sigma\omega\tau\eta\rho$) e.g. Serapis or $\sigma\omega\tau\epsilon\iota\rho\alpha$, e.g. Isis", at any rate as far as first century mystery terminology is concerned. We must suppose therefore that it was the imperial cultus (where the term is much more frequently attested at this period) which was the direct cause of the Hellenistic Christian usage of *soter*.

4. *The Gnostic Redeemer Myth*

The so-called pre-Christian (or Iranian) redeemer myth is not directly attested in pre-Christian sources. It is no more than a scholarly reconstruction. The theory was made possible by the publication of the then recently discovered literary remains of Mandeanism by M. Lidzbarski between 1905 and 1925.[29] R. Reitzenstein submitted Lidzbarski's material to analytical study and produced the following theory. The Mandean literature (which in its present form is dated seventh or eighth century A.D.) and the even later Manichean literature witness to a much earlier myth. It is earlier even than the New Testament, and is derived ultimately from Iranian religion. This myth appears in different expressions in the Christian gnostic systems refuted by the fathers such as Hippolytus and Irenaeus, and in the gnostic remains, such as *Pistis Sophia*, the Odes of Solomon, the Acts of Thomas,[30] and the Hermetic literature. It allegedly underlies the christological presentation of the Pauline and deutero-Pauline writings, the Epistle to the Hebrews and the Johannine literature. It is to be found in certain aspects of Philo's doctrine of the logos, and underlies the *ḥokhma-sophia* tradition in Hellenistic Judaism and in the Old Testament. The value of the Mandean literature according to Reitzenstein was that, despite its late date in its present 'form, it incorporates much older material. This material provides evidence for the oldest accessible form of the gnostic redeemer myth.

The myth as reconstructed is as follows.[31] In the beginning there existed the heavenly or first man, who belonged to the world of light. Creation was a tragic fall, in which the heavenly man underwent at least a partial disintegration. Parts of the body of light of which he was composed sank down into the world of matter and darkness, and were incorporated into the bodies of human beings. We are all— or at least the fortunate ones among us—chips off the old block! Whereupon the heavenly man, or what remained of him, descended personally into the world of matter to rescue the sparks of light which had become detached from his body, re-incorporated them into himself and reascended into heaven.—This theory was taken up by R. Bultmann[32] and given considerable currency. It appears to be accepted without question in the Bultmann school.[33]

Now this theory, if it be substantiated, is of the utmost importance for NT Christology. For it would mean that here is the source of the christological pattern of Hellenistic Christianity, and therefore of Paul, Hebrews, and the Johannine writings. This pattern replaced the older "adoptionist" pattern of the earliest Palestinian church with the pattern of a pre-existent redeemer who becomes incarnate, performs the redemption and reascends into heaven. Nor need we be initially shocked at such a theory. For the Church was looking round for adequate concepts in which to express its basic conviction that "God was in Christ", and everything was grist to its mill. It is this central faith which remains constant, while the expression of it was a matter of trial and, if not of error, then at least a discarding of inadequate concepts and of those which proved to be unsuited to the changed environment in which the gospel had to be proclaimed.[34]

The question is really a historical one. Is the Reitzenstein-Bultmann theory tenable? When parallels are produced between several documents, indicating an obvious relationship between them, it is always possible to explain that relationship in one of two ways. Either there is a direct relationship between them, so that one of the extant documents is the source of the others. Or, alternatively, it becomes necessary to postulate a lost, no longer extant, source behind them all. This latter is the procedure in the widely accepted solution of the synoptic problem, which postulates the lost source Q. It does not exist, but has to be reconstructed from the extant documents. The pre-Christian or Iranian gnostic myth is a solution of the same order as Q. The question is, is this the solution demanded by the facts? It appears not.

When we examine some of the earlier gnostic literary remains, particularly those of early Jewish gnosis, we find that the redeemer figure is not featured.[35] Instead, what happens is that a gnosis or revelation is in some way conveyed directly to human beings. In the Jewish gnostic Adam literature[36] this revelation is first conveyed to Adam, and is then handed on from generation to generation. Adam is here apparently equivalent to the fallen First Man, who then lives on in all his descendants. The same type of myth appears to underly the literary remains of early Jewish Christian gnosticism.[37] The "true prophet" who figures in the Pseudo-Clementine literature is equated with Adam. His function is to pass on the true gnosis. He re-appears in a whole succession of figures, including Jesus, until finally he reaches the "heavenly rest". The early fathers complained of the low Christology of the Elkesaites. This is due to the fact that Jesus in these Jewish Christian gnostic systems is not a redeemer-figure, but one of the successive recipients of gnosis or revelation. In pre-Christian Jewish gnosis this revelation first came with Adam, the fallen First Man. It was then passed on to his OT successors. In the Jewish Christian adaptations Jesus is simply added to the succession.

The Odes of Solomon[38] exhibit a somewhat different type of Jewish Christian gnosticism, less specifically Jewish in form. Here Adam plays some part, but there is still no redeemer figure. The gnosis or revelation is conveyed direct from God to the soul.

Finally, the Mandean *Ginza*,[39] upon which Reitzenstein based his theory of the pre-Christian gnostic redeemer myth, is a highly composite work. There are parts in which the redeemer figure is absent. Here, as in the Odes of Solomon, the gnosis or revelation is conveyed direct to the soul.

There is a further confusion here which does not seem to have been noticed either by the protagonists of the gnostic redemption redeemer myth or by its critics. This concerns the part played by the first man. On the one hand, he is ideal man who undergoes a fall at the beginning of creation. On the other hand, he allegedly descends, apparently for a second time, as redeemer. This dual capacity has never been properly explained. Instead the two figures are merged together in the formula "the redeemed redeemer" (*erlöste Erlöser*).

It seems highly questionable whether the two figures should be merged in this way. Rather, we seem to have a composite myth in two parts. There is the first man who falls from the world of light and enters the thralldom of the material world. He becomes the inclusive head of all the human race. And, secondly, there is the distinct concept of the heavenly wisdom or revelation, which enters the world through a series of emissaries in each successive generation, bringing the gnosis which will release man from his fallen condition. The second part of the myth had firmly embedded itself in Judaism in the *hokhma-sophia* tradition. The first part of the myth was re-formed by Philo (and perhaps by other Hellenistic Jews before him) in the light of the Genesis story and in the interests of his Platonism. Philo split the first man into two. The first or heavenly man he identified with Wisdom-Logos. The second man became fallen man. When we come to the chapter on the Gentile mission, it will be very important to keep this distinction between the two parts of the myth in mind. For the wisdom part of it will provide the tools for affirming the pre-existence and divinity of the Redeemer, and the idea of his descent into the world to redeem it. The second part, that which relates the fall of the first man, will provide the tools for the typological comparison between the first (fallen man) and the second or last man. The first man is the inclusive head of fallen humanity.

The "second" or last man reverses Adam's or the first man's fall by his obedience and by analogy with Adam becomes the head of the new human race.

We may speak therefore of a pre-Christian gnostic myth of a fall of man from the world of heavenly light and of his redemption offered to him by a series of emissaries who bring a revelation from the world of light. But there is no evidence for a pre-existent redeemer who becomes incarnate. Only in second-century "Christian" gnosticism does the incarnate redeemer figure finally penetrate the gnostic tradition. At first, as in the Jewish Christian type of gnosticism mentioned above, the figure of Jesus appears simply as one of a whole series of recipients of the gnosis, not as a redeemer. Later on, when it does appear in the great gnostic systems of the second century, gnosticism is not fully at home with it, and resorts to docetism as the only means of assimilating it. We may welcome the conclusion of Schmithals, coming as it does from within the Bultmann school: "The oldest historical envoy attested is Jesus Christ," and, in the footnote to this quotation:

> The judgment of R. Bultmann in his *Commentary on John*, that "the idea of the incarnation did not penetrate into gnosticism from Christianity, but is itself of gnostic derivation" must, it seems to me, be corrected accordingly. There is no doubt that the redeemer myth is gnostic, but the particular form of this myth, which speaks of the incarnation of the redeemer in a historical person, is not proven for the period prior to Christianity.

It is confusing, however, to continue speaking of a "redeemer myth". Rather we should speak of a pre-Christian gnostic *revelation* myth, though of course the revelation is also redemptive. It is this revelation myth which is constitutive for gnosticism and the "Q" for which Reitzenstein was searching.

5. *The Divine Man*

Finally, we must return to the concept of the divine man, which has already engaged our attention in Hellenistic Judaism. There, we saw that the divine man concept was taken over into Hellenistic Judaism in drastically modified form, strictly controlled by the OT tradition. The most characteristic features of the Hellenistic concept were for the most part rigorously eschewed. Among these omitted features was the divine essence or nature of the θεῖος ἀνήρ ("divine man"). The divine reality was present in him as substance or power, enabling him to enjoy ecstatic experiences, to utter prophecies, to do miracles, and to perform egregious feats.

Now it cannot be denied that most of the evidence adduced for the Hellenistic concept of the divine man by the History of Religions school is later than the NT. This has led, e.g. Prümm[40] to suggest that the miracles attributed to the Hellenistic divine men are often deliberate plagiarisms from the gospel stories. But the polemics of pre-Christian Hellenistic Jewish writers[41] against the Hellenistic divine man concept indicate that the concept was fully established in the Hellenistic world long before the NT. Also, Jewish and pagan opponents of Christianity were not slow to point the similarity between the gospel stories and those of the Hellenistic world, as we know from Origen's Celsus. We must remain open-minded about the possibility that when the tradition of Jesus' miracles was brought from a Palestinian and Hellenistic Jewish to a Hellenistic Gentile environment it took on some of the traits of the Hellenistic divine man.[42]

NOTES ON CHAPTER IV

1. For a bibliography of earlier works of the History of Religions school see A. Schweitzer, *Paul and His Interpreters*, London: Black, 1950, pp. 179–181. More recent treatments will be found in the relevant parts of *Cambridge Ancient History*, vol. VII (Ed. S. A. Cook *et. al.*). Source material is quoted in *TWNT* III, pp. 1045f., s.v. Κύριος by Foerster, and *ibid.* IV, pp. 810–820, s.v. μυστήριον by Bornkamm. K. Prümm's *Religionsgeschichtliches Handbuch*, Rome: Pontifical Biblical Institute, 1954, contains a comprehensive survey, but for primary sources he refers to N. Turchi, *Fontes historicæ mysteriorum aevi hellenisticae*, Rome, 1923. For a recent critique of the History of Religions school see C. Colpe, *Die Religionsgeschichtliche Schule*, Göttingen: Vandenhoeck u. Ruprecht (*FRLANT* NF 60), 1961, which contains an exhaustive bibliography on the gnostic redeemer myth.

2. See Foerster *art. cit.* (note 1 above).

3. Pindar, *Isthm.* 5:33, Ζεὺς ὁ πάντων κύριος.

4. E.g. *BGU* 1834, 6f.: τῶν θεῶν καὶ κυρίων βασιλέων (cited in Foerster, art. cit.).

5. Augustus is called θεὸς καὶ κύριος καίσαρ αὐτοκράτωρ, *BGU* 1197 I 15 (Foerster).

6. Foerster, *art. cit.*, p. 1054.

7. Cullmann, *Christology*, p. 198.

8. κύριος τοῦ πάντος κόσμου Νέρων, A. Deissmann, *Light from the Ancient East*, London: Hodder and Stoughton, 1927², p. 354, n. 4. It is noteworthy that in Acts 25:26 Nero is addressed in a letter as "Lord". "His Imperial Majesty" (*NEB*) misses the religious association of the term. It is not like "our sovereign Lord, King George" (or "Lady, Queen Elizabeth") in the Prayer Book, but a title connoting divinity.

9. See e.g. the quotation given in note 4.

10. See R. Bultmann, *Essays Philosophical and Theological*, London: S.C.M. Press, 1955, pp. 275–286.

11. Deissmann, *Light*, p. 361.

11a. Deissmann, *ibid.*, pp. 346f.

12. *Ibid.*, p. 369; P. Wendland, *ZNW* 5, 1904, pp. 335–353; W. Bousset, *Kyrios Christos*, *FRLANT* NF 21, pp. 240–244; E. Meyer, *Ursprung und Anfänge des Christentums*, Stuttgart and Berlin: Cotta, 1923, III, pp. 390–397.

13. ἐπιφανεία ("epiphany") is also a term used in the imperial cultus. Deissmann, *Light*, p. 373, Bousset, *op. cit.*, pp. 244f.

14. On the mystery cults cf. K. Prümm, *Handbuch*, pp. 215–356.

15. C. H. Dodd, *The Apostolic Preaching and its Developments*, London: Hodder and Stoughton, 1936¹, Lecture 1.

16. Cf. Prümm, *Handbuch*, p. 308; A. E. J. Rawlinson, *The New Testament Doctrine of the Christ*, London: Longmans, 1926, p. 279.

17. Cf. A. Oepke, *TWNT* I, pp. 369f. (s.v. ἀνίστημι), "resurrection for the Greek mind is either impossible, or occasional and exceptional". For πάθη ("sufferings") see Bornkamm, *art. cit.* (note 1), pp. 811f. and the documentary evidence given there.

18. Bousset, *Kyrios Christos*, pp. 99; 240–44; 107–10.

18a. For the theory of the influence of the mysteries on Pauline sacramentalism see Bultmann, *Theology* I, pp. 135–152; G. Bornkamm, *Studien zu Antike und Christentum*, Munich: Kaiser, 1959, p. 172; W. Schmithals, *Die Gnosis in Korinth* (*FRLANT* 66), Göttingen: Vandenhoeck u. Ruprecht, 1956, pp. 209–222.

19. *Art. cit.* (see note 12), p. 353.

20. E. Meyer, *Ursprung und Anfänge*, III, p. 393; A. Schweitzer, *Paul and his Interpreters*, pp. 191f. Schweitzer recognizes that the mysteries already existed in Paul's time. But he considers that they were then still vegetation rites. They developed into redemptive and missionary religions only in the second century. F. C. Grant, *Roman Hellenism and the New Testament*, New York: Scribners, 1962, pp. 77f., writes: "The main period of *floruit* of the mystery religions was not the first century, but the second and third—much too late to have provided Christianity with

sacraments, or the fundamental doctrines of salvation, regeneration, or the death and resurrection of a divine Saviour."

21. These dates are as given by Prümm, based on the evidence of N. Turchi.

22. *CIG* 4897a quoted Foerster, *art. cit.* (note 1), p. 1048.

23. *Ditt. Or.* 608 (from *ibid.*).

24. P. Wendland, *art. cit.* (note 12), pp. 336, 337, 352.

25. W. Bousset, *Kyrios Christos*, p. 242, Dölger (1908) first published the inscription.

26. Cf. the use in the imperial cultus, above p. 89.

27. Prümm, *Handbuch*, p. 339, n. 1: "here and there", and, in the index, "occasionally".

28. R. Bultmann, *Primitive Christianity*, p. 158.

29. M. Lidzbarski, *Das Johannesbuch der Mandäer*: I *Text*, Giessen, 1905; II *Einleitung, etc.*, 1915; *Mandäische Liturgien*, Berlin, 1920. *Ginza*, Göttingen, 1925. Until recently Lidzbarski was the only accessible text of the material, and that was in German translated from incomplete MSS. Now however we have in English a complete translation of the Mandean liturgical material from a current copy of the material. This is E. S. Drower, *The Canonical Prayerbook of the Mandaeans*, Leiden: E. J. Brill, 1959. Unfortunately, Drower's system of numerical references is completely different from Lidzbarski's, used by German writers, which makes the Drower difficult to use.

30. The Nag Hamadi literature was of course unknown to Reitzenstein.

31. For the gnostic redeemer myth cf. Bultmann, *Primitive Christianity*, pp. 163ff.

32. First, in *EYXAPIΣTION* (Gunkel *Festschrift*), Göttingen: Vandenhoeck u. Ruprecht, 1923, II, pp. 1–26, in application to John 1:1–14. Later Bultmann extended the theory to the whole Johannine discourse material (*ZNW* 24 (1925), pp. 100–146). It forms the basic assumption of his commentary on John. It is stated dogmatically in his programmatic essay on demythologizing of 1941 (*Kerygma and Myth*, I, London: S.P.C.K., 1953, p. 8), and is reiterated in his *Primitive Christianity* and in his *Theology of the New Testament*.

33. E.g. E. Käsemann, *Leib und Leib Christi* (*BHTh*, Tübingen: J. C. B. Mohr, 1933 (where the doctrine of the body of Christ in Eph. is derived from the gnostic redeemer myth), and *idem.*, *ZThK* 47 (1950), pp. 313–360 (where it is argued that the gnostic redeemer myth underlies Phil. 2:6–11); H. Braun, *ZThK* 54 (1957), pp. 341–377.

34. The substance of this paragraph is from G. E. Wright and R. H. Fuller, *The Book of the Acts of God*, London: Duckworth, 1960 (American edition, 1957, p. 274), pp. 221f.

35. Cf. M. Dibelius, *Botschaft und Geschichte* II, p. 69: "In many of the gnostic sects the figure of the redeemer is as yet absent"; W. Bousset, *Hauptprobleme der Gnosis* (*FRLANT* 10), Göttingen: Vandenhoeck u. Ruprecht, 1907, p. 321: "It is worth noting that the figure of the redeemer is not yet present in many of these sects" (viz. Ophites,

Nicolaitans, Archontics). C. Colpe, *Die religionsgeschichtliche Schule*, is particularly insistent on discriminating between the various types of gnostic myth.

36. *Vita Adae* 25–29; *Apoc. Mos.* 3 (both in Charles, vol. II).

37. Ps.–Clem. *Hom.* III, 20, 2; Rec. I, 52; VIII 59 (text in Ante-Nicene Fathers). "But the true prophet is not a redeemer figure sent from heaven, but the fallen first man himself, whose 'knowledge' rests upon recollection" (W. Schmithals, *Das kirchliche Apostelamt, FRLANT* NF 61, Göttingen: Vandenhoeck u. Ruprecht, 1961, p. 108). Cf. also Hipp. *Ref.* 9:9—H. J. Schoeps, *Theologie und Geschichte des Judenchristentums*, Tübingen: J. C. B. Mohr (P. Siebeck), 1949, p. 103, and *Urgemeinde, Judenchristentum und Gnosis* (same publisher), 1956, pp. 52–54, denies that the true prophet in the Jewish-Christian literature has any connection with gnosticism. I believe however that this is due to his uncritical acceptance of the view of gnosticism promulgated by the History of Religions school. The ultimate Jewish origin of the second century gnostic systems is becoming increasingly clear. Cf. R. M. Grant, *Gnosticism and Early Christianity*, New York: Columbia Univ. Press, 1961. Grant's theory that gnosticism is Jewish apocalyptic run to seed does not, however, carry conviction.

38. Odes of Solomon 15 (An ode to "the Lord" as the Sun, i.e. the source of revelation); 26. Texts in *The Odes and Psalms of Solomon*, ed. J. Rendel Harris, Cambridge University Press, 1909. Rendel Harris denies the gnostic affinities of these psalms (against Harnack). Though not always apparent, a gnostic background is clear, e.g. at Ode 15:2 ("His light hath dispelled all darkness from my face" and "It suffices to know and to rest").

39. Schmithals, *Apostelamt*, pp. 108f. cites several passages from the left *Ginza* as translated by Lidzbarski.

40. *Handbuch*, pp. 458–464.

41. E.g. *The Letter of Aristeas*.

42. See below, p. 228. Cf. also my *Interpreting the Miracles*, London: S.C.M. Press and Philadelphia: Westminster Press, 1963, pp. 48–68.

Chapter V

THE HISTORICAL JESUS: HIS SELF-UNDERSTANDING

1. *Preliminary Considerations*

IN the introductory chapter we asserted that Christology is essentially the church's response to the history of Jesus. The church understood that history as the eschatological act of God and confessed and proclaimed that understanding in terms of Christology. This view of the nature of Christology is not an *a priori* theological judgement. It rests upon the modern critical understanding of the nature of the gospels, and of the history of the gospel tradition. Prior to the rise of gospel criticism it was natural and inevitable to regard Christology as part of, and indeed the essential content of, the actual historical teaching of Jesus. By and large the traditional view rested upon an acceptance of the historicity of the fourth gospel. For it is only in this gospel that Jesus' proclamation is (almost) purely christological. Once the historicity of the fourth gospel was abandoned—in the sense that the Johannine discourses contain the *ipsissima verba* of Jesus[1]—we were thrown back upon the synoptic gospels as the main evidence for the proclamation and teaching of Jesus.

In the synoptic tradition generally, and particularly in the primary strata, (Mark, Q, the special Lucan and special Matthean material) the central content of Jesus's proclamation is not himself, but the kingdom of God. It is true, of course, that the synoptic tradition contains christologically impregnated material. The bulk of this material however, is contained in the *narration* (e.g. the infancy narratives, the baptism, the miracle stories and temptation, Peter's confession at Caesarea Philippi, the transfiguration, the passion narrative, and the resurrection stories). On any view, these stories took shape after the resurrection. And since they reflect the christological beliefs of the post-resurrection church it is not historical scepticism, but sound critical method, to assign these stories in their present shape (whatever factual basis they may have) to the theology of the community.

We are left, then, with a small body of christological material in the synoptic sayings of Jesus.[2] In the primary sources, there is one passage where Jesus asserts that he is the Christ (Messiah) (Mark 14:62), three passages where he uses the term "the Son" or the "Son of God" with ostensible reference to himself (Mark 12:6; 13:32, Matt. 11:27 par.), and a larger body of sayings (some 33 in all) in which he uses "Son of man" as a self-designation. Even if we accept all of these sayings as authentic, their proportion in relation to the teaching of Jesus as a whole is significantly small. This suggests that if Jesus did impart any teaching about his own person in christological terms, such teaching was at best peripheral to his public ministry. In order to come to grips with Jesus' self-understanding it will, therefore, be well to concentrate first on the more characteristic parts of his teaching and seek to probe the self-understanding which that teaching implies. We will then submit the explicit christological utterances to critical analysis, and endeavour to discover an authentic minimum compatible with the implicit self-understanding already extracted from his more characteristic teaching.

2. The Words and Deeds of Jesus

It is widely agreed today that Jesus' message was centred upon the proclamation of the kingdom of God, and that this term is to be understood in eschatological terms within the framework of a "reduced apocalyptic" (R. Bultmann).[3] In its more recent phases the debate has centred not so much upon the meaning of the term kingdom of God itself, as upon Jesus' understanding of its timing. Did he proclaim that the kingdom of God was only imminent,[4] that it was future but already dawning,[5] that it had already come,[6] or that it was both present and future-imminent?[7] In his discussion of this problem in the Mission and Achievement of Jesus, the present writer settled upon the formula "proleptic eschatology". The "kingdom of God has not yet come, but it is near, so near that it is already operative in advance".[8] For some time now—and long before Perrin's criticism of my position[9]—I have felt that this went too far in reaction against Dodd's position (a reaction which was perhaps understandable in Britain at a time when "realized eschatology" was widely taken for granted without qualification).

There can be no doubt that in Jesus' perspective the kingdom was future—as indeed it had to be, since it was conceived in apocalyptic terms. Yet it is doing less than justice to ἔφθασεν ("has come") in Matt. 12:28 par. to say that there the Kingdom is not actually present, but merely casting its shadow before it. There is in Jesus' sayings about the kingdom a very delicate balance between the present and the future aspects.[10] And now that the excesses of realized eschatology have been redressed it is clear that the balance should be shifted slightly, yet perceptibly, to the side of the present aspect of the kingdom in Jesus' ministry. Let us say, therefore, that the message of Jesus proclaims the *proleptic presence* of the future kingdom of God. In Jesus' ministry God is already beginning his eschatological action, and will shortly consummate it. But the future consummation is not of a different quality from the present beginning. It only manifests the final quality of that which is already hiddenly present. Jesus does not offer teaching about the future, but enforces the decisiveness of the present for the future.

Jesus' proclamation of the kingdom is not, then, an abstract idea but the proclamation of an event. But it is an event that is already happening precisely and concretely in Jesus himself, in his words and his works. Now as Bultmann has said in an oft-quoted statement, Jesus' call to decision (i.e. for his message of the kingdom) "implies a christology".[10a] It is because Jesus proclaims the kingdom that the future kingdom is proleptically present. This is brought out in the formula Ἀμὴν λέγω ὑμῖν "Truly, I say to you". In this "Amen", Jesus pledges his whole person behind the truth of his proclamation.[11] This formula has certainly been added secondarily to some of Jesus' sayings, as a synoptic comparison will show. But it cannot be doubted that it was characteristic of the historical Jesus. Now it is noteworthy that one of the two main contexts in which Jesus uses the formula is in sayings which speak of the polarity between the presence of the kingdom and its futurity: "accept the kingdom now in my message, and you will be accepted in the kingdom; reject it now and you will be rejected then."[12] It is precisely in the message of Jesus that a man is confronted with the proleptic presence of the future kingdom of God: "Blessed are the . . . ears which hear what you hear" (Matt. 13:16 par.).

In his exorcisms and healings[13] the future kingdom of God is proleptically present: "If it is by the finger of God that I cast out demons, then the kingdom of God has come upon you" (Luke 11:20 par.). Note the implicit christological concentration here: the kingdom of God is not present when the sons of the Pharisees cast out demons (v. 19), but only when Jesus does so or when his disciples do so in direct commission by him, Matt. 10:7 par. The same implicitly christological understanding of the miracles is shown in the saying, "Blessed are the eyes which see what you see" (Matt. 13:16 par.). The things that they "see" are precisely Jesus' miracles.[14] It becomes more explicit in the saying (in a context where Jesus is speaking of his words and works) "Blessed is he who takes no offence *at me*" (Matt. 11:6 par.).[15]

Jesus understands his activity in eating with publicans and sinners in the same concentrated way. The parables of the lost sheep, the lost coin and the prodigal son (Luke 15) all interpret Jesus' consorting with the lost as the action of God seeking out and forgiving sinners.[16]

Jesus' deeds, then, like his proclamation, are present actualizations of the future kingdom of God. In his works, as in his words, God is present, acting eschatologically through Jesus. Such is Jesus' understanding of his own words and works. It is demonstrated by logia which pass all the criteria of authenticity.

The ethical teaching of Jesus points in the same direction. Jesus backs his ethical demand with the same formula as his eschatological message: "Truly I say to you."[17] That is the sole ground of his authority. Throughout his ethical teaching Jesus confronts men with the direct demand of God. In him that demand is immediately uttered. He is not reporting or interpreting a tradition, like the Rabbis. Nor is he reporting a message received from a distant God, like the OT prophets. God is directly present in the word of Jesus, actively demanding unreserved obedience to his will from those who have accepted the eschatological message and its offer of salvation.

Jesus' teaching about God has an immediate quality about it, too. For Jesus, God is not a distant God, but a near God. This he expressed by the use of the intimate address, "Abba",[18] and in his teaching about God's providential care which removes all ground for anxiety (Matt. 6:25–34). In his emphasis on the nearness of God Jesus is not substituting an earlier metaphysic of transcendence by one of immanence, as the Bishop of Woolwich[19] would substitute an abstract conception of "God out there" by an equally abstract conception of the "God down there" as the ground of existence. The nearness of God is *now* a reality precisely in his drawing near in Jesus' eschatological ministry, which is therefore implicitly christological. Jesus can call God "Abba" because he has known him as the one who has drawn nigh in his own word and deed, and he admits to the same privilege those who have responded to his own eschatological message.[20]

An examination of Jesus' words—his proclamation of the Reign of God, and his call for decision, his enunciation of God's demand, and his teaching about the nearness of God—and of his conduct—his calling men to follow him and his healings, his eating with publicans and sinners—forces upon us the conclusion that underlying his word and work is an implicit Christology. In Jesus as he understood himself, there is an immediate confrontation with "God's presence and his very self", offering judgment and salvation.

The majority of Jesus' sayings about his death contain either an explicit Christology (notably the predictions of the passion, which will be discussed later) or an explicit soteriology (so Mark 10:45b and the cup word at the supper, Mark 14:24). They must therefore on grounds of traditio-historical criticism be assigned to the early church, rather than to Jesus himself. But there are two other passages which pass the test of our critical methods.

The first is Luke 13:32f. Here we follow Wellhausen's reconstruction:[21]

Behold, I cast out demons and perform cures today and tomorrow. Nevertheless, I must be on my way the day after that, for it cannot be that a prophet should perish away from Jerusalem.

Jesus' understood his exorcisms and healings, as we have already seen, as part of God's eschatological action in him. Here, his death at Jerusalem is stated, in terms devoid of any church theology, to be the ultimate outcome of this action. Jesus goes up to Jerusalem, not simply in order to die, which as J. Knox[22] has contended would be morbidly pathological and tantamount to suicide, but in order to continue his eschatological ministry. Specifically, as both Bornkamm and Conzelmann insist,[23] it was to issue his eschatological challenge at the heart and centre of Judaism. But he knows that this will assuredly involve his death. Why? Because martyrdom was at that time considered to be inherent in the prophetic vocation[24] and because Jesus had before him the example of his immediate predecessor, John the Baptist.[25] Jesus, therefore, accepts the possibility, if not the inevitability, of death as part of his eschatological ministry. His death is part of the coming of God's salvation.

This comes out even more clearly in the eschatological saying in the supper tradition. This saying, unlike the bread and cup words, suffered progressive atrophy in the church's liturgical tradition, and is therefore not open to suspicion as a church formation.[26] In its Marcan form it runs:

Amen, I say to you, I shall not drink again of the fruit of the vine until that day when I drink it new in the kingdom of God. (Mark 14:25).

In this saying Jesus makes a distinction between himself and his disciples. The meal is for him (though not for them) the last meal on earth. He is to be taken from them and will die. But on the other side of death he will feast in the Messianic banquet. Between Jesus at the supper and the consummation of the kingdom lies the decisive event of his own death. Here Jesus brings his death into direct association with the eschatological message of the kingdom of God which he had proclaimed throughout his ministry. This association is even more explicit than Luke 13:31–33, where his death was to be the outcome of his deeds. His death, as understood by himself, is a part of God's eschatological action in him. In other words, Jesus' death, like his words and deeds, implies a Christology.

3. *The Christological Titles*

Thus far we have seen that the proclamation, teaching and deeds of Jesus were not directly christological in content. The Christology is contained "in, with and under" them. But, as we noted earlier, there is a residuum of sayings in which a direct Christology is asserted. Do these sayings in any way add to the evidence for Jesus' self-understanding?

The present writer dealt with this subject at some length in *The Mission and Achievement of Jesus*, in a chapter entitled "The Raw Materials of Christology" (pp. 79–117). Broadly, the thesis of this chapter was that Jesus understood himself to stand in a unique relation of sonship to God, involving election and call, responsibility and obedience in a ministry of eschatological proclamation and deed. This ministry he conceived in terms of the Deutero-Isaianic servant as portrayed in Isa. 42, 35, 61, and 53. He believed that his obedience to this programme would lead to his vindication as the glorified Son of man, whose functions he was already exercising in a partial and proleptic manner in his earthly ministry. Behind this thesis lay a twofold purpose. On the one hand it sought to rescue a basis for the kerygma in the historical Jesus, which appeared to have been denied by Bultmann.[27] On the other hand it was intended to be a cautious revision of the view, popular in Britain,[28] that Jesus understood himself without qualification to be the apocalyptic Son of man, interpreted in the light of Deutero-Isaiah's suffering servant. The present writer is glad to find that the "post-Bultmannians"[29] now share his basic concern to find a point of contact in Jesus' history for the subsequent kerygma of the church. But it appears now that the implicit Christology which the post-Bultmannians have found in the words and works of Jesus is sufficient to rescue a historical basis for the kerygma. It is also more scientifically based on the methods of traditio-historical criticism.[30]

We must therefore embark upon a re-examination of the

seven titles used or implied in the sayings of Jesus. They are: (i) the Christ (i.e. Davidic Messiah), (ii) Son of David, (iii) Son of God, (iv) Servant, (v) Kyrios, (vi) Son of man: (vii) Prophet.

(i) *The Messiah*

The Q material does not contain any example of the title "the Christ" on Jesus' lips as a self-designation. In Mark it appears only in the obviously secondary passage, Mark 9:41 (contrast Matt. 10:42).[31] This leaves two important passages where the title is proffered to Jesus by others and where his reaction is recorded.

The first passage is the Petrine Confession, Mark 8:27–33. As it now stands, Peter's confession is followed by (1) a command to silence (v. 30); (2) a passion prediction (vv. 31–32a); (3) a mutual rebuke of Peter and Jesus, following closely upon and motivated by the passion prediction (vv. 32b–33).[32] (1) is a typical Marcan theme (Messianic secret), and must be eliminated as a Marcan redaction.[33] The passion prediction (2) had doubtless been combined with the Petrine confession before Mark, but did not belong originally to the scene. For it belongs to the same layer of tradition as the other passion predictions in Mark and is therefore detachable.[34] In (3) v. 32a is clearly constructed as a link between the passion prediction and Jesus' rebuke of Peter. Subtracting (1), (2) and v. 32a we are left with a straight pronouncement story in three parts:

1. The setting: Jesus at Caesarea Philippi asks the disciples who they say he is (vv. 27f.).
2. The action: Peter answers "you are the Christ", v. 29.
3. The pronouncement: Jesus rebukes Peter, "Get behind me, Satan", v. 33.

Jesus rejects Messiahship as a merely human and even diabolical temptation.[35] When we remember that "Messiah" meant the Davidic Messiah of a religious-national kind, this becomes intelligible. The same rejection is discernible in the third temptation in Matt. 4:8–10(Q).

The second important passage is in the preliminary investigation of Jesus before the Sanhedrin (Mark 14:61f.).

Incidentally, it is wrong to call this scene a trial. Its purpose was to establish a charge to bring before Pilate in the trial proper. The whole episode has recently been under fire as pure fabrication.[36] It is alleged to be entirely a christological composition of the church. However, it is undeniable that Jesus was crucified as a Messianic Pretender,[37] a fact which is clinched by the title on the cross (Mark 15:26). Jesus must therefore have been condemned as such by Pilate, and the preliminary investigation by the Sanhedrin must have been staged to get Jesus to incriminate himself in this sense. The high priest's question, "Are you the Christ?" (the addition, "the Son of the Blessed One", is probably an early Christian addition, though the reverential periphrasis, "Blessed One", shows its Palestinian origin) is historically plausible.

How did Jesus actually reply? We may ignore the second half of the reply for the moment, since it concerns a very different christological complex—the Son of man, his session at the right hand of God and parousia. This leaves us with "I am", which in view of Jesus' reaction at Caesarea Philippi is unlikely to be authentic. We must therefore either follow Cullmann[38] and others and fall back on the Matthean form, "You have said so", interpreting it in the sense, "It's your word, not mine".[39] This would be understood either as a non-committal answer or as an outright denial. And in view of Caesarea Philippi it would have to be a denial. Or alternatively we must suppose that Jesus actually remained silent throughout the investigation, as at Mark 14:61 and 15:5 (before Pilate). Yet the motif of silence may have been suggested by Isa. 53:7. So we cannot be quite sure how Jesus reacted to the charge. But on either view Mark 14:62 cannot be used as evidence for Jesus' own acceptance of the title Messiah.

It has frequently been asserted, even by critical scholars, that Jesus took the term Messiah, divested it of its Jewish associations and "spiritualized" it in a general sense.[40] More specifically, it is alleged that he reinterpreted it in terms of the suffering Son of man.[41] The first suggestion is vague, and lacks any concrete support from the texts. The second is supported by the Petrine confession in Mark 8:27–33 and by Jesus' reply to the high priest in their present Marcan form. But, as we have seen, both these passages in their present form must be judged by the rules of traditio-historical criticism to be reflections of the church's Christology. The passion prediction in Mark 8:31 is not an integral part of its pericope. And Mark 14:62b not only contains the problematical self-identification of Jesus with the Son of man (still to be discussed) but uses Ps. 110:1, one of the apologetic *testimonia* of the early church. The evidence suggests that it was the early church which "spiritualized" the term *Christos*[42] rather than Jesus himself, though of course the church did so under the impact of Jesus' history.

(ii) *The Son of David*

That Jesus came from a family which (through Joseph) traced its descent from the royal line of David need not be doubted.[43] But did this tradition contribute anything to his self-understanding?

The story of the birth in David's city of Bethlehem is the end-result of a long christological development and will be examined later.

Only once in the synoptic tradition does the title Son of David occur on Jesus' lips, viz. in Mark 12:35–37. If genuine, this passage can only be regarded as an academic discussion on Messianic doctrine.[43a] But it is more likely a reflection of the debates of the early church. Note too that it is based on the LXX text. It is therefore more likely to be of Hellenistic Jewish Christian provenance.

Twice in Mark Jesus is proffered the title Son of David, once explicitly and once by implication. The first of these occasions is the twice uttered cry of blind Bartimaeus. "Son of David, have mercy on me" (Mark 10:47 and 48). It is to be recalled, as we have already noticed, that miraculous healing was *not* associated in Judaism with the Davidic Messiah. Also, this appeal of the sick becomes almost stereotyped in Matthew (repeated at Matt. 9:27; 15:22). It looks as though we have here a specific theme of the church's Christology, in which the Davidic sonship expresses Jesus' function as the merciful healer. But, as we shall see, in the earlier Palestinian tradition the Davidic sonship of Jesus was first connected with his parousia. The earthly Davidic sonship is a later development in Hellenistic Jewish Christianity.

The story of blind Bartimaeus marks the beginning of this Hellenistic Jewish Christian development. In the first occurrence the wording is, "*Jesus*, Son of David, have mercy upon me" (v. 47). In the second occurrence in v. 48 the name, Jesus, is dropped. This circumstance suggests that at an earlier stage in the tradition the cry occurred only once, and in the form, "Jesus, have mercy upon me" (cf. Luke 17:13).

The second passage to be considered occurs in the triumphal entry at Mark 11:10, "Blessed is the kingdom of our father David that is coming." This acclamation is sandwiched into a quotation from Ps. 118:25f. and serves to interpret it. The "coming one" of the psalm is identified with Jesus and his coming is then equated with the coming of the "kingdom of our father David". Jesus is thus the one who brings the kingdom of David, and is therefore, David's son.

Mark 11:9f. presents a complicated combination of different traditions. It begins with the Aramaic "Hosanna", and follows with a quotation of Ps. 117(118):25f. LXX in which ὁ ἐρχόμενος ("the Coming One") is individualized to refer not (as in the original Jewish usage) collectively to the pilgrims, but christologically to Jesus (the Coming One). The use of the LXX suggests that this part of the acclamation comes from the Hellenistic Jewish Christian tradition.[44]

The christological reference is then interpreted by the words, "Blessed be the kingdom of our father David 'that is coming." The phrase "father David" is not paralleled elsewhere in pre-Christian Jewish literature.[45] Moreover, Jewish tradition does not speak of the "coming" of David's kingdom, but rather of its restoration.[46] Clearly, we have here a church formation. Its perspective on the Davidic kingdom is future. And this, as we shall see later, is a characteristic not of the Hellenistic Jewish church, which introduced the LXX quotation, but of the Aramaic speaking Palestinian church. We must conclude, therefore, that the acclamation is a floating tradition, possibly of liturgical origin, and certainly emanating from the Palestinian church.

We can now venture to reconstruct the history of the tradition behind the acclamation.

(1) In the original Palestinian version of the triumphal entry, the acclamation ran: "Hosanna! Hosanna in the

highest." Whether Ps. 118:25f. in the MT version followed we can no longer say, though the use of this psalm by the pilgrims at Tabernacles and Passover makes this quite probable. In that case, however, "he who comes" would have been understood collectively of the pilgrims, and not to refer specifically to Jesus. As John 12:16 suggests, the meaning of this scene was not perceived until after the resurrection.

(2) At the same time there existed a quite separate liturgical acclamation, deriving from the Palestinian Aramaic church, and looking to the coming of the Davidic kingdom (Christianly understood) at the parousia.

(3) To (1) the Hellenistic Jewish community added Ps. 117(118): 26. Alternatively it replaced the MT version by LXX.

(4) Next, the Hellenistic Jewish community inserted (2) into the psalm quotation to secure the christological interpretation of ὁ ἐρχόμενος ("the Coming One"). This involved a shift, characteristic of Hellenistic Jewish Christianity, from the parousia to the exaltation of Jesus as the moment of the inauguration of the (Christianly understood) Davidic kingdom. (4) therefore, like (3), was the work of the Hellenistic Jewish church.

Consequently, in its original form (which may well rest upon authentic memory), Jesus was not hailed as the Davidic Messiah at the triumphal entry, but simply acclaimed as a pilgrim. To complete the history of the tradition, it may be noted that Matthew has altered the indirect allusion to Jesus as the Son of David to a direct acclamation (Matt. 21:9, 15). This results in a further shift: Jesus' Davidic sonship is no longer inaugurated at the parousia, as in the original, detached, Palestinian form of Mark 11:10, nor yet at the exaltation, as in the Marcan form, but already in the humility of his earthly life—a typical trait of Matthean Christology.[47] Similarly Luke, writing for a gentile audience, has removed all reference to the Davidic sonship and substituted, "Blessed is the king who comes in the name of the Lord" (19:38). Thus, like Matthew, Luke pushes back Jesus' kingship into the earthly life, though in more universal terms typical of his own theology.

What then was the historical intention of Jesus in the

triumphal entry? It is often held[48] that Jesus deliberately staged it as a demonstration against a national-political interpretation of his Messiahship, replacing this by a concept of Messiahship in terms of Zech. 9:9. Since, however, Zechariah's prophecies played a prominent part in the apologetic of the early church, we may safely conclude that Mark 11:1–6 (which, though it does not actually quote Zech. 9:9, is generally recognized to have it in mind) is a church formation. It tells us nothing of the intention of Jesus. While the story of the discovery of the ass may be legendary, as Bultmann and his school believe,[49] we need not doubt that Jesus did ride on an ass on Palm Sunday. If the combination of the triumphal entry with the temple cleansing is pre-Marcan and rests on authentic memory, then we may take it that Jesus' intention was to go to the temple to lay down the final challenge of his eschatological message at the heart of Judaism. This, as we have seen, was his purpose in breaking off the Galilean ministry and going up to Jerusalem. He had no explicit "Messianic" intention, either in the Davidic sense, or in the re-interpreted sense of Zech. 9:9.[50]

(iii) *The Son of God*

In the synoptic *logia* of Jesus the term Son of God is surprisingly rare, though it does occur in both of the primary strata, Mark and Q. Let us first look at the parable of the vineyard (Mark 12:6). If this parable is accepted as authentic,[51] the "son" must not be allegorized into a direct self-designation. It simply stands for God's final, eschatological mission. It must, however, be admitted that this attempt to eliminate the allegorical element from the interpretation is not very successful. So perhaps it would be better with Kümmel[52] to regard the vineyard not as a parable of Jesus, but as an allegory of the church on the history of salvation. In either case, it falls out as a self-designation of Jesus.

In Mark 13:32 the term "Son" is used absolutely in Jesus' disclaimer of knowledge of the date of the End. This is an apocalyptic context, and probably represents an original "Son of man".[53]

In Q there is a "Son" saying in the famous "synoptic thunderbolt from the Johannine sky" (Matt. 11:25–27 par.,

Q). I have discussed this passage at length elsewhere.[54] While rejecting a Hellenistic origin for it, I hesitated in pronouncing a decisive verdict in favour of its authenticity, but inclined to think it a church-formation representing a bridge between the synoptic Jesus and the Jesus of the fourth gospel. If Hahn is right (see above, note 54), the "thunderbolt" would appear to be a creation of the very early (? Palestinian) church. Yet it is based directly on Jesus' use of Abba, and his admission of others through his eschatological message to the privilege of calling God Abba. So although we cannot accept the "thunderbolt" as directly from Jesus, it is an indirect witness to his self-understanding. While he asserted no explicit Messianic claim and displayed no direct Messianic consciousness, he was certainly conscious of a unique Sonship to which he was privileged to admit others through his eschatological ministry. For, although there is no indubitably authentic logion in which Jesus calls himself the "Son", he certainly called God his Father in a unique sense. That Father-Son relationship, we have argued elsewhere, was one involving "choice and response, authority and obedience".[55]

(iv) *The Servant*

It was further suggested in *The Mission and Achievement* that Jesus filled out the pattern of this obedience from the figure of the Isaianic Servant.[56] This was true despite the fact that Jesus never used the term "Servant" as a self-designation. Since 1954, the case for the influence of the Servant of Yahweh concept has been supported by Cullmann.[57] But it has been vigorously contested at various points by H. E. Tödt, C. K. Barrett, M. D. Hooker, and F. Hahn.[58] It is therefore necessary to review the subject in the light of the subsequent discussion.

First, with regard to the baptism, even Miss Hooker allows, though "somewhat dubiously", that in the three key words, υἱός, ἀγαπητός and εὐδόκησα ("son", "beloved" and "I am well pleased") the language of Isa. 42:1 may have coloured the voice from heaven. Hahn is more certain of this.

This conclusion may stand. But this does not warrant Cullmann's conclusion that "Jesus became conscious at the moment of his baptism, that he had to take upon himself the *ebed Yahweh* role."[59] For, as Cullmann himself later contends: "in the most ancient period of early Christianity there existed an explanation of the person and work of Jesus which we could characterize somewhat inaccurately as a Paidology . . . we may therefore assert that this is probably the oldest known solution to the Christological problem."[59a]

With the first part of this statement we are in complete agreement, although, as we shall see, the second part will require some modification. There *was* a paidological interpretation of Jesus in the earliest Palestinian church. Now at the beginning of his work Cullmann announces his intention to follow the form-critical method.[60] But this means, among other things, that where a saying or a tradition about Jesus in the gospels reflects the theology of the post-resurrection church, that saying or tradition must be placed to the credit of the church, rather than to Jesus himself, or to his original history. Let us apply that principle here. The earliest Palestinian church interpreted Jesus's earthly ministry in terms of a "paidology". The heavenly voice at the baptism (in its Palestinian form, where υἱός appeared as "my servant") expresses this "paidology". Therefore the heavenly voice must be set to the credit of the earliest Palestinian church, rather than to Jesus' personal reminiscence of his baptismal experience. It cannot be used as evidence for Jesus' self-understanding.

How then did Jesus understand his baptism? We can answer this question from two types of evidence: (1) his subsequent behaviour; (2) his indubitably authentic references to John the Baptist.

(1) It was after his baptism that Jesus embarked upon his eschatological ministry of preaching, teaching, exorcism and healing, of calling men to follow him and consorting with the outcast. The evident effect of his baptism upon Jesus was to cause him to embark upon this ministry. It was, if you like, his "call" to this particular ministry.

(2) Among Jesus' authentic sayings about the Baptist, there are some which throw considerable light on his understanding of his baptism.

The first is the question about Jesus' authority (Mark

11:27–33): "Was the baptism of John from heaven or from men?" Jesus' own ἐξουσία ("authority") was inseparably bound up with that of John. In other words, it was in his baptism by John that Jesus received the ἐξουσία ("authority") "from heaven" (i.e. from God) for his eschatological ministry.

The second passage is Matt. 11:12—"From the days of John the Baptist until now the Kingdom of heaven has suffered violence (βιάζεται), and the men of violence take it by force." The exact interpretation of βιάζεται is highly problematical. But the saying makes it clear that, for Jesus, John the Baptist stood at the "watershed of the aeons". John marked the point where the future kingdom of God became a present factor in history. Thus, it was through his baptism by John that Jesus considered himself to have crossed over into the proleptic presence of the age to come.

But this does not mean that Jesus merely continued John's eschatological ministry. This is made clear in the third passage, Matt. 11:16–19, the similitude of the children playing funerals and weddings. John's eschatological ministry was a stern and preparatory ministry of repentance. Jesus' ministry was the joyful and positive ministry of salvation. Here again for Jesus, his baptism marks the point when the eschatological salvation burst through. The paidological interpretation of the baptism, including the opening of the heavens (cf. Isa. 64:1), the descent of the Spirit (Isa. 42:1c) and the voice from heaven in the Palestinian form is the subsequent christological articulation of the implied Christology of the original event.

We cannot therefore use the original Palestinian form of the baptism narrative to prove that Jesus understood himself to be the Servant of God in the sense of Isa. 42:1. Still less, in view of the atomistic interpretation of the OT current at that time, can we infer that this carries along with it an identification with the suffering, atoning servant of Isa. 53.

That in the answer to John (Matt. 11:2–6 par.) Jesus interprets his healing as well as his preaching ministry in terms of Isa. 35 and 61 cannot be doubted.[61] This does not, however, entitle us to infer that Jesus understood himself to be the suffering and atoning servant of Isa. 53. The atomistic interpretation again rules out that possibility. The answer to John simply indicates that he interprets his preaching and healings as the beginnings of God's eschatological action as promised in Isa. 35 and 61.

In *The Mission and Achievement*[62] the Marcan passion predictions (Mark 8:31; 9:12; 9:31; 10:33f. and 10:45) were analysed in an attempt to lay bare two strata: (1) an original substratum in which Jesus speaks of his sufferings in terms of Isa. 53. (2) the residue as a series of *vaticinia ex eventu*.

Since then H. E. Tödt[63] has shown that the alleged derivations from Isa. 53 are from other sources. πολλὰ παθεῖν could only have originated in Greek, for it is not possible in Aramaic. It is perhaps derived from Ps. 33(34):20 LXX and, therefore belongs not to an earlier, but to a later stratum. ἀποδοκιμασθῆναι in Mark 8:31 and ἐξουδενηθῆναι in 9:12 are synonymous, and variant translations of Ps. 118:22. In quoting this psalm verse the first rendering is used in Mark 12:10 and the second in Acts 4:11. Since this psalm played a prominent part in the passion apologetic of the earliest Aramaic speaking church, Tödt accredits the primary stratum of the passion predictions to this stratum rather than to Jesus himself. Only at Mark 10:45b does he find (thus agreeing with me against Barrett and Miss Hooker) an allusion to Isa. 53:11 MT. This is certainly Palestinian, but a secondary expansion of v. 45a, which was originally a "present" saying. Elsewhere, throughout the passion predictions the death of Jesus is interpreted, not redemptively in terms of Isa. 53, but in terms of Ps. 118:22, as the Jews' rejection of Jesus which was subsequently reversed by the resurrection. This, Tödt maintains, is the earliest interpretation of the passion and resurrection in the post-Easter Palestinian community. We may call this the No-Yes interpretation—the Jew's No in the cross and God's Yes in the resurrection. So we cannot use the Marcan passion predictions as evidences for Jesus's self-understanding, but only as evidence for the kerygma of the earliest Palestinian church. Finally, there is the eucharistic cup word (Mark 14:24). Here Tödt, followed by Hahn, does recognize in ὑπὲρ πολλῶν an allusion to Isa. 53:11 (MT). But this, Tödt holds, is a creation of the liturgical tradition of the Palestinian church, not an original logion of Jesus.

Though many will doubtless shrink from the conclusion as excessively sceptical, we must surely now agree that between them Tödt and Miss Hooker have demolished the thesis that Jesus understood himself as the Servant of the Lord. Still less did he understand himself as the suffering atoning servant of Isa. 53. But against Miss Hooker, we must recognize that this interpretation did come into the Palestinian church very early, though not quite at the beginning. I have suggested elsewhere[64] that the church's explicitly soteriological interpretation of the death of Jesus originated with the first Christian passover celebration of A.D. 31. It may well have been this occasion which introduced the cup-word in the eucharistic tradition. The soteriological interpretation, far from being an arbitrary imposition on the history of Jesus, unfolds the implications of the authentic eschatological prediction of Mark 14:25.[65]

(v) *Kyrios*

Apart from removing Mark 12:35-37 (for the reasons stated above) from the relevant evidence for Jesus' attitude to the honorific addresses, *maran(a)* and rabbi, there is no need to alter what was written on this subject in *The Mission and Achievement of Jesus*. It should however be emphasized that as the disciples began to appreciate the tremendous authority of Jesus already during his earthly life, these terms of address must already have acquired something more than a purely honorific significance even before the rise of the post-Easter faith. Thus, the up-grading of both terms, and especially of *maran(a)*, which followed the Easter experiences, was not entirely unprepared for in the ministry of Jesus. Jesus appears to countenance this heightening of the meaning in the original form[66] of the Q saying, in Luke 6:46—"Why do you call me 'Lord, Lord' and not do what I tell you?" To call Jesus *mar* means not only to accord to him an honorific title, but to recognize the authority of his enunciation of God's final, absolute demand.

(vi) *Son of Man*

The volume of discussion upon this subject has been enormous.[67] There are two main problems involved here. The first is the derivation of the term as used in the gospels.

The second is whether Jesus used it as a self-designation. We have already decided the first question in favour of its derivation from later Jewish apocalyptic tradition (see above pp. 34ff.). With regard to the second question, the difficulty is that the usual methods of source and form criticism yield an inconclusive answer.

Source criticism indicates that the "suffering sayings"[68] are found only in Mark. While this does not warrant Bultmann's conclusion that they are Marcan creations (for Tödt's demonstration of their origin in Palestinian Aramaic Christianity see above), their absence from Q suggests that they belong to a somewhat later stratum. The "parousia" and "present" sayings are found in both Mark and Q. They may both therefore be accepted as representing very early Palestinian tradition. The earliest Palestinian church believed that Jesus had spoken of his coming again as the Son of man, and of his working during his ministry as Son of man, and that he had used the term as a self-designation in both senses.

It is when we submit these two traditions to the test of traditio-historical criticism that we get an uncertain answer. The crucial question is, did the early church use Son of man as a christological title? There are only a few isolated passages where the NT writers themselves use Son of man as a title for Jesus outside of sayings attributed to Jesus. These are: Acts 7:56 (Stephen at his martyrdom); Heb. 2:5-7 (quotation of Ps. 8:5 applied to Jesus—note that in the ensuing exegesis the author does not pick up the term, but refers to "him" and "Jesus"); and Rev. 1:13 (apocalyptic language lifted directly from Dan. 7:13). It is also frequently claimed that the Pauline "second Adam" is derived directly from the term Son of man,[69] and sometimes that the christological pattern of pre-existence-humiliation-exaltation comes from the same source.

Lohmeyer[70] went so far as to postulate the existence of a Galilean Christianity with a distinctive "Son of man" Christology, in contrast to the Davidic Messiah of the Jerusalem Church, But this theory has not commanded wide acceptance. Again, J. M. Robinson concludes that the "varied and imaginative ways in which the term and concept were used by the primitive Church weaken considerably the argument that the Church could not have initiated the identification of Jesus with the Son of Man whose coming he predicted". Actually, however, the evidence is not quite as strong as Robinson suggests. The application of Ps. 8:5 in Hebrews may represent an earlier tradition (cf. the use of v. 7 in 1 Cor. 15:27). But to apply a scripture text to Jesus is not the same as ascribing to him a title. This only happens when the term in question is used outside the scripture and independently. The same consideration applies to Rev. 1:13. And, as Hahn has rightly insisted,[71] the derivation of the Pauline Adam/Christ typology from the Palestinian Son of man Christology should not be too hastily assumed. The pre-existence-incarnation-exaltation pattern is actually a combination of the wisdom and Kyrios christology. The patristic references (e.g. Eusebius, *Ch. Hist. II*, 23 from Hegisippus) are too late to base anything certain upon. We are left with Acts 7:56 as the sole evidence for the independent use of Son of man in the church as a designation for Jesus. But in itself this is a highly problematical passage,[72] and hardly invalidates Hahn's conclusion: "All the Son of man sayings are formulated in the third person and are put into the mouth of Jesus. We never meet Son of man in an invocation or a confession of faith." Thus, the strict application of traditio-critical principles will not allow us to eliminate the "present" and "future" Son of man sayings from the authentic *logia*.

But, as Bultmann pointed out,[73] there is an inner inconsistency within the Son of man sayings. There are some in which a clear distinction is drawn between Jesus and the Son of man (Mark 8:38; Luke 12:8, Q). In the rest of the future sayings the identification of the Son of man is an open question. Yet again, the "present" sayings clearly involve a self-identification. Could Jesus have been so inconsistent as sometimes to equate himself with the Son of man, and sometimes to distinguish between himself and that figure? It is on the grounds of this inconsistency that Bultmann concludes that only the passages in which the distinction is drawn, or the identification not asserted, are authentic. Those, however, in which Jesus identifies himself with the Son of man are creations of the church, which after the resurrection identified Jesus with the Son of man.

In *The Mission and Achievement of Jesus* I tried to take the passages in which the distinction is drawn very seriously, and it is a fault of conservative scholarship that these passages are either ignored or brushed lightly aside.[74] This will not do. They must be the starting point of any investigation, since they have the highest claim to authenticity. In *The Mission and Achievement* I tried, however, to retain all the other sayings by interpreting them in a manner compatible with this distinction. Thus, I reached the conclusion that while Jesus distinguished himself from the future Son of man who was to come in glory (since he was then upon earth) he nevertheless regarded himself as proleptically performing the functions of the coming Son of man.

This thesis had the merit of compatibility with Jesus' conception of the kingdom as future, though proleptically active (cf. *ibid.*, ch. II). But it must be pronounced a rather artificial attempt to paper over the undeniable inconsistency within the Son of man sayings. My basic concern was to refute Bultmann's conclusion that the life of Jesus was un-Messianic, and that he looked for the Son of man as a figure completely detached from his own person, to which he bore merely the relation of the forerunner.

More recently, however, H. E. Tödt has opened up a new understanding of Mark 8:38, Luke 12:8, which obviates Bultmann's negative conclusions. Mark 8:38, Tödt contends, is a developed form which has received further apocalyptic and Christian colouring.[75] The Q form, Luke 12:8f., is nearer to the original:

> Everyone who acknowledges me before men,
>> the Son of man also will acknowledge before the angels of God;
> But he who denies me before men
>> will be denied before the angels of God.

On this saying Tödt comments: "The mystery of this saying lies in the relation which exists between the fellowship of the disciples with Jesus and their participation in the salvation with the Son of man." There is thus, he adds, a "soteriological continuity, though not a christological identity, between Jesus and the Son of man".

I believe we can go further than this. Luke 12:8f. asserts that a man's acceptance of Jesus and the salvation which he brings determines his participation in the final kingdom of God: his rejection of that offer determines his exclusion from it. The distinction between Jesus and the coming Son of man corresponds to the distinction between the kingdom as it is breaking through in Jesus and its final consummation. Jesus is not concerned to impart teaching about the future Son of man, any more than he imparts teaching about the future kingdom or indulges in apocalyptic elaboration. As in his words about the future kingdom (cf. "Blessed are [now] you poor, for yours is [now] the [future] kingdom of God"), the Son of man is brought in simply to reinforce the decisiveness of his present offer. The Son of man merely acts as a kind of rubber stamp at the End for the salvation which is already being imparted in Jesus. Despite the distinction between Jesus and the Son of man, the *ultimate import of this saying is therefore implicitly christological*. So far from driving a wedge—as Bultmann tries to do—between Jesus and the coming Son of man, it brings them as close together as it was possible to bring them within the framework of the Jewish apocalyptic. For Jesus could not identify himself with the coming Son of man, since that figure was to come at the End on the clouds of heaven.[76]

Tödt also accepts as probably authentic five other future Son of man sayings, viz. Matt. 24:27 par., Matt. 24:37 par. (Q); Luke 17:30; Luke 11:30; Matt. 24:44 par. (Q).[77] These sayings are devoid of apocalyptic elaboration, and like Mark 8:38; Luke 12:8 they introduce the Son of man as a sanction for the present and challenge offer of Jesus.

Only at one point does it seem necessary to demur from Tödt's treatment. This is his rejection of Matt. 19:28 in its entirety as a post-Easter creation of the church. His reasons are (1) the Hellenistic word παλιγγενεσία ("regeneration"); (2) the absence of "Son of man" in the Lucan parallel (Luke 22:28–30), which has βασιλεία ("kingdom") instead; (3) the phrase, "throne of his glory" which is apocalyptic colouring absent from the genuine sayings of Jesus; (4) κρίνειν means to rule, and in the authentic Son of man sayings the Son of man is only the rubber stamp (advocate), never ruler of the coming kingdom. It is hard, however, to believe that the post-Easter church, which identified Jesus with the Son of man, and created the "present" and "suffering" sayings to express this identification, should have created a saying which preserved the distinction. To reject this saying is to abandon the form-critical method. While agreeing therefore that points (1)–(3) are church elaborations, we must widen Jesus' conception of the future Son of man to include the function of his ruling in the kingdom of God.

It is significant that in this saying Jesus is so completely and self-effacingly absorbed in his eschatological work that he does not raise the question of his own place in that coming kingdom—a fact which will leave open the possibility for his identification with the Son of man in the post-Easter church.

As regards the present sayings, many will find it difficult to eliminate these altogether from the teaching of Jesus. The Marcan sayings (Mark 2:10 and 28), it is true, are easily dismissed as church formations, for they reflect the concerns of the Palestinian church. But the Q sayings, Matt. 8:20 par. ("The Son of man has nowhere to lay his head") and Matt. 11:19 par. ("The Son of man came eating and drinking") have a freshness about them and a firm anchoring in the situation of Jesus' ministry which makes it difficult to reject them outright. The real difficulty about them is that it is impossible to account for these sayings within the framework of Jewish apocalyptic, where the Son of man is a transcendent figure coming on the clouds of heaven. It is this consideration which has led many to search for another source for the concept in Jesus and to take these sayings as the starting point, even at the cost, if necessary, of eliminating the future apocalyptic sayings.[78] Alternatively, it has been maintained that although Jesus took over the term from Jewish apocalyptic, he profoundly modified it to make it applicable to himself as a historical figure.[79] Such ways of escape, however, leave unexplained the passages where Jesus clearly distinguishes between himself and the coming, apocalyptic Son of man. The latter introduce an intolerable inconsistency. And at the same time they cannot be dismissed as church formations since they are contrary to the post-Easter faith, which made the identification. We have therefore no alternative but reluctantly to regard these "present" Q sayings *in their existing form* as church formations. At the same time we may admit the possibility that in both cases an original "I" stood in place of the Son of man: "*I* have nowhere to lay my head" and "*I* came eating and drinking".

One other Q saying needs discussion, namely Matt. 12:32 par., "And whoever says a word against the Son of man will be forgiven." Tödt takes this as a church formation.[80] He interprets it to mean that those who did not follow Jesus in his earthly life will be forgiven, whereas those who now refuse to follow the Holy Spirit (the exalted Lord) will not be forgiven. Its creative milieu would thus be the church's mission to the Jews in Palestine. The saying presupposes two epochs: first the period of the Son of man on earth; and second, the period of the Spirit or exalted Lord. The Marcan form (Mark 3:28f.) on this view is a secondary alteration of the Q form. T. W. Manson's[81] interpretation is, however, to be preferred. According to Manson the Marcan form is original and authentic. Its meaning is that the one unforgivable sin is to reject Jesus' eschatological message. Q's substitution of "Son of man" (singular) is a mistake for "sons of men" (plural).

(vii) *Prophet*

In any effort to recover Jesus' self-understanding it is usual to begin with a discussion of Jesus as a prophet on the ground that this is the lowest estimate of his person. We have deliberately left the good wine until now, for three reasons. First, in the course of our investigation of the other titles we have already discovered indubitably authentic material which bears relevantly upon Jesus' understanding of his mission in prophetic terms. This has notably been the case in our search for the Servant concept in Jesus' *logia*. Our investigation of his proclamation and miracles as he understood them did not yield altogether negative results. Second, it is true that the post-Easter church interpreted Jesus as the Mosaic-servant-prophet. But, as we shall see later, there is a small body of material in the gospels which presents Jesus as a prophet in more general, non-Mosaic terms. This material should not, therefore, be eliminated with the other titles as formations of the post-Easter community.

Some of Jesus' contemporaries certainly regarded him as a prophet.[82] In one of the primary sources, Mark 6:15 and 8:27f., it is reported that some people (not disciples) regarded Jesus as εἷς τῶν προφητῶν ("one of the prophets"). The word εἷς ("one") is a semitism meaning not one particular prophet, but *any* (τις) prophet, i.e. a man belonging to the general prophetic type. This popular estimate of Jesus is confirmed by Simon the Pharisee's observation that if Jesus were a prophet (as presumably some held him to be) he would have known the shady past of the woman who anointed him (Luke 7:39, Special Luke). The tradition of this contemporary estimate has perhaps survived in two of Matthew's editorial additions (Matt. 21:11 and 46) to the Marcan narrative. Again, in Luke 24:19 it is reported that the Emmaus disciples had regarded Jesus as a prophet during his lifetime. It is possible, however, that these last three cases reflect the later church's understanding of Jesus as *the* eschatological prophet man in the explicitly christological sense.[83] Undoubtedly, προφήτης μέγας ("a great prophet") in the choric ending of the raising of the widow's son at Nain (Luke 7:16) is intended christologically[84] and must therefore be regarded as a church formation. There is no passage in Q to support this popular view of Jesus as an ordinary prophet, but this is probably due to the almost complete absence of narrative material from that tradition. Despite the absence of evidence from Q, there is, however, sufficient evidence to establish the popular estimate of Jesus as a prophet.[85]

There are a number of passages where it is reported that Jesus was regarded by some of his contemporaries as a specific OT prophet *redivivus*. Most of these are clearly secondary.[86] But the report that Jesus was John the Baptist or Elijah *redivivus* occurs in a primary source (Mark 6:14f.; 8:28). Now there is no evidence that the post-Easter church ever interpreted Jesus as John the Baptist *redivivus* or even as Elijah *redivivus*, although certain traits from the Elijah tradition were taken up into the later conception of Jesus as an eschatological prophet. Rather, in Christian tradition John the Baptist himself became Elijah *redivivus* (Mark 9:13). It would seem then that on traditio-historical grounds, Mark 6:14 and 8:28 should be taken as genuine historical reminiscence. There were evidently some among Jesus' contemporaries who regarded him as an eschatological prophet; not indeed in the sense that the End was breaking through with him, but in the sense that he was the immediate herald of the End. In no sense is this a christological confession. For Christology asserts that the eschatological salvation *has actually broken through* with Jesus.

But did Jesus understand himself as a prophet? That is the crucial question. There are two passages in which he compares his fate with that of a prophet, namely Mark 6:4 par. and Luke 13:33. In neither case is "prophet" a self-designation. Each time Jesus is quoting a proverb or a commonly accepted truth. As Friedrich, however, has pertinently remarked[87] about the second passage—and it applies equally to the first—"By not only identifying himself with this view point, but engaging himself to make it a reality he is ranging himself in the company of the prophets." In other words, without using "prophet" as a direct self-designation, Jesus clearly indicates that he understood his role in prophetic terms in so far as it involved rejection and martyrdom.[88]

Dr. C. H. Dodd[89] has assembled fifteen prophetic characteristics in the style and content of Jesus' ministry in word and deed. To them, Dr. Barrett adds, somewhat tentatively, sayings in which Jesus speaks of his mission as a coming ($\mathring{\eta}\lambda\theta o\nu$, "I came") or sending ($\mathring{\alpha}\pi\epsilon\sigma\tau\acute{\alpha}\lambda\eta\nu$, "I was sent").[90] In his form-critical analysis of these sayings, Bultmann[91] admits that "There is no *a priori* objection against the possibility that Jesus should have spoken of himself and his coming in the first person. After all, that would accord with his prophetic self-consciousness." But he then proceeds to eliminate most of them as church formations on grounds of content, leaving only Luke 12:49, Mark 2:17 and Matt. 15:24. He then eliminates these also, on the ground that they all look back upon Jesus' ministry as a completed fact of the past. He seems to be determined to get rid of these sayings at all costs! But in Luke 12:49 Jesus is clearly speaking of his ministry as still in process and of his tension until it is completed. The saying does not look back upon that ministry as complete. Mark 2:17 speaks, too, of his Galilean ministry to the outcast, not necessarily of his whole saving work including the cross. Matt. 15:24 is certainly more dubious in its attestation, for it occurs only in the narrowly Judaistic Special Matthean material.[92] Bultmann also suspects that this saying originates in the debates of the Palestinian church about the gentile mission. But quite apart from the problem as to whether this represents the precise attitude of the Palestinian church towards the gentile mission,[93] it may be questioned whether this was in fact the original application of the saying. It could very well have referred originally to Jesus' ministry to the outcast. In that case it is very similar in import to Mark 2:17. In addition, it will be remembered that we suggested (above p. 125) that in the Q saying Matt. 11:18f. par., "Son of man" may have replaced an original "I" and that in this form it may have been an authentic saying. If so, it would refer again to Jesus' eating with the outcast. Accordingly, we may postulate an original nucleus of ἦλθον ("I came") and ἀπεστάλην ("I was sent") sayings which formed the model for the later church formations.[94]

Now it will be noted that nearly all of this residual nucleus concerns Jesus' ministry to the outcast. It was in this connection that his consciousness of mission was most clearly expressed. Yet it is precisely here that his activity passed beyond that of a prophet, even of an eschatological prophet in the sense of one who was merely proclaiming salvation which was yet to come. Here he is the herald of a salvation which is *already breaking through* in his own conduct.

Jesus' understanding of his own proclamation and healings points in a similar direction. The answer to John (Matt. 11:4–6 par. (Q)) employs, as we have seen, the language of Isa. 61:1 and 35:5f. to show that these activities have an eschatological significance. We can no longer infer from this passage (in view of the current atomistic exegesis) that Jesus is interpreting his role in terms of the Isaianic suffering servant. But it is legitimate to infer that he understood his proclamation (εὐαγγελίζεσθαι!) and healings in prophetic terms derived from the Servant passages of Deutero-Isaiah. His ministry was eschatological-prophetic in the sense that he was not merely proclaiming a future salvation, but was actually inaugurating it.

It has also been widely acknowledged that the ἐξουσία ("authority") of Jesus is a prophetic trait.[95] Moreover, if we follow T. W. Manson's thesis that Mark 3:29 is the original form of the saying about blasphemy (see above, p. 125), we may go a step further. Jesus here indicates that his words and works are the work of the Holy Spirit. This again points to Isa. 61:1. Could it be, too, that Jesus understood his baptism a little more specifically than we suggested above (pp. 116f.)? Did he regard it as his anointing with the Spirit for an eschatological-prophetic mission in terms of Isa. 61:1? If so we can trace three stages in the growth of the baptism pericope as recorded in Mark 1: (1) Jesus' own interpretation of his baptism in terms of Isa. 61:1; (2) the Palestinian inter-pretation of it in terms of Isa. 42:1 (an explicit paidology); (3) the Hellenistic interpretation of it in terms of the Son of God-divine man concept.[96] If Jesus himself attributed his words and works to a charismatic anointing with the Holy Spirit, this does not signify a "Messianic" self-understanding. But he did understand his mission in terms of eschatological prophecy.

Finally, there is a collection of sayings in the Q material in which Jesus ranges his own mission in the prophetic succession, viz. Matt. 23:29f. par., 34-36 par., and 37. The finality of the judgments pronounced over Israel at the end of each of these sayings (vv. 31, 36 and 38) indicates that Jesus thought of his mission not only as belonging to the same class as that of the OT prophets, but as representing the final prophetic mission to Israel, and of his own rejection (and possible martyrdom) as the culmination of Israel's rejection of the word of Yahweh. Here we penetrate the heart of the matter. Jesus thought of his own mission not simply as one in the prophetic series, but as the final mission, bringing God's last offer of salvation and judgment. Jesus does not identify himself *expressis verbis* with the eschatological prophet in any of the current forms of Jewish expectation. But he does interpret his mission in terms of eschatological prophecy.[97]

4. Summary

We are accordingly led to revise our interpretation of Jesus' self-understanding as formulated in *The Mission and Achievement of Jesus*. There we said that Jesus, while not dictating any interpretation of his person, understood himself to be called to a mission of obedience in terms of the suffering servant, the fulfilment of which would lead to his vindication as Son of man. Revised, it now runs: Jesus understood his mission in terms of eschatological prophecy and was confident of its vindication by the Son of man at the End. As eschatological prophet he was not merely announcing the future coming of salvation and judgment, but actually initiating it in his words and works. It is the unexpressed, implicit figure of the eschatological prophet which gives a unity to all of Jesus' historical activity, his proclamation, his teaching with ἐξουσία ("authority"), his healings and exorcisms, his conduct in eating with the outcast, and finally his death in the fulfilment of his prophetic mission. Take the implied self-understanding of his role in terms of the eschatological prophet away, and the whole ministry falls into a series of unrelated, if not meaningless fragments.

Two *caveats* should be entered here. First, this interpretation of Jesus's self-understanding must be sharply differentiated from the interpretation of Jesus as a prophetic social reformer, a view which has been championed in American scholarship from the time of Rauschenbusch down to the present day.[98] The roots of Jesus' message in the eschatology of a reduced apocalyptic is the indubitable refutation of all such views.

Second, it must not be inferred that "eschatological prophet" is the definitive understanding of Jesus' person. This concept cannot be used as a corrective either of the christological responses of the New Testament church or of the subsequent metaphysical development of Christology which culminated in Chalcedon and Nicea. Jesus did not *define* his own person as that of an eschatological prophet. It was simply the working concept which guided him in the tasks of his earthly ministry. The basic datum of NT Christology is not the concept of Jesus as eschatological prophet, but his proclamation and activity which confront men and women with the presence and saving act of God breaking into history and his utter commitment and entire obedience to the will of God which made him the channel of that saving activity. To interpret this datum in terms of explicit Christology was the task of the post-Easter church, in whose *kerygma* the Proclaimer became the Proclaimed.

NOTES ON CHAPTER V

1. This is not to deny that the Johannine discourses do enshrine traditional logia, some of which may well go back to Jesus himself. But Jesus' christological utterances in the fourth gospel are beyond all doubt church formations. Nor, again, would we deny that the fourth gospel enshrines early and valuable narrative and even factual traditions. See my *The New Testament in Current Study*, London: S.C.M. Press, 1963, pp. 125f., 141–143.

2. Passages which are clearly redactional are omitted from this list.

3. For a report on modern discussion of the kingdom of God since Ritschl see N. Perrin, *The Kingdom of God in the Teaching of Jesus*, London: S.C.M. Press, 1963, pp. 13–157.

4. E.g. J. Weiss, *Die Predigt Jesu vom Reich Gottes*, Göttingen: Vandenhoeck u. Ruprecht, 1892; A. Schweitzer, *The Mystery of the Kingdom of God*, London: A. & C. Black, 1925 (Eng. Tr. of *Das Abendmahl* Part II, "*Das Messianitäts- und Leidensgeheimnis*", 1901); The Swiss liberal school (M. Werner, F. Buri) also follows Schweitzer's "thoroughgoing eschatology" (*konsequente Eschatologie*).

5. R. Bultmann, *Theology* I, pp. 6–9; *Primitive Christianity*, pp. 86–90.

6. "Realized eschatology", associated with the name of C. H. Dodd, (*The Parables of the Kingdom*, London: Nisbet, 1936[2], pp. 41–51). This view has been widely accepted in Britain and to some extent in the U.S.A. It is only fair to add that Dodd himself has somewhat modified his position since: see his *The Coming of Christ*, Cambridge: University Press, 1951, pp. 13f.; *The Interpretation of the Fourth Gospel*, p. 447 and note 1.

7. W. G. Kümmel, *Promise and Fulfilment* (*SBT* 23), London: S.C.M. Press, 1957, pp. 19–87, 105–140. Cf. Jeremias' formula, first suggested by Haenchen, "sich realisierende Eschatologie" ("eschatology in the process of realization", perhaps "process eschatology"), *The Parables of Jesus*, London: S.C.M. Press, 1954, p. 159 and O. Cullmann's formula, "D-Day and V-Day", *Christ and Time*, London: S.C.M. Press, 1951, p. 84.

8. *The Mission and Achievement of Jesus* (*SBT* 12), 1954, p. 25.

9. *Op. cit.* (note 3), p. 87. Cf. also R. F. Berkey in *JBL* 82 (1963), pp. 177–187.

10. Since the proclamation of Jesus is not the direct concern of this book, there is no need to justify this position exegetically in the text. It is based on the fact that authentic logia of Jesus sometimes represent the kingdom as future, sometimes as present, cf. above all ἤγγικεν, Mark 1:15 and Matt. 10:7, par., with ἔφθασεν, Matt. 12:28 par.

10a. *Theology* I, p. 43. It is curious that this concession occurs not in Chapter I which deals with the historical Jesus, but only in Chapter II, which deals with the relation of the church's kerygma to the historical Jesus.

11. Cf. H. Schlier in *TWNT* I, s.v. 'Aμήν, pp. 341f.: "In the ἀμήν before the λέγω ὑμῖν of Jesus the whole of Christology is contained *in nuce*." Schlier's thesis has been employed by G. Ebeling, *ZThK* 55 (1958), pp. 99–102, in his pioneering essay in the post-Bultmannian "new quest" of the historical Jesus.

12. E.g. Matt. 10:15, 42. See G. Bornkamm, *Jesus of Nazareth*, London: S.C.M. Press, 1960, p. 93.

13. For the general historicity of Jesus' exorcisms and healings, see my *Interpreting the Miracles*, London, S.C.M. Press, 1963, pp. 18–29.

14. For the interpretation cf. *ibid*. p. 28.

15. For the authenticity of this saying, see R. Bultmann, *History of the Synoptic Tradition*, Oxford: Blackwell, 1963, p. 151.

16. See Jeremias, *Parables*, pp. 99–120; E. Fuchs, *Studies of the Historical Jesus* (*SBT* 42) London: S.C.M. Press, 1964, pp. 19–25. Here the post-Bultmannians have gone decisively beyond Bultmann. Jesus not only demands a decision but actually brings the eschatological salvation. This provides a more adequate basis for an implicit Christology than the mere demand for a decision, which really only yields a self-understanding of Jesus as an eschatological prophet of a salvation still entirely future.

17. E.g. Matt. 5:18. The antithetical formula in the Sermon on the Mount: "You have heard that it was said . . . but I say" is peculiar to Matt. and probably an editorial construction, for it is absent where parallels occur elsewhere (contrast Matt. 5:31f. with Mark 10:11f.; Luke 16:18). But it catches the point of "Amen, I say to you". The antithesis "Love your enemies" is introduced at Luke 6:27 with the formula ἀλλὰ λέγω ὑμῖν ("but I say to you"). This shows how little change was needed to produce the Matthean formula. Cf. E. Klostermann, *Das Matthäusevangelium* (*HNT* 4), 1927, p. 42.

18. For the significance of the form, Abba, see G. Kittel in *TWNT* I, pp. 5f.; J. Jeremias, *ET* 71 (1960), p. 144. Jeremias claims with the help of his assistants to have examined the whole later Jewish literature of prayer and to have found not a single instance of Abba as an address to God.

19. J. A. T. Robinson, *Honest to God*, London: S.C.M. Press, 1963, pp. 11–18. A Christian doctrine of God must be christologically oriented. That is to say, it must arise out of the encounter with God in Jesus of Nazareth. As presented by Dr. Robinson, the "God beneath" appears as an abstract, metaphysical concept, replacing another, equally abstract and metaphysical concept of the "God out there". Of course, God is also

"near" in the OT. Yet here again, it is not an abstract metaphysical doctrine but a confession arising from encounter with his mighty acts in Israel.

20. Cf. N. Perrin, *Kingdom*, p. 192: "The disciples are being told to use the child's word, Abba, of God, a practice specifically avoided by the Jews, *and this can only be the result of their response to the kingly activity manifest in Jesus and his ministry*" (italics mine). All the more surprising is it to find Hahn, *Hoheitstitel*, p. 327, saying that originally in the teaching of Jesus "everyone could say 'Father', whereas in Matt. 11:27 a christological contraction (*Verengung*) has taken place." On the contrary, in the teaching of Jesus it is not "everyone" but precisely and only those who have accepted his eschatological message who can say "Abba". Matt. 11:27 is not a "christological contraction," but an explicit expression of the implicit Christology of Jesus' own use of Abba.

21. J. Wellhausen, *Das Evangelium Lucae*, Berlin: G. Reimer, 1904, pp. 75f., followed in *Mission and Achievement*, p. 62, and subsequently also by G. Bornkamm, *Jesus of Nazareth*, p. 154. Note that Jesus calls himself "a prophet".

22. J. Knox, *The Death of Christ*, New York: Abingdon Press, 1958, pp. 72–76.

23. Bornkamm, *ibid.*, pp. 154f.; H. Conzelmann, *RGG³*, s.v. "Jesus Christus".

24. J. Jeremias in *The Servant*, pp. 101 and 471.

25. So E. Fuchs, *op. cit.*, p. 26; J. Knox, *The Death of Christ*, p. 120. R. Bultmann, *Glauben und Verstehen* III, Tübingen: J. C. B. Mohr, 1960, pp. 176f., n. 6 has protested against this as a psychological speculation. But it is rooted in the historical and contextual situation of the saying: it occurs in a warning against Herod, who had recently put John the Baptist to death. I see no reason why the church should have created that setting.

26. Bornkamm, *Jesus of Nazareth*, p. 160.

27. Bultmann, *Theology* I, p. 27. "The synoptic tradition leaves no doubt about it that Jesus' *life and work*, measured by traditional ideas, *was not Messianic*." It is only fair to note the qualification, "measured by traditional ideas". Yet, all that Bultmann concedes in this chapter is that Jesus was *an* (not *the*) eschatological prophet. His more positive statement that Jesus' call to a decision "implies a Christology" occurs not in his chapter on Jesus, but in the following chapter (p. 43) on the earliest church!

28. E.g. C. H. Dodd, *According to the Scriptures*, pp. 116–119; V. Taylor, *Jesus and His Sacrifice*, London: Macmillan, 1937, esp. p. 48: "He reinterpreted the Son of Man in terms of Isa. liii,"; W. Manson: *Jesus the Messiah*, esp. p. 112: "The glorification of the Son of Man can only come about through the endurance of the sufferings predicted of the servant in Isa. liii." A. M. Hunter, *Introducing New Testament Theology*, London: 1957, S.C.M. Press, esp. p. 62: "God has ordained that Jesus the Son of Man shall fulfil the destiny of the suffering Servan (*sic*) of the Lord."

29. For their work see J. M. Robinson, *A New Quest*, pp. 12–19.

30. For the methods of traditio-historical criticism, see chapter I, pp. 18f.

31. In *Mission and Achievement*, pp. 110f., it was stated that Mark 12:35–37, if authentic, could only be an academic debate about Messiahship. But the use of Ps. 109(110):1 LXX points to the origin of this pericope in the Hellenistic Jewish Church. Matt. 23:10, peculiar to Matt., is a late reflection of the dominical saying in v. 8 (Klostermann *ad loc.*). The title is significantly absent from the Q material.

32. The Matthean expansion (Matt. 16:17–19) is clearly secondary (*contra* Bultmann, *Tradition*, pp. 258f.) in its present position though it is demonstrably of independent Palestinian origin, belonging to the Supper tradition according to O. Cullmann, *Peter*, London: S.C.M. Press, 1953, pp. 183f., or to a post-resurrection scene according to E. Stauffer, *New Testament Theology*, London: S.C.M. Press, 1955, pp. 32f.—the latter more plausibly.

33. See W. Wrede, *Das Messiasgeheimnis in den Evangelien*, Göttingen: Vandenhoeck u. Ruprecht, 1913, *passim*, esp. pp. 61, 66, 141f. Wrede does not think that Mark invented the idea, but he does attribute its insertion into the tradition to Mark, here and wherever else it occurs. For an important corrective to Wrede, see H. Conzelmann, *RGG³*, s.v. "Jesus Christus". This matter will be discussed later.

34. See M. Dibelius, *From Tradition to Gospel*, New York: Scribners, 1935, pp. 115, 275.

35. Cf. Cullmann, *Peter*, 174. Cullmann, however, regards the passion prediction as part of the original pericope. But it not only belongs to a different stratum, it destroys the clear cut form of a pronouncement story. Hahn would also remove 27b–29a from the original pericope on the ground that it belongs to an independent tradition surviving also at Mark 6:14–16 (*Hoheitstitel*, pp. 226–230), but this reduces the pericope to a torso, and removes the setting for Jesus' question.

36. P. Winter, *On the Trial of Jesus*, Berlin: De Gruyter, 1961, pp. 20–30 renewing the objections of H. Lietzmann, *Der Prozess Jesu*, *SBA* 14 (1931), pp. 313–322. For a critique of Lietzmann see G. D. Kilpatrick, *The Trial of Jesus*, Oxford University Press, 1953. Cf. also T. B. Burkill in *Vig. Chr.* 12 (1958), pp. 1–18. Burkill considers that the trial scene has been constructed out of the original authentic *titulus* (see below, note 37) and that the oldest stratum of the Marcan passion narrative contained only a brief mention of a matutinal assembly to prepare the charge against Jesus (cf. Mark 15:1). In that case, it is at least arguable that the question "Are you the Messiah?" was put to Jesus at the matutinal assembly.

37. There has been weighty support for the historicity of the *titulus* in recent years against Bultmann, *Tradition*, p. 284. See e.g. Dibelius, *Botschaft und Geschichte* I, p. 256; Burkill, *op. cit.*, p. 16; P. Winter in *ZNW* 50, 1959, pp. 250f., and *op cit.* (above, note 36), pp. 107–110; N. A. Dahl in H. Ristow and K. Matthiae, *Der historische Jesus und der kerygmatische Christus*, Berlin: Evangelische Verlagsanstalt, 1961, pp. 149–169, esp.

pp. 159f. There can be no doubt that Jesus was executed not simply as a Messianic prophet (Bultmann), but as a Messianic pretender. The *titulus* cannot be a Christian creation, for βασιλεὺς τῶν 'Ιουδαίων was not a Christological title current among the early Christians.

38. Cullmann, *Christology*, pp. 118f.; Taylor, *Mark* (see below note 48) favours the reading σὺ εἶπας ὅτι ἐγώ εἰμι (Θ fam 13 etc.).

39. Hahn denies the feasibility of this interpretation (*Hoheitstitel*, pp. 182, n. 1, 195, n. 6) but without offering any grounds for his denial.

40. According to Hahn (p. 159, n. 3) this suggestion is as old as F. C. Baur.

41. According to Hahn this more specific suggestion goes back to Holtzmann (*Hoheitstitel*, p. 159, n. 4). This view is widely accepted by British scholars today.

42. Cf. R. P. Casey, *JTS* n.s. 9 (1958), pp. 258–260, who shows that where in Mark the title *Christos* is authentic it is used in a Jewish sense. Where it has been re-interpreted it is the work of the post-Easter Christian community.

43. Cf. *Mission and Achievement*, p. 115. But my attempt to show that this family tradition influenced Jesus' self-understanding as the Ebed Yahweh (linking Isa. 9 and 11 with 42 and 53) ignores the atomistic exegesis of the period, and must be abandoned.

43a. So *Mission and Achievement*, p. 113.

44. B. Lindars, *New Testament Apologetic*, London: S.C.M. Press, 1961, p. 112. This work is a valuable contribution to traditio-historical criticism from one line of approach, viz. the OT quotations, though the author sometimes shrinks from the full traditio-historical consequences of his analyses.

45. W. G. Kümmel, *Promise and Fulfilment*, London: S.C.M. Press (*SBT* 23), 1957, p. 115, following *SB*; Lindars (*op cit.*, p. 171) miscon-strues the evidence provided by *SB* to support the Jewish character and authenticity of this acclamation.

46. Kümmel, *ibid.*

47. On the Matthean Christology see G. Bornkamm in *Tradition and Interpretation in Matthew*, London: S.C.M. Press, 1963, pp. 32–51.

48. V. Taylor, *The Gospel According to St. Mark*, London: Macmillan, 1952, p. 452, "Messianic for Jesus, but not Messianic for the people" (following Schweitzer).

49. Bultmann, *Tradition*, p. 261; Hahn, *Hoheitstitel*, p. 172: like the similar episode in Mark 14:12–16 the discovery of the ass suggests supernatural prescience of the Hellenistic divine man.

50. For a denial of a messianic intention on the part of Jesus in the triumphal entry cf. Lindars, *op cit.*, p. 112: "It seems that the action of Jesus was not so much making a claim concerning himself as giving a sign of the immediate fulfilment of his preaching about the kingdom of God." The positive part of this interpretation, however, rests upon Lindars' acceptance of the authenticity of the acclamation in v. 10.

51. C. H. Dodd, *Parables*, pp. 124–132; Jeremias, *The Parables of Jesus*, pp. 55–60; Taylor, *Mark*, pp. 472f. Dodd and Jeremias admit that the

authentic parable has undergone subsequent allegorization, and seek to recover an authentic nucleus by the omission of certain verses (Dodd: 4 (?5) and 9b; Jeremias: 5b, 10f.).

52. Kümmel, *Promise and Fulfilment*, pp. 82f., and more fully in *Aux sources de la tradition chrétienne*, pp. 120–131. Kümmel shows (1) that there is no ground for deducing a non-allegorical *Urform* owing to the absence of linguistic criteria for the differentiation of the allegorical and non-allegorical parts; (2) that υἱὸς ἀγαπητός belongs to the same stratum as the heavenly voice in the baptism and transfiguration narratives; and (3) that in the authentic teaching of Jesus judgment falls upon Israel not because of their murder of him, but because of their rejection of his eschatological message.

53. *Mission and Achievement*, p. 83.

54. *Ibid.*, pp. 89–95. Hahn (p. 325, n. 1) expresses general agreement with my treatment except that he considers my attempt to link it with the Servant of Yahweh concept "*abwegig*". It does, however, have some support from L. Cerfaux (Hahn, p. 328, n. 3). More recently S. Schulz has found in πάντα παρεδόθη μοι ὑπὸ τοῦ πατρός μου a connection with the Son of man tradition (*Untersuchungen zur Menschensohnchristologie im Johannesevangelium*, Göttingen: Vandenhoeck u. Ruprecht, 1957, pp. 124ff.). Hahn prefers himself to regard it as an inner-Christian development from the filial consciousness of Jesus expressed in his use of Abba, and his admission of others to that privilege. None of these three suggestions is exclusive and it seems preferable to regard the passage as a combination of all three strands: (1) Jesus' use of Abba; (2) the servant; and (3) the Son of man concept. It is then clearly a church formation. But its precise *Sitz im Leben* (Palestinian-Aramaic or Hellenistic Jewish Christian?) is as yet undetermined.

55. *Mission and Achievement*, p. 85.

56. *Ibid.*, pp. 86–95.

57. Cullmann, *Christology*, pp. 60-69; 158-164.

58. H. E. Tödt, *Menschensohn*, pp. 143–161.

59. Cullmann, *Christology*, pp. 66f.

59a. *Ibid.*, p. 73.

60. "In order to arrive at Jesus's self-consciousness we shall make use of the form-critical examination of the Gospel tradition in that we shall attempt to distinguish between the places where the Gospel writers obviously express their own view and the places where they report the words of Jesus himself." This statement is difficult to reconcile with the statement on the following page: "The early Church believed in Christ's Messiahship only because it believed that Jesus believed himself to be the Messiah." Apart from the imprecise use of the term, Messiah, in this sentence, it involves the abandonment of the form-critical method announced on the previous page.

61. So even Hooker, *Servant*, pp. 85f.

62. *Mission and Achievement*, pp. 55–64.

63. See above, note 58. In addition to the points mentioned in the text, Tödt also discovers semitisms in εἰς χεῖρας ἀνθρώπων (Mark 9:31);

in the use of ἀποκτανθῆναι rather than the Hellenistic σταυρωθῆναι in Mark 8:31; 9:31; 10:34, and in the use of ἀναστῆναι. He would agree that παραδοθῆναι has no OT background, and maintains that γέγραπται in 9:12b must refer to Ps. 118:22. In Mark 10:45a διακονηθῆναι etc. refers not to Isa. 53, but to Jesus' service at table (cf. Luke 22:27). Tödt's conclusions may sound sceptical. But they represent an important gain over Bultmann, who relegated the passion predictions to the Hellenistic church. These are shown now to be definitely Palestinian, though not authentic to Jesus.

64. In a paper entitled "The Double Origin of the Eucharist", *BR* 8, (1963), pp. 60-72.

65. E. Schweizer, *RGG*³, s.v. *"Abendmahl"*.

66. The evidence is surprisingly scanty. In the primary sources only at Mark 7:28, Matt. 8:8 par. (Q), both on the lips of gentiles. But its use in Jesus' lifetime as an honorific address is clinched by Matt. 7:21 par., where the Lucan form is probably original, against Hahn pp. 97f. Hahn thinks that the Matthean form is original, and that it is an eschatological invocation of Jesus as the coming one in the parousia, and therefore a church formation. He does agree, however, that Jesus was actually addressed as *Maran(a)* in his lifetime.

67. For a recent report on discussion see A. J. B. Higgins in *New Testament Essays*, pp. 119–135. This essay was written too early to take full account of the recent developments in the Bultmann school, except for a brief mention of Bornkamm, p. 133, n. 24. For further reports on these developments cf. my *New Testament in Current Study*, pp. 44–49, and N. Perrin, *Kingdom*, pp. 109–111, 124f.

68. For a tabulation of the Son of man sayings according to Bultmann's now commonly accepted threefold classification (not originally suggested by Bultmann, but by K. Lake and F. Jackson, *The Beginnings of Christianity*, pp. 368–384), see *Mission and Achievement*, pp. 96–98.

69. E.g. A. E. J. Rawlinson, *New Testament Doctrine*, pp. 122–136; Cullmann, *Christology*, pp. 166–181; J. M. Robinson, *A New Quest*, p. 102, n. 2.

70. E. Lohmeyer, *Galiläa und Jerusalem*, Göttingen: Vandenhoeck u. Ruprecht, 1936, pp. 68–79.

71. Hahn, *Hoheitstitel*, p. 21. See below, pp. 233f.

72. Stephen's vision cannot be used as evidence that the early church confessed or proclaimed Jesus as the Son of man, but only that it looked for his return as such. On Acts 7:56 see H. P. Owen, *NTS* 1 (1955), pp. 224–226, who explains Christ's standing as an indication of the immediacy of his return. Stephen is granted an advance vision of the parousia and thus of his own vindication, cf. Mark 9:1.

73. *Theology* I, pp. 29f.

74. "Anyone who accepts these sayings as genuine, but tries to explain them by the theory that Jesus designates someone other than himself as the coming Son of man, raises more problems than he solves." Cullmann, *Christology*, p. 156. But Tödt has shown that the problem is by no

means insoluble, whereas Cullmann fails to do justice to the inconsistency of Mark 8:38; Luke 12:8f. with the sayings where Son of man is a clear self-designation of Jesus. Cf. A. Richardson, *An Introduction*, p. 134, who simply comments on my taking seriously the distinction between Jesus and the Son of man in these passages, "even the sure-footed Fuller stumbles here". He then tries to eliminate the inconsistency by taking his start with the suffering passages and reading their meaning into Mark 8:38 etc., and accusing Bultmann of reading Mark 8:38, etc., in the light of his own prejudice against Jesus' Messianic consciousness. But the distinction is plain for all to see in the text, and it is the identification of Jesus with the Son of man which is being read into it.

75. καὶ τοὺς [λόγους] ἐμούς is probably not part of the original saying. It spoils the parallelism, and seems to reflect the later church's interest in the sayings of the historical Jesus. ἐπαισχύνθησεται is certainly Pauline, and perhaps part of the missionary vocabulary of the Hellenistic churches (Rom. 1:16, 2 Tim. 1:8, etc.). ἐν τῇ δόξῃ is added apocalyptic colouring (so also Taylor, *Mark*, pp. 383f. and J. A. T. Robinson, *Jesus and His Coming*, London: S.C.M. Press, 1959, p. 54. τοῦ πατρὸς αὐτοῦ is a christianization. In Jewish apocalyptic God does not appear as "Father" (Hahn, p. 33).

76. P. Vielhauer in *Festschrift für G. Dehn*, ed. W. Schneemelcher, *Neukirchen*, 1959, pp. 51–79, eliminates *all* the Son of man sayings from the authentic *logia* of Jesus on the grounds that they never occur in combination with Kingdom of God, a combination also absent in Judaism. For a refutation of Vielhauer's thesis see E. Schweizer in *ZNW* 50 (1959), p. 186 and Tödt, *Menschensohn*, pp. 298–316. Vielhauer thinks that the original form of the saying, Luke 12:8f., is betrayed by the second half of the *parallelismus membrorum*, so that the first half ran thus:

> Everyone who denies me
> will be denied before the angels of God.

Schweizer, who wishes to eliminate all of the parousia sayings from the authentic *logia* (see below, note 78) is inclined to agree with Vielhauer here. But it would seem most unlikely that the post-Easter church, which certainly accepted the identity of Jesus with the Son of man, should have created a saying which distinguished between them. In fact the principles of traditio-historical criticism actually vindicate the authenticity of Luke 12:8 in its present form.

77. *Menschensohn*, p. 206.

78. E.g. J. A. T. Robinson, *Jesus and His Coming*, and, rather similarly, Schweizer *art. cit.* Robinson starts with the present sayings as authentic. He then accepts the future sayings in so far as they speak of Jesus' vindication, but eliminates the ideas of a *return*. In this last point he is correct in so far as the concept of a "return" was only possible after the resurrection when the church had identified Jesus with the coming Son of man. But Jewish apocalyptic does not provide a starting point for Jesus' self-identification with the Son of man in his earthly life. Therefore,

Robinson's thesis could only be sustained if Jesus' use of the Son of man had some other origin, which is most unlikely.

Schweizer holds that Jesus adopted the term Son of man primarily as a simple self-designation equivalent to "I" and filled it with the content of humiliation-exaltation. In fact he is inclined to take the suffering sayings as his starting point. He then endeavours to eliminate the future sayings from the authentic *logia*. But the use of הָהוּא בַּר־נָשָׁא as a simple self-designation in Aramaic has not been demonstrated (see Dalman, *Words of Jesus*, pp. 249f.), despite the attempt of J. Y. Campbell in *JTS* 48 (1947), pp. 145–155, to show that Jesus used it as such.

79. E.g. by those who hold that Jesus combined the apocalyptic Son of man with the Deutero-Isaianic Suffering Servant. See, above all, W. Manson, *Jesus the Messiah*, pp. 110–113; similarly J. W. Bowman, *The Intention of Jesus*, London: S.C.M. Press, 1945, pp. 126–136.

80. Tödt, *Menschensohn*, pp. 109–112.

81. T. W. Manson, *The Sayings of Jesus*, London: S.C.M. Press, 1949, p. 110.

82. The classical treatment of Jesus as a prophet is by C. H. Dodd in *Mysterium Christi*, ed. G. K. A. Bell–A. Deissmann, London: Longman, 1930, pp. 56–66. See also C. K. Barrett, *The Holy Spirit and the Gospel Tradition*, London: S.P.C.K., 1947, pp. 94–99; V. Taylor, *The Names of Jesus*, London: Macmillan, 1953, pp. 15–17; O. Cullmann, *Christology*, pp. 30–38. Also the following articles: P. E. Davies, *JBL* 64 (1945), pp. 241–254; F. W. Young, *JBL* 68 (1949), 285–299; H. M. Teeple, *op. cit.* (see ch. II, note 75); G. Friedrich, *TWNT* VI, pp. 842–849, s.v. προφήτης.

83. So Friedrich, p. 847. That the Lucan occurrence is intended to be christological is indicated by v. 21 (λυτροῦσθαι).

84. So Friedrich, *ibid.*, and Hahn, *Hoheitstitel*, p. 393 against Cullmann, *Christology*, p. 30, who appeals to the anarthrous form. But the force of this is cancelled out by the adjective μέγας.

85. Friedrich quotes H. A. Guy, *New Testament Prophecy*, 1947 (not accessible to me), p. 82, who thinks that the original tradition must have contained more frequent references to Jesus as a prophet than our present sources have preserved.

86. Luke 9:8 contrasted with Mark 6:15; Luke 9:19 contrasted with Mark 8:28. In each instance Luke has changed Mark's εἷς τῶν προφήτων to προφήτης τις τῶν ἀρχαίων; Matt. 16:14 contrasted with Mark 8:28, where Matt. has added "Jeremiah".

87. P. 843. Contrast Barrett, *Spirit*, p. 98: "Jesus did not think of himself as a prophet—because he thought of himself as more than a prophet"; Taylor, *Names*, p. 15: "whether he thought of himself as a prophet is more open to question".

88. For the apocryphal tradition of the martyrdom of the prophets see above, p. 107.

89. *Mysterium Christi*, pp. 57–65. The fifteen points are conveniently summarized by Barrett, *Spirit*, pp. 94f. Dodd includes the institution of

the eucharist as an instance of prophetic symbolism, following Wheeler Robinson. The bread and cup words, however, are not symbolic but realistic (see G. Bornkamm, *Studien*, pp. 156ff.) and are also church formations, see above p. 107. As an eschatological meal the Last Supper has, however, like the earlier Galilean meals, the character of prophetic symbolism.

90. ἦλθον sayings:

Mark 1:38 par.; 2:17 par.; 10:45

Matt. 5:17; 10:34–36, Luke 12:49 (Q?); Matt. 11:19f. par. (Q)

ἀπεστάλην sayings:

Mark 9:37 (τὸν ἀποστείλαντά με); cf. Matt. 10:40

Luke 10:16 (Q?); Matt. 15:24.

91. *Tradition*, p. 153 (author's translation).

92. B. H. Streeter, *The Four Gospels*, London: Macmillan, 1926[2], p. 425, attributes the saying to Matthew's redaction, but admits that it is of the same type as the "M" material.

93. See J. Munck, *Paul and the Salvation of Mankind*, London: S.C.M. Press, 1958, pp. 26–28, esp. 26, n. 2, which offers important linguistic evidence for the Palestinian character of Matt. 15:24.

94. This is an application of the important principle of traditio-historical criticism enunciated by Hahn, see above, note 35.

95. E.g. Dodd, *Mysterium Christi*, p. 57; Barrett, p. 94; P. E. Davies, *ibid.* (see note 82), p. 251.

96. The explicit quotation of Isa. 61:1 in the Lucan version of the sermon at Nazareth (Luke 4:17f.) is almost certainly not a redactional composition (against Bultmann, *Tradition*, pp. 31f., apparently favoured by H. Conzelmann, The *Theology of St. Luke*, London: Faber, 1960, pp. 31–38) but taken from Luke's special material. This is shown by the dislocated reference to earlier miracles in v. 23, and by the composite form of the LXX quotation from Isa. 61:1, 58:6 and 62:2a, which suggests that Luke drew it from an already existing compilation of testimonia, whether written or oral. The text is almost entirely LXX, but κηρῦξαι instead of καλέσαι at v. 19 from Isa. 62:2 follows MT קְרָא. This suggests the possibility that the application of the Isaiah text to Jesus was originally made in the Palestinian church, and then taken over by the Hellenistic Jewish church. For the testimonium see Lindars, *Apologetic*, p. 152, and for the composite form of the quotation see A. R. C. Leaney, *The Gospel According to St. Luke* (Black's NT Commentaries), London: Black, 1958, p. 53.

97. Cullmann, *Christology*, p. 37 denies that Jesus identified himself with the eschatological prophet. His case rests on Jesus' identification of John the Baptist with Elijah in Matt. 11:14. This, he argues, shows that Jesus did not identify himself with Elijah and consequently not with the eschatological prophet. But (1) Matt. 11:14 is hardly an authentic logion, for it reflects the Baptist community's and the church's interpretation of John the Baptist, and with Hahn (*Hoheitstitel*, p. 376) must be taken as a "compositional addition"; (2) there was not one, but a

number of varying forms of the expectation of the eschatological prophet, and even if Jesus identified John the Baptist with the *redivivus*
type, it would not preclude his own understanding of his mission in terms
of another type of eschatological prophet.

98. For a summary and critique of the views of these American scholars
see Perrin, *op. cit.*, pp. 148–157. In an earlier form it is to be found in
H. J. Cadbury and S. J. Case; in later forms in C. C. McCown and
F. C. Grant, modified by J. Knox and A. N. Wilder.

Chapter VI

THE KERYGMA OF THE EARLIEST CHURCH: THE TWO FOCI CHRISTOLOGY

1. *The Beginnings of Christology*

(i) *The Resurrection: The Proclaimer becomes the Proclaimed*

WE are not concerned here with the historical problems which underlie the NT assertion that God raised Jesus from the dead. That within a few weeks after the crucifixion Jesus' disciples came to believe this is one of the indisputable facts of history.[1] The whole subsequent history of the church rests upon this fact, and is inexplicable without it. How the disciples came to believe in the resurrection is only slightly less certain. The claim that Jesus had appeared to Peter, to the Twelve and the five hundred brethren is contained in one of the earliest post-Easter traditions in the New Testament,[2] possibly going back to the year 33, i.e. within three years of the actual events recorded.

The appearances may be categorized as "visions", but in the New Testament they are understood not as merely pious experiences, but as the revelatory acts of God. That they were so is a decision which faith alone can make. That the experiences did occur, even if they are explained in purely natural terms, is a fact upon which both believer and unbeliever may agree. According to the testimony, however, what occurred in the "visions" is not merely that God produced faith in the resurrection. Rather, he revealed to them Jesus as the One he had raised from the dead. The Easter testimony asserts an act of God not merely upon the disciples but a prior act of God upon Jesus himself, whereby he has taken Jesus out of the past of history and inserted him into his own eternal now. Henceforth encounter with Jesus is not limited to those who saw him in his earthly ministry, or to his post-resurrection appearances or to the memories of these experiences. This means that the salvation which was inclosed in the words and deeds of Jesus is not a mere past memory, but is a salvation which continues to be offered always in the here and now.

This is why the proclamation of the church is not just an extension of Jesus' own proclamation of the kingdom of God as the eschatological act of God which was beginning in his earthly ministry. It is rather the proclamation of Jesus himself as the One in whom God began to act eschatologically, in whom he acted eschatologically in the supreme crisis of Jesus' death and resurrection, in whom he continues to act eschatologically in the church's kerygma, and in whom he will consummate his eschatological action at the End. In this way the proclaimer became the proclaimed, and the implicit Christology of Jesus becomes the explicit Christology of the church.

It is true that the earliest church continued Jesus' own proclamation, ἤγγικεν ἡ βασιλεία τοῦ θεοῦ ("the kingdom of God has drawn nigh"), Matt. 10:7 par., cf. Mark 1:15. Otherwise this proclamation would not have been enshrined in Q material and Mark—for the church was not merely concerned with recording past history. Yet the very fact that it continues Jesus' own proclamation means that side by side with it the church proclaimed his resurrection. For Jesus' eschatological message had been radically called in question. An apparently unanswerable question mark had been placed against it by his crucifixion. Jesus' own proclamation could only have been continued by the vindication of Jesus and his message through the resurrection. So although the Q material does not contain the kerygma of the resurrection it presupposes it all the way through.[3] The earliest church could have continued Jesus' own proclamation only alongside of its own proclamation that God had raised him from the dead.

(ii) "The Most Primitive Christology of All"

Jesus had declared that his own eschatological word and deed would be vindicated by the Son of man at the end. Now his word and deed had received preliminary yet certain vindication by the act of God in the resurrection. The earliest church expressed this new-born conviction by identifying Jesus with the Son of man who was to come. He would come as his own rubber stamp, vindicating his own word and deed, as he had already done in a preliminary way in the resurrection appearances. In preserving those sayings in which Jesus speaks of the coming Son of man, the church identifies Jesus with the coming Son of man. So sayings such as Mark 8:38, Luke 12:8f. are now repeated, but on the assumption that it is Jesus who is the coming Son of man, and who will appear at the End to vindicate his word and work openly as he had already appeared in his resurrection appearances to his disciples.

The church also formed new "future" Son of man sayings. It modelled them on Jesus' own sayings to the extent that they were couched in the third person and were circulated as sayings of Jesus—a fact, which, as Hahn pointed out,[4] is a clear indication that sayings about the coming Son of man in the third person were embedded in the authentic tradition of Jesus' sayings. Nowhere, apart from Acts 7:56,[5] does the Son of man figure in the church's own independent christo-logical statements. We may reasonably expect that the earliest type of Son of man sayings created by the church were those which were closest to Jesus' own sayings, i.e. sayings which spoke of the future coming of the Son of man. Since, too, the church now identified Jesus with that coming Son of man, the intention behind these creations is explicitly christological. In these new sayings Jesus is purporting to be speaking not about another figure, but about himself.

These secondary future Son of man sayings differ from the authentic future Son of man sayings in two further ways. First, they elaborate the apocalyptic imagery. Jesus himself, as we saw, introduced only the bare minimum of apocalyptic imagery. For his intention was not to give apocalyptic instruction about the future, but simply to invoke an ultimate sanction for his own word and work. The centre of gravity in his proclamation was what God was actually doing in him. The early church's proclamation, however, is oriented to the future because it looks for the coming precisely of *Jesus* as the Son of man. It is faith in Jesus which gives rise to the apocalyptic elaboration in earliest Christianity.[6] Therefore, this elaboration is not due merely to apocalyptic fantasy run riot; it is an expression of explicit Christology. The second trait is the introduction of Old Testament phraseology into the Son of man sayings (which again was not characteristic of Jesus' own Son of man sayings). The reason for this was again christological. The early church had to defend its proclamation of the death and resurrection of Jesus as the saving act of God by "proving" it from the OT. It had also to show that the final completion of his work would likewise be the fulfilment of scripture.

The Q material contains no clear example of any secondary future sayings. Those future sayings which occur in Q are probably all of them authentic,[7] although they may have received certain secondary modifications here and there.[8]

The Marcan material contained one genuine Son of man saying, viz. Mark 8:38. But as we saw,[9] this saying has, compared with the Q version in Luke 12:8, undergone apocalyptic elaboration. The two other Marcan future Son of man sayings exhibit the characteristics, not of Jesus, but of the Palestinian church. Mark 13:26 is not a detached saying, but integral to the apocalyptic context in which it occurs. It is not beyond the bounds of possibility that the whole section, 13:24–27, has been taken over bodily from a pre-Christian Jewish apocalypse,[10] including the reference to the coming Son of man. Alternatively Mark 13:26 is a new creation modelled on Jesus' own Son of man sayings. It differs from the authentic sayings not only in its apocalyptic elaboration, but also in its OT phraseology. Note the use of Dan. 7:13 ("coming on the clouds of heaven"), and the allusion to Dan. 7:14 ("with power and great glory"). The christological intention is clear—Jesus is identified with the coming Son of man. For in the face of Jesus' own Son of man sayings on the one hand and of the cross on the other, the church would neither have borrowed nor created this saying had it not believed that Jesus' word and work had been vindicated in the resurrection.

In the previous chapter[11] it was argued that the second part of Jesus' answer to the high priest (Mark 14:62) is a secondary formation. It combines the session at the right hand of God from Ps. 110:1 with the picture of the parousia from Dan. 7:13. The Palestinian origin of this saying is secured by the reverential periphrasis "power" for "God". It has frequently been argued[12] that the "coming" of the Son of man refers not to a coming from heaven, but to the coming to God in the ascension. This has support from Dan. 7:13f., where the Son of man is brought *to* the Ancient of Days. The obvious objection that the session at the right hand is mentioned before the coming is overcome by J. A. T. Robinson's[13] brilliant suggestion that the session at the right hand and the coming on the clouds of heaven are alternative expressions of the same thing, viz. the ascension or exaltation. Dr. Robinson proceeds to eliminate as unauthentic and to interpret all the other parousia sayings in the same way, thus eliminating the parousia from the teaching of Jesus.[14]

In a certain sense this elimination of the parousia is quite justified. For, as we have seen, Jesus only invoked the Son of man as the ultimate sanction, for his own word and work, and it was not his intention to speak of his *own* return. But there is a further difficulty in taking the second half of the saying as a reference to the parousia. It requires ὄψεσθε to be taken in two different senses, as Glasson pointed out.[15] On the one hand, in reference to the heavenly session it must mean mental perception,[16] whereas in reference to the parousia it must mean literal sight. For the parousia is essentially an event plain for all to see: "Every eye shall now behold him." Glasson therefore proposes to take ὄψεσθε throughout the verse as referring to inward vision. But it is doubtful whether ὄψεσθε can bear this sense at all. This was brought out years ago in the discussion of C. H. Dodd's interpretation of ἴδωσιν in Mark 9:1.[17] Both parts of the reply must be visible portents and the second half must refer to the parousia, exactly as in Mark 13:26. As a visible portent, the sitting at the right hand must refer to the first act in the parousia. The Son of man is revealed first, sitting at the right hand of God, and then leaving that position and coming on the clouds of heaven. This will mean that this earliest statement about the heavenly session as yet contains no reflection about an interval (which Glasson found to be a difficulty in McArthur's interpretation). The Palestinian church believes that it—and Jesus' enemies —will shortly see Jesus sitting on the right hand of God and coming on the clouds of heaven. The church believes that Jesus is now in heaven, but as yet it has not reflected upon his activity in the interim prior to his return. The end is coming too soon for that. This view of a non-active waiting in heaven we shall come across in other places in the evidence for the beliefs of the early Palestinian church.[18]

The special Matthean material contains one saying about the parousia of the Son of man, namely Matt. 10:23. It will be remembered that A. Schweitzer not only took this saying as authentic to Jesus, but found in it the whole clue to his interpretation of Jesus: it announced the first delay in the parousia.[19] Others since Schweitzer have argued for the authenticity of Matt. 10:23.[20] The saying, however, clearly presupposes the post-resurrection mission of the Palestinian church.[21] It testifies to the church's expectation of an imminent parousia in the early days of its mission. Tödt concludes his discussion of this saying:

> Of great significance is the fact that this prophetic saying for primitive Christian missionaries follows close in form upon the Son of man sayings of Jesus. As a promise it is put into the mouth of the earthly Jesus and so his authority is claimed for it. The prophet hears the risen One in the words of the earthly One. Both the earthly and the risen One speak of the coming of the Son of man in the same way.[22]

The secondary future Son of man sayings are clearly modelled on the authentic Son of man sayings, and express the earliest church's identification of Jesus with the coming Son of man. But what about the other classes of sayings, the present and the suffering Son of man sayings? These have to be seen alongside of the earliest church's continuation of Jesus' own proclamation. This continuation implies that that proclamation has now been validated. Certain of Jesus' sayings, in which his implicit Christology was most clearly expressed, are accordingly transformed in terms of the church's own explicit Christology. This is how the present son of man sayings (which are attested in both Mark and the Q material and are therefore quite early) apparently arose. In these sayings Jesus identifies himself in his earthly ministry with the Son of man.

147

We saw in the previous chapter that it was difficult to account for the present sayings as authentic if he took the term "Son of man" from the apocalyptic tradition. But for the earliest Palestinian church this difficulty no longer existed. Jesus had claimed that his message and offer of salvation would be vindicated at the End by the Son of man. That vindication has now taken place through the appearances of Jesus as risen. Jesus has therefore been manifest in his resurrection appearances as his own rubber stamp: he *is* the coming Son of man. It is he who will return as the triumphant Son of man—very shortly. Therefore, Jesus' proclamation in his earthly ministry has now been rubber-stamped by the coming Son of man, and so the term Son of man can be transferred as it were to the other side of the equation, to the earthly "I" of Jesus. As Tödt has shown,[23] however, this does not mean that Jesus in his earthly life was the transcendental majestic figure of the Son of man already appeared on earth. The contrast between Jesus and the *coming* Son of man is still maintained. By identifying Jesus in his earthly life with the coming Son of man the early church was making an affirmation about the *authority* of the earthly Jesus in his word and work. His claim to exousia was now vindicated. It *was* the eschatological word: his offer *was* the offer of the eschatological salvation. This is what the so-called present sayings in the Q material and in the conflict stories in Mark are designed to express. Let us take a closer look at them.

Matt. 8:20 par. (Q) is a challenge to discipleship.[23a] To follow Jesus is to follow One who is rejected. It is important too that this Son of man saying occurs in the context of criticism of Jesus by his contemporaries. That criticism has now been reversed by the resurrection. In the call of Jesus the call to the eschatological salvation has really gone out— despite its criticism and rejection by his contemporaries, criticism and rejection which, as Q knows full well, has culminated in the cross. To be a disciple is to follow One who was not only rejected, but vindicated out of that rejection.

In Matt. 11:19 par. (Q) Jesus is eating with publicans and sinners and is again criticized by his adversaries. He is "a friend of publicans and sinners"—a reproach which has a force very similar to "nigger-lover" in the Southern States. But it is precisely as the Son of man that he does this. In eating and drinking with the outcast Jesus is not acting as a rebel against the conventions of society, but by his conduct as vindicated by the resurrection has brought the eschatological salvation. Indeed, Jesus' eating with the outcast is an anticipation of the Messianic banquet. This is not a new interpretation of Jesus' conduct. It simply makes explicit what he had himself asserted, in the light of his subsequent vindication. "Son of man" expresses the vindicated *exousia* of Jesus on earth.

In the Marcan group of *conflict* stories (the context is significant) there are also two present sayings. The first occurrence is the saying (Mark 2:10) about remission of sins in the secondary insertion (Mark 2:6–10)[24] into the story of the paralytic. The Palestinian origin of the saying—which may well have circulated independently prior to its insertion into this story—is clear. The early Palestinian church would be particularly concerned to vindicate against Pharisaic criticisms their claim to mediate the eschatological remission of sins through baptism. Like the sayings in Q it is asserting the *exousia* of Jesus against his critics, an *exousia* which had been radically called in question by the defeat of the cross, but which had been vindicated by the resurrection. Jesus' word of forgiveness pronounced on earth is a proleptic utterance of the word which he as Son of man will pronounce at the last judgment.[25]

The second Marcan saying is Mark 2:28. It serves as a comment on 2:27, the latter itself an originally detached saying, as the renewed introduction καὶ ἔλεγεν αὐτοῖς ("and he said to them") shows.[26] That the sabbath was made for man and not man for the sabbath is probably an authentic pronouncement of Jesus. It was not an expression of liberalism, but asserted that the sabbath was the symbol of the eschatological salvation which Jesus was now bringing to man.[27] The sabbath was for man because the eschatological salvation is for man. Verse 28 gives this statement a different twist. It justifies the early church's[28] claim to freedom from the sabbath laws, and seeks Jesus' authority for doing so. Here, "lord" is not christological, but simply denotes the *authority* of Jesus to dispense his church from the sabbath laws.

The Marcan material contains one further present Son of man saying, Mark 10:45a, the word about service which precedes the λύτρον ("ransom") saying. This is a clear example of the replacement of an original "I" by "Son of man". For the "I" form occurs in Luke 22:27b: "*I* am in the midst of you as one who serves", and, if not actually authentic to Jesus, is almost certainly earlier.[29] As Tödt has pointed out, this saying is somewhat different from the ones we have examined thus far. Whereas the other sayings speak of the *exousia* of the Son of man over against the criticisms of Jesus' adversaries, as vindicated by the resurrection, the saying about service speaks of Jesus' voluntary humiliation. It thus forms a bridge to the suffering Son of man sayings. Here is a slight but perceptible christological development.

There are also later editorial creations of present sayings which are formed on the analogy of the earlier ones.[30]

The present sayings are definitely Palestinian in origin. First, they reflect the Palestinian church's conflict with the Jewish religious authorities. Second, the presence of these sayings in both Q material and Mark points to their early origin. They occur in both strata alongside of sayings in which Jesus speaks of the future Son of man in a way which distinguishes him from the Son of man or avoids identifying him with that figure. This points to a different origin of the present sayings. These future Son of man sayings are authentic, while the present sayings are the church's creations or modifications of authentic "I" sayings. Yet there is a subtle connection between them. In the future Son of man sayings the Son of man appears in order to vindicate the authority of Jesus in his earthly word and work. In the present Son of man sayings, Jesus is made to assert directly his own *exousia*. Tödt points out[31] that the predicates of the future Son of man, such as his appearance in glory, are not transferred to the earthly side of Jesus. The church is not claiming that Jesus is the incarnation of the pre-existent son of man, but that in his earthly life he was exercising proleptically the functions of the future, eschatological Son of man. The "most primitive christology of all" revolves around two poles, the earthly work of Jesus as proleptic Son of man and his future coming in glory as the transcendent Son of man. By speaking of Jesus as already on earth the Son of man the church was underlining his *exousia* in word and work. He had truly brought, as he had claimed, the final eschatological word and deed of God.

(iii) *The Suffering Son of Man*

As we saw in the previous chapter, Tödt upholds against Bultmann the basically Palestinian origin of the suffering Son of man sayings.[32] But they are slightly later in origin than the present sayings. Their absence from Q does not in itself militate against an early origin. For Q does not contain a passion narrative, to which these sayings are all integrally related, though, as we have seen, it presupposes the resurrection and contains hints of the passion (e.g. Matt. 23:29–36 par.: Jesus' ministry as the culmination of Israel's rejection of the prophets).

Hahn, who agrees with the Palestinian origin of the basic tradition and of the suffering Son of man sayings, carries Tödt's analysis somewhat further,[33] and finds within the Palestinian tradition two different types of suffering sayings:

1. The simplest and earliest form of the type: the Son of man is delivered into the hands of men (Mark 9:31 cf. 14:41b). This type of saying contains no reference to scripture fulfilment or to the resurrection. The word-play Son of man/men (in Aramaic *bar naša/bᵉne naša*[34]) indicates that this type of Son of man saying has been developed out of the "present" sayings, which featured the opposition to and the rejection of the son of man by his human enemies. These sayings then underwent a development by the addition of references to the killing and rising again of the Son of man. Both terms ($\dot{a}\pi o \kappa \tau a \nu \theta \hat{\eta} \nu a\iota$, "to be killed", and $\dot{a}\nu a \sigma \tau \hat{\eta} \nu a\iota$ "to rise") are remarkable. For in passion formulae the usual terms are $\dot{a}\pi o \theta \nu \acute{\eta} \sigma \kappa \epsilon \iota \nu$ ("to die") and $\dot{\epsilon} \gamma \epsilon \rho \theta \hat{\eta} \nu a\iota$ ("to be raised"). Hahn suggests that the verb $\dot{a}\pi o \kappa \tau \epsilon \acute{\iota} \nu \epsilon \iota \nu$ ("to kill") is connected with the late Jewish tradition of the killing of the prophets,[35] while $\dot{a}\nu a \sigma \tau \hat{\eta} \nu a\iota$ ("to rise") suggests the *exousia* of the Son of man—he is not raised by God but rises by his own power as Son of man (cf. John 10:18). Thus, according

to Hahn, the basic conception of the Son of man (*exousia*) is carried to its logical conclusion.

Once this development had taken place, the passion predictions sometimes receive secondary expansions from the details of the passion narrative, notably at Mark 10:33f., which Hahn considers to be a Marcan formulation on the basis of Mark 9:31.

2. The second type of passion prediction is dominated by the idea of the fulfilment of scripture. This idea, according to Hahn, was not originally connected with the concept of the Son of man and he therefore designates it a "mixed form". It should be noted that the idea of scripture fulfilment had already entered the *future* Son of man sayings constructed by the Palestinian church, viz. Mark 13:26 and 14:62. This first occurs in a passion saying at Mark 14:21, which shows that the theme of scriptural fulfilment originally attached itself to the earliest form of the first type. Here an authentic Son of man theme is expressed: the opposition between the Son of man and "that man" Judas, the representative of all Jesus' human enemies who reject him.

The element of scripture fulfilment is further developed by (1) the words ἀποδοκιμασθῆναι, "to be rejected", (Mark 8:31) or ἐξουδενεῖσθαι, "to be set at nought" (Mark 9:12), both from Ps. 118:22; (2) δεῖ, "it is necessary" (Mark 8:31)[36] and (3) πολλὰ παθεῖν, "to suffer many things" (Mark 8:31; 9:12).[37] (2) and (3) are not LXX, nor do they represent any possible Semitic word. Hahn also regards Mark 9:12 together with Mark 9:9, as a redactional composition. But the application of Ps. 118:22 to the passion is surely Palestinian, so this part of Mark 9:12 must be early. Apart from this however his contention that the scripture-fulfilment suffering sayings have undergone further development on Hellenistic soil is well grounded. These sayings, we may add, have also undergone expansion under the influence of the passion narrative (e.g. "by the elders and the chief priests and the scribes", Mark 8:31).

Both Tödt's analysis and Hahn's further development of it indicate that the suffering Son of man sayings arose quite naturally out of the present sayings. And in both of Hahn's basic types they suggest the Palestinian earliest church's distinctive interpretation of the death of Jesus. It is the rejection of Jesus as the eschatological bringer of salvation by "men" and the vindication of his *exousia* by God. At a very early date the Palestinian earliest church sought scriptural confirmation for this idea in Ps. 118:22. This is the earliest interpretation of Christ's death and resurrection.

The definitely soteriological interpretation of Jesus' death, found in the primitive gospel traditions only at Mark 10:45b and Mark 14:24 and in the kerygmatic formula, 1 Cor. 15:3, is also Palestinian.[38] It should be taken as firmly established that Isa. 53 is constitutive for Mark 10:45b, and 14:24. Yet the absence of allusions to Isa. 53 in the other suffering Son of man sayings, and the possibility that 1 Cor. 15:3 ($\kappa\alpha\tau\grave{\alpha}$ $\tau\grave{\alpha}\varsigma$ $\gamma\rho\acute{\alpha}\phi\alpha\varsigma$, "according to the scriptures") did not originally refer to Isa. 53 but rather to Ps. 118:22, invite the conclusion that the expressly soteriological interpretation of Jesus' death, while early and Palestinian, was not part of the very earliest tradition. How did it arise? Is it a questionable and dubious addition to the earliest form of the kerygma?

It will be remembered that we found evidence that Jesus himself ascribed a soteriological significance to his work as a whole. He also faced death at Jerusalem as the culmination of that work. The very earliest Son of man Christology was intended to assert that the soteriological significance of Jesus' ministry, radically called in question by Jesus' crucifixion at the hands of his enemies who rejected his soteriological offer, was triumphantly vindicated by the resurrection. Thus the suffering Son of man sayings, even apart from Mark 10:45b, already imply that the cross is the culmination of Jesus' soteriological ministry, the rejection of that soteriological offer by Jesus' enemies, and its vindication in the resurrection. There was never a period, not even a very short one, after the resurrection, when the saving significance of the cross was not implicitly recognized. It was only gradually, however, that it received explicit formulation.

Perhaps the earliest line of thought was not derived from Isa. 53, but from the general idea of the atoning significance of the death of the martyrs. As Lohse[39] has demonstrated, the idea of vicarious atonement by death was widespread in

Palestinian Judaism, though it was never based on Isa. 53. This general late Jewish idea produced the statement that Jesus died ὑπὲρ τῶν ἁμαρτιῶν ἡμῶν, "for our sins", or simply ὑπὲρ ἡμῶν "for us". Once, however, this step had been taken, it was not long before Isa. 53 was brought in, as we see from Mark 10:45b and Mark 14:24 (note πολλῶν, "many", in both verses, from Isa. 53:11f.). Further, the fact that, apart from Mark 10:45b, the Son of man sayings contain no reference to the atoning significance of Jesus' death is a clear indication that the doctrine of the atonement was not originally associated with the Son of man concept, but arose in a different context. This is further indicated by the absence of the "Son of man" from Mark 14:24 and 1 Cor. 15:3. Where then did the doctrine of vicarious atonement arise? Mark 14:24 suggests that it was in the context of the liturgical tradition.[40] Now the saying about the Son of man's service in Mark 10:45a already lent itself to liturgical application (Jesus as host at the eucharistic table). This attracted to itself Mark 10:45b, which was liturgical in origin, as we see from Mark 14:24).

The Son of man tradition thus witnesses to a christological pattern in earliest Palestinian Christianity which is focused upon two poles: (1) the earthly work including the death of the historical Jesus understood as the saving act of God—and including, at a later stage, the soteriological interpretation of the death of Jesus as a vicarious atonement in terms of Isa. 53; and (2) his return to consummate that saving work. The resurrection is not as yet thought of as inaugurating a period of further soteriological activity by Jesus in his exalted state, but merely as inaugurating a brief interval of inactivity before the parousia.

Obviously the church could not long remain content with this rudimentary Christology. For it said nothing positive about the interval and nothing about what Jesus was doing between the resurrection and the parousia. Nor did it say anything about God's revelatory and saving activity prior to his saving act in Jesus. The earliest Palestinian Church had neither the motivation nor the tools to answer this question. That was left to the Hellenistic church, Jewish and Gentile. But before we embark upon these succeeding phases of christological development, a certain terminological shift within Palestinian earliest Christianity calls for notice.

2. *The Terminological Shift*

"Son of man" was not a satisfactory term for kerygmatic proclamation, for confession of faith, or for use in Christian instruction and worship. For it naturally lent itself to use only in sayings of Jesus. Other terms had to be found for these purposes, and already in Palestinian Christianity these terms replace "Son of man" to cover Jesus' earthly ministry and his coming again.

(i) *Rabbi*

Jesus was undoubtedly addressed as Rabbi (Rabbouni) and maran(a), the honorific titles accorded to a Jewish teacher of the law.[41] But in Judaism the relationship between teacher and disciple was temporary. After "graduation" the disciple set up on his own. The relation basically was not to the person of the Rabbi, but to what the Rabbi taught. With the relation between Jesus and his disciples the situation becomes very different. Even after his death they remain disciples,[42] and disciples of Jesus exclusively (Matt. 23:8). Whether this saying is a creation of the post-Easter church or is authentic to Jesus makes no difference. Its preservation and circulation in the church indicates that Jesus continued to be regarded as their Rabbi even after the resurrection; cf. also Matt. 10:24 par. (Q). The exclusive and permanent character of this relationship indicates that even the term Rabbi as applied to Jesus acquired a higher meaning than it ever had in Judaism. No doubt, as we have seen, this was already to some extent the case even during Jesus' earthly ministry. For he gave the impression of one with *exousia*, and not as the scribes. But his *exousia* had been vindicated by the resurrection, and with it the permanence and exclusiveness of its claims.

Thus "Rabbi" as applied to Jesus after the resurrection came to have something of the same christological weight as "Son of man" in the present sayings. It came to denote the continuing authority of the word of the historical Jesus in the post-Easter church.[43] Yet the term was of little use for the kerygma. For a Jewish audience it could only put Jesus on the same level as any of the rabbis, and could not draw out his eschatological significance. Nor was the title transferred to the parousia context. The church did not pray, Rabbi, come! Etymologically this would have been quite possible, since the original meaning of Rabbi was "great one". But by NT times, as we have seen, it had come to be restricted almost exclusively to a teacher of the law. Hence it was suitable only as an expression of the *exousia* of the word of the historical Jesus.

(ii) *Mari, maran(a)*

Mari, maran(a), "my lord", "our lord", was also, as we have seen, undoubtedly applied to Jesus during his earthly life. On the lips of outsiders it would be merely a polite form of address, like "sir". On the lips of his own disciples, it would already, during his lifetime,[44] have acquired a higher meaning, as the disciples began to appreciate the authority of his call and word. But after the resurrection that authority is vindicated in its permanence and exclusiveness so that *mari, maran(a)* are still used of the earthly Jesus, with reference to his continued authority in the church. Like Rabbi-*didaskalos* ("teacher"), it is used both as an address to Jesus and as a title in narrative about him. Actually the evidence for this narrational use of "Lord" in the gospels is very scanty. Apart from its use as a direct address it occurs at Mark 11:3, and in Luke, where it is impossible to be sure whether it is not redactional. It is not surprising that many scholars have denied its use in Palestinian Christianity except in the eschatological sense (*marana tha*). However, we may call Paul in here as evidence. He speaks of James, etc. as ἀδελφοὶ τοῦ κυρίου, "brothers of the Lord" (1 Cor. 9:5; Gal. 1:19). This clearly relates to the earthly Jesus, not to the heavenly as in the characteristic Hellenistic usage. It is therefore certainly Palestinian in origin. As a second witness we may cite Eusebius to the effect that Jesus' family were called δεσπο-σύνοι, "belonging to the Lord" (Eus. *Ch. Hist.* I, 7, 14).[45] This unusual adjective may well be an independent translation from the Aramaic. We may therefore infer that the expression "brothers of the Lord" is not a Pauline creation, but a firmly established term in Palestinian Christian usage.

This leads to an important conclusion. The use of the title *kyrios* for the earthly Jesus is not due to the reading back into the earthly ministry of the Hellenistic Christian usage in application to the exalted Lord, but is Palestinian. Its roots lay in the earthly lifetime of Jesus, and it was heightened in meaning as a result of Jesus' vindication at Easter. Its meaning is very similar to that of "Son of man" in the present sayings. But it has the advantage over "Son of man" in that it can be used of Jesus by others.[46]

Unlike "Rabbi" however, *mar(i)*, *maran(a)* could be extended to cover the coming Son of man, as we see in the well-known Aramaic formula, *marana tha*[47] (1 Cor. 16:22, Did. 10:6). From the discussion inaugurated by Bousset, the following points have emerged and may now be taken for granted:

1. The formula is Aramaic.
2. It comes from earliest Palestinian Christianity.
3. It is a liturgical formula like Amen, Hosanna, and Abba.
4. Its *Sitz im Leben* was the eucharist. Cf. the context where it occurs in Did. 10:6 and Rev. 22:20, and its connection in 1 Cor. 16:22 with *anathema*, which is a warning against unworthy communion.[48]

Still uncertain is whether it is an invocation to the Lord to come in the supper celebration[49] or at the parousia[50] or both.[51] But surely this is a false dilemma. In the perspective of the Palestinian community there is really only one coming of the Lord Jesus, and that is the final parousia. There is not a series of repeated eucharistic comings between the resurrection and the parousia, any more than there are repetitions of the once-for-all sacrifice of Calvary in the Pauline-anamnesis type of eucharist. But in the Palestinian meals there is an anticipated experience of the parousia, as is indicated by the term ἀγαλλίασις ("joy") in Acts 2:46.[52] Even Hahn, who is most concerned to uphold the exclusively future reference of *marana tha*, admits that in the Palestinian meal there was "an enthusiastic anticipation of the end-time coming", and that it was this sense of present anticipation which provided the basis for the later Hellenistic Jewish Christian development of the idea of the present Lordship of Christ.

At the same time, however, the Palestinian use of *maran(a)* contains no christological affirmation of the present Lordship of Christ,[53] but only of his expected and anticipated revelation as Lord-Son of man. Hence it is illegitimate to infer that *marana tha* is "an expression of the cultic veneration of Christ by the original Aramaic-speaking church".[54] Even in the later Hellenistic church the exalted Jesus was never the direct object of worship. As the later liturgies show, Christian worship is not Jesus-worship, but the worship of the Father through the Son in the power of the Spirit. Where it does occur (e.g. in some of the liturgical hymns of the Apocalypse) the direct invocation of Jesus in worship is "para-liturgical" in character, and strictly exceptional. As regards the Palestinian church, all we can conclude from *marana tha* is that the cultus was the creative milieu in which the Lord was invoked to come again at the parousia.

This early Palestinian and strictly eschatological use of Kyrios survives in a number of synoptic passages: in the secondary form[55] of the Q saying Matt. 7:21; in the following verse, which is also secondary (contrast Luke 13:26f.); in Luke 13:25, paralleled by Matt. 25:11; and in the secondary application[56] of crisis parables to the parousia of Jesus— Matt. 25:14–30 par. (talents or pounds), and the waiting servants (Mark 13:33–37) with its Q parallel (Matt. 24: 45–51 par.). How close in meaning the term *kyrios* is in these contexts to the future use of Son of man is shown by the occurrence of the latter in the earlier (yet no less secondary) interpretation of the same parable in the Q version in Matt. 24:44 par.

In conclusion, then, we may say that as a christological title, Lord (*maran(a)*) was firmly embedded in Palestinian Christianity. There it was used in two senses. It covered the authority of Jesus in his earthly ministry, and in liturgical invocations his coming again as Son of man. These two senses correspond to the two main poles of Palestinian Christology.

(iii) *Mašiaḥ*

While, in view of the preceding section, it is hardly correct to suggest that Peter's speech in Acts 3:12–26 contains "the most primitive Christology of all",[57] Dr. J. A. T. Robinson is undoubtedly right in finding there a *more* primitive Christ-ology than in Peter's speech in Acts 2. In other words, we cannot say[58] that the earliest Palestinian Christology held that Jesus became the Messiah at his resurrection (Acts 2:36). Rather, it held that at the parousia Jesus will return as "the Christ appointed for you" (Acts 3:20). Thus, the term *Mašiah* must have entered the Palestinian church as an equivalent to Son of man in its future sense. The christo-logical pattern of the speech in Acts 3 is exactly the same as that which we have discovered in Palestinian Aramaic Christianity thus far. It oscillates between two poles, the earthly work of Jesus (here interpreted in terms of the Mosaic prophet-servant, see below) and his parousia. There is as yet no christological assessment of Jesus' continued activity in his exalted state. The interim is purely of a waiting character: "whom heaven must receive until the time (*sc.* of the parousia)" (v. 21).

How came it about that the church appropriated for Jesus the very term *Mašiah* which he himself had rejected as a diabolical temptation? The answer is that the whole situation had now changed. Until his programme had been fulfilled "Messiah" could only suggest the traditional Jewish national-political king. But when it is used of Jesus by others after his assumption into heaven and in the specific context of his return it is crystal clear that the term Christos-*Mašiah* is an equivalent for the apocalyptic title, Son of man. In this context there was no danger of confusing the title with the political type of Messiah. The Palestinian church was forced to use the word which Jesus had avoided, because only so could it proclaim, to Jews, Jesus as the end-time ruler. For "Son of man" could only be used in sayings of Jesus.[59] It should also be remembered that there was already a tendency within Jewish apocalyptic for the Son of man to take over elements from the Davidic messianology, particularly, as we have seen, in the Book of Enoch. The church could either continue to reject the whole concept, as Jesus had done, or alternatively it could take the bull by the horns and christ-ianize it. It chose the latter course, with far-reaching conse-quences for later christological development, particularly, as we shall see, in Hellenistic Jewish Christianity.

The same re-interpretation of the term *Mašiah* occurs in the Marcan form of Jesus' answer to the high priest (Mark 14:62). As we have seen, the earliest tradition probably represented Jesus as parrying the question with a non-committal "You have said so". The Marcan form of the answer, "I am; and you will see the Son of man sitting at the right hand of Power, and coming with the clouds of heaven" reaches back into the Palestinian tradition. This is already apparent on linguistic grounds. Note the use of the reverential periphrasis "Power" of God. We can now see how perfectly the expanded answer to Caiaphas expresses the re-interpreted Messianology of the Palestinian community, especially if the καί ("and") following ἐγώ εἰμι ("I am") is adversative.[60] Jesus is now made to accept the title Christos, but only as an equivalent to the future apocalyptic Son of man.

(iv) *The Death and Resurrection of the Messiah*

The Palestinian character of the kerygmatic formula in 1 Cor. 15:3b–5 has been firmly established by the analysis of J. Jeremias,[61] and has met with general acceptance. Here the kerygma of the death of Jesus for our sins according to the scriptures, his burial, his raising on the third day according to the scriptures and his appearances has "Christos" as its subject. Two connected problems arise here: (1) Is the anarthrous Χριστός ("Christ") here used as a title, or as a proper name? (2) Is it part of the original Palestinian formula?

The prevailing opinion is that Paul always uses Christos without the article as a proper name.[62] Since, however, *Mašiah* cannot be used in Semitic as a proper name,[63] this would mean that Χριστός is not part of the original formula, but an addition either of Paul himself or of his Hellenistic Jewish Christian predecessors. However, the anarthrous *titular* use in Semitic speech *is* established. It occurs in Dan. 9:25 in the phrase *'adh mašiah naghidh*, "until (the) Messiah prince" (Messiah here is not an adjective qualifying prince: the two nouns are in apposition). John 4:25 reflects the same usage. Strack-Billerbeck give early examples from Palestinian midrash.[64] Thus the recent claims of N. A. Dahl[65] and

Hahn appear to be fully justified. $X\rho\iota\sigma\tau\acute{o}s$ in 1 Cor. 15:3b is part of the Palestinian tradition. And it is used as a title not as a proper name.

How did this come about? We have seen how Son of man was first used of the future coming, and slightly later, though very early in the Palestinian tradition, shifted first to Jesus' earthly ministry and then to the passion. The adoption of *Mašiaḥ* in the context of the passion is a parallel and probably concurrent process. Note that the theological interpretation of the passion in 1 Cor. 15:3b is the same as that of the synoptic suffering Son of man sayings: it is $\kappa\alpha\tau\grave{\alpha}$ $\tau\grave{\alpha}s$ $\gamma\rho\acute{\alpha}\phi\alpha s$, "according to the Scriptures", (cf. Mark 8:31; 9:12b) and $\acute{v}\pi\grave{\epsilon}\rho$ $\tau\hat{\omega}\nu$ $\acute{\alpha}\mu\alpha\rho\tau\iota\hat{\omega}\nu$ $\acute{\eta}\mu\hat{\omega}\nu$, "for our sins" (cf. Mark 10:45b). Now, as we have maintained, this soteriological interpretation of Christ's death was achieved not right at the beginning, but probably at the first Christian passover in A.D. 31. Hence the formula in 1 Cor. 15:3b must have been crystallized between passover A.D. 31 and Paul's conversion in A.D. 33. Within this period, the term *Mašiaḥ* thus acquired a use in Palestinian Christianity in connection with the soteriological interpretation of Jesus' death. Since "Son of man" could not be used kerygmatically, but only in dominical sayings, an alternative title was needed as soon as the church began to reflect on Jesus' death. So it settled for *Mašiaḥ* which had already been adopted as a substitute for "Son of man" in the parousia context.

In this second terminological shift the fact that Jesus was crucified as a Messianic pretender must have played an important part.[66] This can be seen from the secondary colouring of the trial scene before Pilate and the mockery and from the way in which the theme, "King of the Jews", derived from the titulus, is spun out (Mark 15: 2, 9, 12, 18).[67]

These are the only Palestinian passages where the suffering Christos Christology is evidenced. But there are many NT passages which witness to its survival in Hellenistic circles. First, there are many passages, too numerous to cite, where Paul speaks of the dying or rising again of $X\rho\iota\sigma\tau\acute{o}s$, either anarthrously and alone, or anarthrously before "Jesus". These passages are commonly taken as examples of the use of $X\rho\iota\sigma\tau\acute{o}s$ as a proper name. But they should all now be

attributed to the continuing influence of Palestinian christological conception. It also appears in Hebrews, 1 Peter, and
in the Lucan writings. On the Lucan usage, Dr. J. A. T.
Robinson[68] has contended that the specific combination $\pi a\theta\epsilon\hat{\iota}\nu$
$\tau\grave{o}\nu$ $X\rho\iota\sigma\tau\acute{o}\nu$ ("that the Christ should suffer") is a Lucan
speciality (Luke 24:26f., 45f.; Acts 3:18; 17:2f; 26:22f.).
He thus distinguishes it from the anarthrous use of Christos
in 1 Peter. While he is right in his main contention, viz. that
Acts 3:18 is not part of the earliest christological formula in
the speech, his thesis needs qualifying at two points. First,
the anarthrous $X\rho\iota\sigma\tau\acute{o}s$ in 1 Peter is not to be interpreted as
a proper name, but is a survival of the titular anarthrous use
in the Palestinian tradition enshrined in 1 Cor. 15:3b.
Second, and consequently, the Lucan usage also is not a
Lucan invention but a continuation of early Palestinian
usage. $X\rho\iota\sigma\tau\acute{o}s$ in these contexts, whether with the article or
without it, means the same thing and is always a title.[69]

(v) *The Son of David*

Once Jesus had been identified in the Palestinian tradition
with the *Mašiaḥ* this inevitably brought along with it the
other features of Jewish Messianology, particularly the use of
"son of David" and "Son of God". At first, these titles would
be associated purely with the parousia.

We have already[70] come across one example of the Davidic
Messianology in the acclamation of the crowds at the
triumphal entry, Mark 11:10. It was suggested that this was
an originally detached fragment with a *Sitz im Leben* in the
liturgical usage of the Palestinian church. "The kingdom of
our father David" is looked for at the parousia. Another
Palestinian[71] fragment in a similar vein is to be found in
Luke 1:32f. In its early Christian application this fragment
must have referred to the enthronement of Jesus as the
transcendental Davidic Messiah at the parousia. Note here
the complete absence of any reference to Jesus' earthly
ministry. Also the first part of the Benedictus was probably a
pre-Christian Jewish eschatological hymn.[72] In its original
Jewish usage it would have referred to the this-worldly
political kingdom. If it came directly from Judaism into
Christian usage (and not *via* the Baptist community) it must

have been first applied to Jesus' future rule after the parousia.[73] A survival of the parousia application of Son of David is to be found in the Apocalypse (Rev. 3:7; 5:5; 22:16).

The claim that Jesus would inaugurate a transcendental Davidic kingdom left the church with a formidable apologetic task on its hands. Deeply embedded in Jewish Messianology was the expectation that the Messiah would be a physical descendant of David. Was this true of Jesus? As we have already seen, Jesus' family may well have believed in its Davidic descent,[74] although that belief cannot have played any significant role in Jesus' earthly ministry. Now, however, the Palestinian church takes up this tradition and constructs genealogies of Jesus to substantiate it. The genealogies in Matthew and Luke (Matt. 1:1–17 and Luke 3:23–38) differ in many respects, but they agree in tracing Jesus' descent through David. Probably this is as far as they originally went, and the extensions in Matthew and Luke to Abraham and Adam respectively are reflections of the Evangelists' own theologies. As the location of the Lucan genealogy after the Baptism shows, the genealogies are not integral to the infancy narratives, but have an independent origin.[75] Probably their original purpose was to show that Jesus was qualified to appear as the Davidic Messiah at the parousia, and so to justify the church's christological claim.

While the infancy narratives as such are the product of the Hellenistic Jewish Christian community,[76] the tradition of Jesus' birth at Bethlehem is probably older, and had been established as the outcome of a controversy in the Palestinian church. Surviving traces of the controversy appear in John 7:40–42, although this is a torso and breaks off before it offers any solution to the problem. But in the wording of v. 42b (cf. Nestlé's text) there is at least a hint that Mic. 5:2 played a part in this controversy. Now Mic. 5:2 is quoted in Matt. 2:6 as one of the "reflection-quotations" which the evangelist has introduced into the narrative. As he not infrequently does, Matthew quotes not from the LXX, but in a "pesher" adaptation. The purpose of this adaptation is to make crystal clear that Jesus satisfies the qualifications for the Davidic Messiah.[77] It is likely that this pesher-adaptation had been made already in Palestinian Christianity. In that case, the words "who shall rule my people Israel" would have originally applied to the post-parousia kingdom. The application of this quotation to Jesus in the Palestinian church then provides the basis for the formation of the infancy narratives in Hellenistic Jewish Christianity.

It has frequently been pointed out that the Pauline Epistles, Mark, and the speeches in Acts are apparently unacquainted with the birth at Bethlehem, a circumstance which is often used to deny its historicity. But these writings all know the christological assertion which that tradition expresses, viz. the Davidic descent of Jesus. The fourth gospel, which appears to deny it, is working from a very different set of christological traditions.

(vi) *The Son of God*

It will be remembered that this title was probably just coming into use as an element in the Jewish this-worldly Messianic expectation. It is accordingly to be expected that if and when it was adopted as a christological title in Palestinian Christianity it would, like the other Davidic terms, be first applied in connection with the parousia. Yet, as Hahn pointed out, where the use of this term is postulated for the Palestinian church, it has hitherto been invariably associated not with the parousia but with the resurrection, and in a supposedly adoptionist sense.[78] The passages usually cited in favour of this theory, however, are to be ascribed not to the Palestinian but to the Hellenistic Jewish Christian tradition. Accordingly, Hahn has suggested that in Palestinian Christianity the term Son of God was employed at the outset in a parousia context. But is there any evidence for this? He cites Luke 1:32f., Mark 14:61f. and 1 Thess. 1:9f., the last as an example of its survival in a parousia context in Hellenistic Christianity. Luke 1:32f. we have already interpreted in a parousia sense (above p. 34). Mark 14:61f. is not very strong evidence, since it occurs in the question of the high priest and may antedate the Marcan formulation of Jesus' reply. If so, then at the earliest stage it must have been intended to refer to the earthly Messiahship, which Jesus rejected in the words "You have said it". But when the reply of Jesus was reformulated, it must have carried with it a re-interpretation in the parousia sense of "Son of God", as well as of "Christos". So with some initial hesitation we can accept Hahn's interpretation as applicable to the second stage of the tradition. Much less certain is 1 Thess. 1:9. There seems to have been a tendency in some places to substitute "Son" for Son of man. This is evident at Mark 13:32, and more noticeably in part of the tradition underlying the fourth gospel.[79] Thus it would seem preferable to regard 1 Thess. 1:9 as another instance of this terminological shift, rather than as an instance of the Davidic "Son of God", interpreted in a parousia sense.

At this point we must raise the question of Rom. 1:3–5. It is widely recognized that the section beginning with γενο-μένου ("born") and extending through νεκρῶν ("the dead") is a pre-Pauline formula.[80] J. Weiss[81] took it as evidence for the earliest (Palestinian) Christology, and in this too he has been followed, notably by Bultmann.[82] In order to fit his thesis that the Palestinian Christology was not "adoptionist" but focused on the two poles of the *exousia* of Jesus in his earthly ministry and his coming again in the parousia, Hahn is compelled to locate Rom. 1:3f. in Hellenistic Jewish rather than in Palestinian Christianity.

This is an important question and requires further investigation. The chief evidence for a Hellenistic provenance is the antithesis σάρξ/πνεῦμα ("flesh/spirit") meaning the contrast between the earthly and the heavenly sphere. But is there an original Palestinian nucleus? Working backwards we may begin by eliminating ἐν δυνάμει ("in power") as a Pauline addition made necessary by his insertion of περὶ τοῦ υἱοῦ αὐτοῦ (v. 3) ("concerning his son.") Following Schweizer,[83] we may next eliminate κατὰ σαρκα ("according to the flesh") and κατὰ πνεῦμα ἁγιωσύνης ("according to the spirit")[84] as Hellenistic additions. Thus we are left with the antithetical formula:

γενομένου ἐκ σπέρματος Δαυείδ,
ὁρισθέντος υἱοῦ θεοῦ ἐξ ἀναστάσεως νεκρῶν.
Born of the seed of David;
Appointed Son of God from the resurrection of the dead.

Linguistically, there is nothing against a Palestinian origin for this formula. Now it seems quite unnecessary to interpret ὁρισθέντος ("appointed") in terms of an enthronization Christology (Christ enthroned as Davidic Son), as is done both by those scholars who wish to find here evidence of such a Christology in the Palestinian earliest church (Weiss, etc.) and by Hahn, who accordingly locates this formula in *Hellenistic* Jewish Christianity. ὁρισθέντος here may mean, not "appointed" to an office exercised from this moment on (note incidentally that nothing is said about exaltation; only the resurrection is mentioned), but "predetermined *from the time of* (ἐξ) the resurrection to be the eschatological Son of God at the parousia. There is an exact parallel to this conception in Acts 10:42; "And he commanded (viz. in the apostolic commissioning in the resurrection appearances) to . . . testify that he is *the one ordained* by God (ὁ ὡρισμένος) to be the judge of the living and the dead." Cf. also Acts 17:31: "Because he has fixed a day on which he will judge the world in righteousness by a man *whom he has appointed* (ᾧ ὥρισεν), and of this he has given assurance to all men by raising him from the dead." Acts 3:20, "the Christ appointed for you" (τὸν προκεχειρισμένον Χριστόν) belongs to the same christological conception. In the Palestinian formulae Jesus is not *adopted* at the resurrection to a new status or function, but *pre-destined* to be the eschatological judge at the parousia.

Returning to Rom. 1:3f., we can now see that the original form we have postulated exactly expresses the Christology of the Aramaic speaking church as we have reconstructed it thus far. The Davidic descent of Jesus serves the purpose of legitimating his destined appearance as the eschatological judge and saviour at the parousia. No evaluation of the Davidic sonship for Jesus' earthly ministry is suggested, nor is there any hint of active rule as exalted Son in the interval between the resurrection and the parousia. The Hellenistic and Pauline expansions change the whole meaning. The Davidic sonship now characterizes his whole historical ministry (κατὰ σάρκα, "according to the flesh"), while the divine sonship from the time of the resurrection becomes one of active rule in an exalted state (ἐν δυνάμει . . . κατὰ πνεῦμα ἁγιωσύνης, "in power . . . according to the spirit of holiness.").

Here it is worth raising the question about the place of Ps. 2:7 (and 2 Sam. 7:14) in the Palestinian Christology. Concerned as he is to deny an enthronement-adoptionist Christology to Palestinian Judaism, Hahn allocates the earliest Christian use of the psalm to Hellenistic Jewish Christianity.[85] But it is difficult to suppose that the Palestinian church could have adopted "Son of God" as a christological title from any other source than from Ps. 2:7; 2 Sam. 7:14. However, the earliest evidence we have for the application of these passages comes from the exaltation-Christology of the Hellenistic Jewish Christianity.[86] On the other hand, the critics from Weiss onwards who have postulated an enthronement-adoptionist Christology for Palestinian earliest Christianity have assumed without any real evidence that Ps. 2:7 was there used in an adoptionist sense from the earliest times. These scholars must certainly be right in their conjecture that Ps. 2:7 was already applied christologically in that stratum, despite the lack of evidence; for only so can its use of the title Son of God be explained at all. But are they right in supposing that it was used in an exaltation-adoptionist sense? Now all our evidence (under Kyrios, Christos, Son of David, and Son of God thus far) indicates that this christological conception had not yet developed. We would accordingly hazard the suggestion that when first applied christologically Ps. 2:7 was used not in reference to Jesus' institution to an office exercised from the moment of the resurrection-exaltation. Rather it was used in the sense in which we have interpreted Rom. 1:3f., i.e. in the sense that from that moment Jesus was *pre-destined* to exercise the office of eschatological judge at the parousia. This is admittedly only conjectural, since we have no surviving evidence for the use of Ps. 2:7 in the earliest Palestinian stratum. But it is a question which calls for an answer.

(vii) *Mosaic Servant-Prophet*

We have seen that without adopting any specific self-designation, Jesus appears to have conceived his earthly mission in terms of eschatological prophecy. The early Aramaic speaking church interpreted Jesus' earthly ministry explicitly in terms of the Mosaic prophet servant. The primary evidence for this is again the Petrine speech (Acts 3:12–26).[87]

In this speech, while the post-earthly life, as we have seen, is conceived as an inactive waiting in heaven after an assumption, followed by an appearance as the Christos at the parousia (v. 20f.), the earthly ministry is interpreted almost entirely in terms of the Mosaic prophet-servant, based on a combination of Deut. 18:15–19 with Isa. 52:13 and 53:11. The speech opens with a reference to God as the God of Abraham, Isaac and Jacob, recalling the story of Moses' call (v. 13a, cf. 7:32). Then follows the phrase "glorified his servant" based on Isa. 52:13 (LXX).[88] "The holy and righteous one" is prophetic servant[89] vocabulary. "Denied" in v. 13 occurs in Stephen's speech in connection with Moses' fate at the hands of Israel (7:35). This is not an explicit feature of the exodus story, but represents the general late Jewish tradition of the rejection and martyrdom of the prophets. In v. 15 "the prince ($\dot{a}\rho\chi\eta\gamma\acute{o}s$) of life" recalls Acts 7:35, where Moses is called "ruler ($\ddot{a}\rho\chi o\nu\tau a$) and deliverer ($\lambda\upsilon\tau\rho\omega\tau\acute{\eta}\nu$)" (cf. also $\lambda\upsilon\tau\rho o\hat{\upsilon}\sigma\theta a\iota$ ("to redeem"), Luke 24:21a, in a context which has in v. 19 just spoken of Jesus as a prophet).

The foregoing interpretation is clinched by the direct quotation of Deut. 18:15 and 18 in vv. 22f. The telescoped form of it is typical of the "pesher". The first part appears in almost identical form in Stephen's speech (Acts 7:37). In the fuller form of the quotation in Acts 3 all the emphasis rests on the decisiveness of Jesus' eschatological proclamation, and on the dire consequences of its rejection. Finally, that this prophecy is directly fulfilled in Jesus and his ministry is directly asserted in v. 26: "Having raised up his servant Jesus." As Robinson notes, only here in Acts is $\dot{a}\nu a\sigma\tau\acute{\eta}\sigma a s$ ("having raised") used of Jesus' historical mission, rather than of the resurrection. The word is taken directly from Deut. 18:15. The word "servant" harks back to v. 13 and to Isa. 53.

The Mosaic prophet-servant Christology serves in this speech to interpret Jesus' ministry as the mission to Israel of the final, eschatological proclamation (vv. 22f.), a mission which is not "merely" prophetic, but soteriological ("prince of life", v. 15). But although Isaiah 53 is drawn upon, nothing as yet is said of vicarious atonement for "the many". We may, if we will, call this with Cullmann a "paidology", but it is *not* a paidology which includes the idea of Jesus' atoning death. It must therefore be earlier than Mark 10:45b. And it is remarkably close to the self-understanding of Jesus, though with the difference that it is worked out explicitly in terms of Deut. 18:15ff. and Isa. 52:13; 53:11. Even if there is no linguistic evidence to support an Aramaic origin of Peter's speech in Acts 3, the author of Luke-Acts is clearly drawing upon a very primitive tradition in close touch with the historical Jesus.

We may take it that the christological term servant, which is found in the liturgical passage Acts 4:27, 30, is a survival of this typology. In v. 27 it is combined with motifs from Ps. 2, and thus with the Davidic Christology; a combination which is made the easier by the fact that David also is the servant of God as he is expressly called earlier in the prayer (v. 25) where Ps. 2 is first introduced. But in v. 30 the Mosaic associations of the term are evident (cf. "signs and wonders"), while the Davidic combination must be pronounced secondary. The Mosaic typology of Acts 7, although it occurs in a Hellenistic Jewish Christian tradition, is clearly a survival of a more primitive Christology.

All through this discussion we have insisted that behind the Mosaic Christology, which ostensibly occurs in a Hellenistic Jewish stratum of Luke-Acts, there lies enshrined a Palestinian tradition. We have offered no proof of this, save the general consideration that this interpretation lies close to Jesus' own self-understanding. But our thesis may be tested by examining other survivals of the Mosaic Christology in the synoptic tradition. Here again, it will be apparent that it is a substratum underlying the later Hellenistic colouring. Let us start with the heavenly voice at the baptism (Mark 1:11). This is widely[90] regarded as a combination of Ps. 2:7 and Isa. 42:1. However, our traditio-critical analysis thus far has left room only for a parousia usage of Ps. 2:7 in Palestinian earliest Christianity. Thus, if Ps. 2:7 is part of the background of the heavenly voice, it can only have become so at the Hellenistic stage. Yet ἐν σοι εὐδόκησα ("in thee I am well pleased") is not from Isa. 42:1 LXX (which has προσεδέξατο αὐτὸν ἡ ψυχή μου, "my soul has accepted him"). It must be from the Hebrew text, and therefore Palestinian-Aramaic in origin. Still, the voice could not have been a torso. So ὁ υἱός μου ("my Son") must represent an original ʿabhdî, "my servant",[91] whether it came through mistranslation, or by a deliberate substitution of part of Ps. 2:7. The motif of the Spirit's descent (v. 10) will likewise have come originally from Isa. 42:1, although, as Hahn suggests, it has in Mark been substantialized in a Hellenistic sense by the addition of "as a dove"—a step that Luke has taken even further by the addition of "in bodily form" (Luke 3:22).

Thus, in its original Palestinian form we may suppose that the baptism narrative expressed a "paidology" based on Isa. 42:1.

The Marcan form of the temptation story, with its allusion to Jesus' forty days' and forty nights' sojourn in the wilderness, suggests the theme of the Mosaic eschatological prophet.[92] For both Moses (Exod. 34:28; Deut. 9:9, 18) and Elijah (1 Kings 19:8) underwent a fast for forty days and forty nights. The two Son of God temptations in the Q version are parried with Mosaic material from Deuteronomy, and it may be suggested that υἱὸς τοῦ θεοῦ, "Son of God" (notice the anarthrous υἱός, "son": is this from an original semitic construct?) may, as in the baptism narrative, come from an original ʿebedh ʾelohîm.[93]

The explicit application of Isa. 61:1 to Jesus in the Lucan sermon in the synagogue at Nazareth (Luke 4:17–19) depicts Jesus as the eschatological servant-prophet, endowed with the Spirit to deliver his proclamation and to perform miracles. This is exactly the Christology of the baptism narrative in its earliest form. So, far from freely composing this sermon, Luke has worked into it much older materials. The allusions to Elijah and Elisha later in the sermon (vv. 25–27) are prefaced by the introduction, "But in truth (ἐπ' ἀληθείας = ἀμήν) I tell you", which indicates that this is a detached saying. This saying is clearly a justification of the gentile mission, and therefore is of Hellenistic Jewish Christian rather than of Palestinian origin. But still, it witnesses to the survival of the prophetic Christology.

Closely connected with the sermon at Nazareth is the

answer to John (Matt. 11:2–6 par.). In chapter V we contended for the authenticity of vv. 4–6 to Jesus and interpreted the answer as implying, rather than explicitly asserting, a self-understanding of Jesus in terms of eschatological prophecy. This implied understanding is now made explicit by the context which has been created for the saying,[94] namely John's question, "Are you the Coming One?" The term ἐρχόμενος ("Coming One") is not just a general term for a coming eschatological figure of any type, but specifically a title for the eschatological prophet.[95] Cullmann conjectures that the Heb. *ha-ba* was actually a technical term for the eschatological prophet.[96]

In Luke 24:19, Acts 2:22 (cf. Acts 7:36), in the sermon in the synagogue at Nazareth and in the answer to John, Jesus' miracles are interpreted in terms of the prophetic servant Christology. How far has this primitive interpretation coloured the miracle stories of the gospels? It would be expected that this was *the* interpretation of the miracles in the Palestinian tradition.[97] There are several indications that this is so, although the miracle tradition has been overlaid by other, later christological interpretations, notably that of the Hellenistic θεῖος ἀνήρ.

Hahn[98] has suggested that the acclamation "the holy one of God" in the healing of the demoniac (Mark 1:24) is an expression of servant Christology (cf. "thy holy servant Jesus", Acts 4:27). Be that as it may, the Mosaic background of the feedings has been frequently noted.[99] Mark's location of both versions of the miracle *in the desert* is clearly intended to recall the manna story of Exod. 16:4ff., as also the concluding comment, "the people ate and *were satisfied*". Elijah's miraculous feeding (2 Kings 4:42ff.) is also a minor influence. The original conception also shines through in the Johannine narration of the feeding, where the crowd exclaims, "This is indeed the prophet who is to come into the world" (John 6:14). Although the phrase εἰς τὸν κόσμον ("into the world") is typically Johannine, the prophetic term ὁ ἐρχόμενος, "the Coming One", again appears. Finally, the discourse on the Bread of Life, despite its Johannine theology, is rooted in the primitive Mosaic (manna) typology.

The transfiguration narrative in Mark 9:2–8 must have

undergone an analogous development to the baptism. The heavenly voice reads, "This is my beloved Son, hear him." It is widely recognized that here we have a combination of Ps. 2:7, Isa. 42:1, and Deut. 18:15. Here again, we are faced with the same problem as in the baptismal voice, a combination of Christologies impossible in the Palestinian tradition. If, however, an original ʿabhdî = παῖς μου stood here, we have the unitary conception of the Mosaic prophetic servant. The voice, in this earlier form, gives point to the appearance of Elijah and Moses. Although there are puzzling questions here, it seems at any rate clear that their appearance is intended to designate Jesus as the eschatological prophet who stands at the end of the prophetic succession and fulfils it. Thus whatever later developments the transfiguration narrative has undergone in a Hellenistic direction (not only in the heavenly voice, but in the metamorphosis, suggesting "substantial" thinking), the basis of the story is the Palestinian Christology of Jesus as the eschatological prophet. The Lucan account of the transfiguration contains notable deviations from Mark, which are such as to suggest not merely editorial modification but the preservation of valuable independent traditions. Among the more notable of these deviations is the statement that Elijah and Moses were talking to Jesus about his "departure" (Luke 9:31), Greek ἔξοδον, "exodus"—another expression of Mosaic typology.

We have seen that there is much to be said for taking the parable of the vineyard as a Palestinian church formation.[101] If so, it is worth asking whether υἱόν, "Son" (Mark 12:6) represents an original ʿebhedh, as in the heavenly voice at the baptism and transfiguration. The adjective ἀγαπητόν ("beloved") which qualifies it suggests again a background in Isa. 42:1. Also, the successive servants (δοῦλοι: were these too ʿabhdim?) are clearly the prophets, and suggest the view, common in early Palestinian prophetic Christology, that Jesus represents the culmination of the mission of the prophets and their rejection.

Mark's identification of the Last Supper with the passover has some background in the typological comparison of Jesus' death with the exodus (cf. also 1 Cor. 5:7; 10:1–5), which is again an aspect of the Mosaic typology.

Finally, the interpretation of Christ's death specifically in terms of Isa. 53:11f. as an atonement for the many (Mark 10:45b; 14:24), when finally it was reached, is a further outgrowth of the identification of Jesus with the eschatological prophet-servant.

3. *Summary*

It is difficult not to admire the christological achievement of the earliest Palestinian church. Its Christology of Jesus as the Mosaic prophetic servant in his earthly life, and as the one who was to come shortly as the Son of man to vindicate openly his word and work as God's eschatological revelation and work, conveyed in terms of an explicit Christology precisely what Jesus had implied about himself throughout his ministry. It enabled the history of Jesus to be interpreted not merely in terms of prophetic proclamation of a future eschatological act, but in terms of the soteriological redemptive event which had already occurred in that history, and which awaited consummation. Professor Cullmann acknowledges that the strength of the "concept Prophet" lay precisely here, in its serviceability as a tool to interpret the earthly work of Jesus.[102] But it is difficult to go along with him when he writes: "Nevertheless it is inadequate even in this regard. It emphasizes too strongly one side of Christ's earthly work, his preaching activity, and this misplaces emphasis." The prophetic Christology brings out fully the soteriological aspects of Jesus' history. And this was precisely its intention. Where it proved inadequate was when the Christian mission shifted to the Hellenistic world. Here not functional but ontic categories were needed to interpret Jesus' earthly work.

Professor Cullmann also points out that the "concept Prophet" is inadequate to express "present work of Christ at the right hand of God", and also of the "pre-existent Christ" —or, as we should prefer to say, the connection between God's eschatological activity in Jesus and his creative, revelatory and redemptive action prior to the history of Jesus. This is true. But then of course the earliest Palestinian church had not come to reflect upon the present work of Christ. For it thought (and in this chapter we have been concerned almost entirely with the period between the crucifixion and the conversion of St. Paul) that the parousia was imminent. It was only after the expectation of the imminent parousia began to fade that the church was led to reflect upon Christ's present work in the church, the work of the exalted Christ. But this was done mainly in Hellenistic Jewish and gentile terminology, as we shall see. Yet in all fairness the "concept Prophet" did, it must be recognized, provide the tools for relating the eschatological act of God in Jesus to the prior acts of God in Israel's *Heilsgeschichte*. For it was just this term that enabled the ministry of Jesus to be related to the exodus and to Israel's rejection of the prophets. But the relation of God's saving activity in Jesus to his activity in "general revelation" and to creation (which raises ontological questions) presented no problem in the Palestinian Jewish environment, and the earliest church (whatever people may say of the church today!) was not given to answering questions which nobody asked. It was only when the Greek speaking church had to face these questions that the prophetic Christology proved inadequate.

Professor Cullmann complains finally that the "concept Prophet" was too narrow to encompass the future work of Christ. But the Palestinian church was conscious of this, and did not try to make it do so. Instead, it combined this concept with the other terms which it used as substitutes for the coming Son of man, terms derived from the Davidic Messianology (*Mašiah*, Davidic kingdom, and perhaps Son of God).

NOTES ON CHAPTER VI

1. So even Bultmann, *Kerygma and Myth* I, p. 42: "all that historical criticism can establish is the fact that the first disciples came to believe in the resurrection".

2. Cf. my article in *BR* 6 (1960), pp. 8–10.

3. To have recognized this is one of the outstanding contributions of H. E. Tödt, *Menschensohn*, pp. 224–231.

4. Hahn, *Hoheitstitel*, p. 38 against Vielhauer.

5. See above, ch. V, p. 120.

6. On the growth of apocalyptic in the post-Easter church see E. Käsemann, *ZThK* 57 (1961), pp. 227–244.

7. See ch. V, p. 123.

8. Luke 12:8 appears to be free from elaboration: ἔμπροσθεν τῶν ἀγγέλων ("before the angels") is necessary to show that this is a judgment scene: cf. its survival also in v. 9. It also completes the *parallelismus membrorum*, corresponding with ἔμπροσθεν τῶν ἀνθρώπων ("before men"). In Matt. 24:27, 37, 39 παρουσία ("coming") is also a Hellenistic redaction, absent from the parallel in Luke 17:24. The original form of the saying must have been either οὕτως ἔσται ἐν τῇ ἡμέρᾳ τοῦ υἱοῦ τοῦ ἀνθρώπου or οὕτως ἔσται ὁ υἱὸς τοῦ ἀνθρώπου ἐν τῇ ἡμέρᾳ αὐτοῦ ("So shall it be in the day of the Son of man", or: "So shall the Son of man be in his day"). Luke's plural ἡμέραι (17: 22, 26) is also redactional, expressing the periodization of the history of salvation. Cf. Leaney, *Luke*, pp. 68–72; Tödt, *Menschensohn*, p. 98; Hahn, *Hoheitstitel*, p. 37, n. 4.

9. See above, ch. V, p. 122.

10. Cf. W. G. Kümmel, *Promise and Fulfilment*, pp. 95ff. Kümmel thinks that Mark 13:26 is compatible with Jesus' own proclamation. But this depends on his accepting Mark 14:62 as authentic to Jesus. If, however, Mark 13:26 is from a pre-Christian Jewish apocalypse, this is evidence for the pre-Christian use of Son of man as a title for the eschatological judge.

11. See above, ch. V, p. 110.

12. E.g. W. K. L. Clarke, *Divine Humanity*, London: S.P.C.K., 1936, pp. 25f.; T. W. Manson, *BJRL* 32 (1950), p. 174 (reprinted in *Studies in the Gospels and Epistles*, Manchester: University Press, 1962, p. 126); V. Taylor, *Mark*, ad loc.; T. F. Glasson, *NTS* 7 (1960–61), pp. 88–93 against H. K. McArthur, *ibid.*, 4 (1957–58), pp. 156–158; J. A. T. Robinson, *Jesus and His Coming*, p. 45.

13. J. A. T. Robinson, *ibid.* I entertained this view myself as a possibility in *The Book of the Acts of God*, London: Duckworth, 1960 (first published in U.S.A. in 1957), p. 211. This interpretation, however, ceases to be necessary or tenable once Mark 14:62b is seen on traditio-historical grounds to be a church formation.

14. *Jesus and His Coming*, pp. 46–58.

15. *Art. cit.* (see note 12 above), p. 90.

16. Cf. Taylor, *Mark*, p. 568. "ὄψεσθε does not necessarily describe a portent, but more probably indicates that the priests will see facts and circumstances which will show that Ps. cxl and Dan. vii. 13 are fulfilled in the person and work of Jesus."

17. J. Y. Campbell, *ET* 48 (1936–37), pp. 91ff; J. M. Creed, *ibid.*, pp. 184f. Cf. my *Mission and Achievement*, p. 27.

18. For the important distinction between assumption and exaltation, to which Hahn has drawn attention, see below, ch. VII, pp. 184ff.

19. In his autobiography Schweitzer has told us how the importance of this text suddenly dawned upon him while reading his Greek NT on military service as a young man.

20. Kümmel, *Promise and Fulfilment*, pp. 63f. Kümmel regards it as a detached logion promising an interval in the disciples' lifetime between

the missionary preaching and the parousia. Following Tödt, however, we consider that Jesus spoke of the parousia of the Son of man only to reinforce the decisiveness of his own offer of salvation.

21. So T. W. Manson, *Teaching*, p. 221: "It may quite well represent the ideas of the Early Church rather than the words of Jesus himself."

22. Tödt, *Menschensohn*, p. 56f. Tödt would assign the saying to Q, but this is speculative.

23. *Ibid.*, p. 114.

23a. We may perhaps postulate as the original and authentic form of this saying: "He who follows me has nowhere to lay his head", which would correspond in content with Mark 8:34. On the authenticity of the latter see E. Dinkler, *Neutestamentliche Studien für Rudolf Bultmann*, Ed. W. Eltester, Berlin: A. Töpelmann, 1957[2], pp. 110–129. Here the interesting suggestion is made that the "cross" originally referred not to the cross of Jesus, but to the *tau*, the sign or seal of God's ownership.

24. The secondary insertion is either 5b–10, so Bultmann, *Tradition*, p. 15; V. Taylor, *The Formation of the Gospel Tradition*, London: Macmillan, 1933, pp. 66f.; *idem, Mark*, p. 191; or, preferably, vv. 6–10, so M. Dibelius, *From Tradition to Gospel*, New York: Scribners, 1935, p. 66; Hahn, *Hoheitstitel*, p. 43, n. 1. For the *Sitz im Leben* see Bultmann, *Tradtion*, p. 16.

25. For the exegesis cf. *Mission and Achievement*, p. 106, except that it is to be ascribed to the earliest Palestinian church rather than to Jesus himself. Yet it is only making explicit the Christology implicit in Jesus' original proclamation.

26. See Taylor, *Mark*, p. 218, who notes that this is the view of Bultmann, Dibelius and Schmidt.

27. Hoskyns in *Mysterium Christi*, pp. 74–78.

28. W. Manson, *Messiah*, p. 116: "The voice of the church. . . rather than the voice of Jesus."

29. For the division of 45a and 45b, first suggested by Klostermann in his commentary on Mark *ad loc.*, see Tödt, *Menschensohn*, p. 127. And for the priority of the "I-form" in Luke 22:27b over the "Son of man-form" in Mark 10:45a, *ibid.*, pp. 127, 190, 192–194. In other respects, however, the Lucan form is less primitive, for it reflects a later concern for church order. See *Mission and Achievement*, p. 57, supported by Leaney, *Luke*, pp. 269f.

30. The following future Son of man sayings are secondary, according to Tödt: Matt. 13:37; 16:13; Luke 6:22; 18:8b. To this list we must add Matt. 12:32, since we prefer Mark 3:28 as the original form (see above, ch. V, p. 125).

31. Tödt, *Menschensohn*, p. 115.

32. Cf. above, p. 118.

33. Hahn, *Hoheitstitel*, pp. 46–53.

34. Already noted by Jeremias, *Servant*, p. 102.

35. Cf. Matt. 23:37; Rom. 11:13; 1 Thess. 2:14.

36. δεῖ only once in LXX, Dan. 2:28f., representing a future in MT.

37. Cf. Tödt on πολλὰ παθεῖν, *Menschensohn*, p. 157.

38. For the Palestinian origin of Mark 10:45 cf. *Mission and Achievement*, pp. 55–57. My linguistic arguments have been criticized by C. K. Barrett and M. Hooker, but they are defended by Hahn, *Hoheitstitel*, pp. 57–59. Cf. also Lohse, *Märtyrer*, pp. 117–122.

39. Lohse, *Märtyrer*, pp. 64–110.

40. See above, p. 107.

41. See above, p. 119.

42. The occurrences of μαθηταί ("disciples") in Acts (6:1, etc.) must reflect primitive usage, for by the time Acts was written, this was no longer a common Christian self-designation (note its absence already in the Pauline epistles).

43. Cf. K. H. Rengstorf, *TWNT* II, pp. 155–160, s.v. διδάσκαλος; also Bornkamm in *Tradition and Interpretation*, pp. 40f.

44. Luke obviously has a predilection for κύριος ("Lord") both as an address and as a title in narrative, for he has frequently inserted it into his known sources (Mark and Q) as a synoptic comparison will show. Its occurrences in the special Lucan material are impossible to check, though we may assume that he has followed the same procedure here. But in one instance from Q (Luke 9:61) it is paralleled in a closely associated context in Matt. 8:21. This suggests that here at any rate he found it in his source.

45. Cf. Rengstorf, *TWNT* II, p. 48, s.v. δεσπότης, followed by Hahn, *Hoheitstitel*, pp. 91f. Hahn also thinks that the Pauline references to the "words of *the Lord*" (1 Cor. 7:10; 9:14; 1 Thess. 4:15 and even partly in 1 Cor. 11:23) reflect the same application of κύριος to the earthly Jesus.

46. "It (*sc.* the κύριος title in Palestinian usage) is closer to the idea of the Son of man in his earthly work, although it is concerned not so much with the opposition to men as with the voluntary submission to Jesus' claim to majesty" (Hahn, p. 95).

47. See K. G. Kuhn, *TWNT* IV, pp. 470–475, s.v. μαραναθά and cf. Cullmann, *Christology*, pp. 209–212. Kuhn adds a third possible pointing in Aramaic to the two possibilities offered by Cullmann, viz., מָרַן אֲתָא, "our Lord, come". Both prefer a pointing which will give this meaning, rather than "our Lord has come".

48. J. A. T. Robinson, *Twelve New Testament Studies*, London: S.C.M. Press (*SBT* 34), 1962, p. 155; and more fully, G. Bornkamm in *Das Ende des Gesetzes* (*Ges. Aufs.* I) Munich: Kaiser, 1952, pp. 123–132. The liturgical context is particularly clear in the Didache.

49. In a private letter addressed to me in 1955 the Rev. A. H. Couratin suggested that *marana tha* was a prayer addressed to Christ at the beginning of the liturgy to come as the true President at the eucharist.

50. H. A. Guy, *The Last Things*, London: O.U.P., 1948, p. 107, and most emphatically by Hahn (*Hoheitstitel*, pp. 105–107) against Cullmann. But his argument holds good only in so far as it is directed against Cullmann's particular thesis that belief in the presence of Christ at the rite is derived from the post-resurrection appearance meals. On this

subject cf. H. Grass, *Ostergeschehen und Osterberichte*, p. 89, n. 2, who contends that the meal-setting of the appearances is a later conception, motivated by the need to prove the bodily character of the resurrection.

51. Cullmann, *Christology*, pp. 210f.

52. See Bultmann, *TWNT* I, pp. 19f., s.v. ἀγαλλίασις, etc.; *idem*, *Theology* I, p. 40; O. Cullmann, *Early Christian Worship*, London: S.C.M. Press (*SBT* 10), p. 15.

53. *Contra* Cullmann, *Christology*, pp. 207f.

54. Cullmann, *Christology*, p. 214.

55. On its secondary character compared with Luke 6:46 see above, ch. V, p. 119 and n. 66.

56. See Jeremias, *Parables*, pp. 38–52; 126–139.

57. J. A. T. Robinson, *Twelve NT Studies*, pp. 139–153. Note that the title of this essay is stated interrogatively. If our analysis of the Son of man sayings is correct, the palm must go to the Son of man Christology.

58. E.g. with Bultmann, *Theology*, p. 43; "Indeed, that is the real content of the Easter faith: God had made the prophet and teacher Jesus of Nazareth Messiah!" Bultmann also adduces as supporting evidence the Petrine Confession and the Transfiguration narrative, on his theory that these were originally post-resurrection appearances. But this theory must be firmly rejected. Cf. *Mission and Achievement*, p. 54 and now also Hahn, *Hoheitstitel*, pp. 226–230 on the Petrine Confession and pp. 334–340 on the Transfiguration.

59. Cf. Cullmann, *Christology*, p. 134.

60. Cf. *Mission and Achievement*, p. 111.

61. J. Jeremias, *Eucharistic Words of Jesus*, Oxford: Blackwell, 1955, pp. 129–131.

62. Taylor, *Names*, p. 21; *idem*, *The Person of Christ*, pp. 41f.; Cullmann, *Christology*, pp. 133f.

63. C. C. Torrey in *Quantulacumque* (Kirsopp Lake *Festschrift*), ed. R. P. Casey *et. al.*, London: Christopher, 1937, pp. 317–324.

64. *SB* I, p. 66; Hahn, *Hoheitstitel*, pp. 208f., n. 6.

65. *Op. cit.* (above, ch. V, note 37), p. 161; also *idem* in *Studia Paulina* (de Zwaan *Festschrift*), Haarlem: Bohn, 1953, pp. 83–95. Dahl brings together Acts 3:20f., 2:36 and 1 Cor. 15:3 as three examples of Christos as a primitive title in three different contexts (parousia, exaltation and passion-resurrection respectively), attributing all three uses to the Palestinian earliest church. But the exaltation passage must be assigned to Hellenistic Jewish Christianity. Tödt also recognizes the titular character of χριστός in the passion-resurrection contexts, though he assigns it to "Hellenistic" tradition (*Menschensohn*, p. 146). This is hardly correct, in view of the Semitic character of 1 Cor. 15:3ff., though of course it was still common in the Hellenistic tradition.

66. On this see Dahl *op. cit.*, p. 161. Dahl, however, finds the influence of the titulus also in Acts 3:20f., and 2:36, which is doubtful.

67. See again T. A. Burkill. *Vig. Chr.* 12 (1958), pp. 14–16.

68. *Twelve NT Studies*, p. 146.

69. Robinson also claims that the "suffering Christos" has no place in

the early kerygma, but is a Lucan specialization. It is true that it is absent from Paul, who prefers the verbs ἀποθνῄσκειν ("to die") and σταυροῦν ("to crucify") from Palestinian and Hellenistic tradition respectively. But note the occurrence of παθεῖν ("to suffer") in the secondary Hellenistic strata of the passion predictions (Mark 8:31; 9:12). Hence the usage παθεῖν τὸν χριστόν ("that the Christ should suffer") in 1 Pet. and Heb. (ignored by Robinson) as well as in Luke-Acts. The evidence suggests that παθεῖν came into Hellenistic usage between Paul and Mark. Robinson is right, however, in excising it from the earliest tradition in Acts 3:12–26.

70. See above, ch. V, pp. 112–114.

71. The Palestinian origin is indicated by the poetic form and by the reverential periphrasis ὑψίστου ("of the Most High") v. 32. Hahn considers it pre-Christian Jewish and thinks that in its Jewish usage it referred to the political national kingdom. But if it was pre-Christian Jewish, it would have come into Christian usage at the Palestinian stage and therefore have been applied to the post-parousia kingdom as in Acts 3:20.

72. See above, ch. II, pp. 33f. and note 32.

73. So Hahn, p. 247. In art. "Magnificat", *HDB*, I ventured to suggest that the Benedictus was taken over later from Baptist circles (cf. P. Vielhauer, *ZThK* 49 (1962), pp. 255–272). If this be the case, then it is more likely that the canticle came into Christian usage in application to the reign of Jesus inaugurated at the exaltation, rather than at the parousia, and in the Hellenistic Jewish rather than in the Palestinian stage.

74. See above, ch. V, p. 111 and note 43.

75. Cf. B. Lindars, *N. T. Apologetic*, p. 200, though no reason is given. Lindars also associates the earliest Davidic Christology with the exaltation rather than with the parousia.

76. See the analysis of Dibelius in *Botschaft und Geschichte* I, pp. 1–78. Attempts have been frequently made to postulate a Hebrew origin for Luke 1–2, notably in a series of articles by P. Winter (e.g. *NTS* I, 1954–55, pp. 111–121 and *Nov. Test.* I, 1956, pp. 184–199. But many of the linguistic phenomena can be accounted for by conscious modelling on LXX (so N. Turner, *NTS*, 2, 1955–56, pp. 100–109). For an admirable summary of recent discussion on Luke 1–2 see R. McL. Wilson, *Studia Evangelica* (*TU* 73), 1959, pp. 235–253. Wilson concludes that a good case for Semitic origin can be made out for the "lyrical" passages, including Benedictus and Magnificat, and for the Baptist nativity cycle, but that for the rest of the narrative conscious modelling on LXX must be assumed. This is the view taken here.

77. For details see Lindars, pp. 192–194, who, however, is not concerned with the traditio-historical aspect of the matter.

78. For further discussion see below, and the literature referred to in notes 80 and 82.

79. John 3:35f.; 5:19–23, 25f., 27, 28f. Except in 5:25–28, where the purely future eschatology has been retained, the tenses have been

altered to the past or present, so as to refer to the enthronement of the Son and to his work in his exalted state.

80. E.g. Dodd, *Apostolic Preaching*, p. 14; C. K. Barrett, *The Epistle to the Romans* (Black's Commentary), 1957, p. 18. According to Hahn, the pre-Pauline origin of the passage was first suggested by J. Weiss (see *Earliest Christianity*, New York: Harper, 1959, p. 119). The limits of the pre-Pauline formula are variously defined: (1) From τοῦ υἱοῦ αὐτοῦ through κυρίου ἡμῶν (Dodd); (2) As in the text (Weiss, and Hahn, p. 252); (3) from γενομένου through ἁγιωσύνης (Barrett, to produce an antithetical couplet). We accept (2) because the first υἱοῦ (v. 3) is used of pre-existence and so clearly Hellenistic, while Ἰησοῦ Χριστοῦ τοῦ κυρίου ἡμῶν is clearly Pauline.

81. *Ibid.* Rom. 1:3f.; Acts 2:36 and Ps. 2:7 applied to the resurrection are all taken as evidence of the earliest Christology, which is alleged to be adoptionist, i.e. asserting that Jesus at his resurrection became Davidic Messiah.

82. Cf. also Schweizer, *Lordship and Discipleship*, p. 59. O. Michel, *Der Brief an die Römer* (*K–EKNT*) Göttingen: Vandenhoeck u. Ruprecht, 1955[10], pp. 30f.

83. E. Schweizer, *TWNT* VI, pp. 414f. (s.v. πνεῦμα); Eng. Tr. *Spirit of God*, London: Black, 1960, pp. 57f. Here Schweizer states his conclusion: the arguments were set forth in *Ev. Theol.* 15 (1955), pp. 563–571, to which he refers, but which is inaccessible to me.

84. πνεῦμα ἁγιωσύνης is a *prima facie* Semitism (רוּחַ הַקֹּדֶשׁ). Cf. Isa. 63:10f., Ps. 51:11, where however LXX translates πνεῦμα ἅγιον. But, as Hahn notes, πνεῦμα ἁγιωσύνης occurs in Test. Levi 18:11, so a Hellenistic Jewish origin is not ruled out, whereas a Semitic origin *is* ruled out by the antithesis σάρξ/πνεῦμα, implying a cosmological rather than an eschatological dualism.

85. In discussing the "returning Son" in Palestinian Christology Hahn proceeds at once to Luke 1:32f. (p. 288). He does not bring Ps. 2:7 into the discussion until p. 291 and there in connection with the exaltation Christology, which on p. 192 had been assigned to early Hellenistic Jewish Christianity.

86. Acts 13:33. This contradicts the Lucan Christology, which dates Jesus' divine sonship from the birth. It is thus clearly pre-Lucan.

87. See esp. J. A. T. Robinson, *Twelve NT Studies*, pp. 149–151; Hahn, pp. 385–387.

88. Heb. has יָרוּם וְנִשָּׂא "shall be exalted and lifted up"; Luke has thus conformed with LXX.

89. For ἅγιος ("holy") cf. Acts 4:27, 30 as a modifier of παῖς ("servant"). For δίκαιος cf. Acts 7:52, in Stephen's speech, which is impregnated with the Mosaic prophet-servant Christology, and occurs in a context which speaks of the OT prophets as foretelling the coming of the δίκαιος ("righteous One").

90. Taylor, *Mark*, p. 162; S. E. Johnson, *The Gospel according to St. Mark* (Black's Commentary), 1960, p. 39. The influence of Ps. 2:7 is

denied in *Mission and Achievement*, p. 55; and minimized by O. Cullmann, *Baptism in the New Testament*, London: S.C.M. Press (*SBT*), 1950, pp. 16–18; *idem, Christology*, p. 66.

91. This suggestion appears to have been first mooted by Bousset (!) *Kyrios Christos*, p. 57, n. 2. Recently, it has received strong support from Jeremias (*Servant*, p. 81f.), and is accepted by Cullmann, *Baptism*, p. 17 and *Christology*, p. 66; also by Hahn, *Hoheitstitel*, pp. 281f.; 340–342.

92. C. E. B. Cranfield, *Mark*, p. 57.

93. Bultmann's theory that υἱὸς τοῦ θεοῦ ("Son of God") here represents the Hellenistic θεῖος ἀνήρ ("divine man") is still accepted within the Bultmann school (e.g. Hahn, p. 175). But the Deuteronomic texts with which Jesus parries the temptations imply precisely a rejection of the θεῖος ἀνήρ understanding of Sonship. Cf. *Mission and Achievement*, p. 82.

94. For the tradition-history, cf. *Interpreting the Miracles*, p. 47.

95. So Hahn, *Hoheitstitel*, p. 393.

96. Cullmann, *Christology*, p. 36.

97. In *Interpreting the Miracles* I loosely described the Palestinian interpretation of the miracles as "Messianic": I would now wish to make this more specific, and to say that it is "Mosaic-prophetic".

98. Hahn, pp. 235–238.

99. Cf. most recently, *Interpreting the Miracles*, pp. 57f.

100. See Leaney *ad loc.*

101. See above, ch. V, p. 114.

102. Cullmann, *Christology*, pp. 43–50.

Chapter VII

THE HELLENISTIC JEWISH MISSION: THE TWO STAGE CHRISTOLOGY

1. *Preliminary Considerations*

ACCORDING to the narrative of Acts (Acts 6:1ff.), Hellenistic Jewish Christianity first arose in Palestine, and in very close touch with the original Aramaic speaking community. We may presume that it was here that the Aramaic christological terms were first translated into the Greek language. To begin with, the change would have been purely linguistic: *rabbi* became διδάσκαλος ("teacher"), *maran(a)* became κύριος (ἡμῶν), Son of man became υἱὸς τοῦ ἀνθρώπου, *mašiaḥ* became χριστός, *'ebhedh* became παῖς, ben David became υἱὸς Δαυ(ε)ιδ, Son of God became υἱὸς (τοῦ) θεοῦ. The fact that what we˙have been able to discover about Aramaic speaking earliest Christology has been filtered through the medium of Greek documents suggests that at first the Greek speaking Jewish Christians simply took over and preserved inviolate the Christological perspectives of the earliest Aramaic speaking community.

At first, then, the two poles of christological thought continued to be (i) the earthly life of Jesus, interpreted as the eschatological presence of God (his *exousia* in word and deed, valid not only for the earthly life itself, but projected into the present life of the Christian community); and (ii) the vindication of this authority at the parousia. All of the christological titles used by the Aramaic speaking community, translated into Greek dress, would at first be continued and used in the service of the same christological conception as that of the Aramaic speaking community. Thus Son of man would express the *exousia* of Jesus in his earthly ministry, his *exousia* in his passion and its atoning significance, and his second coming to vindicate his word and work.

Christos would be used in connection with the passion and for the parousia. The complex of Davidic christology would be used at first, partly to indicate Jesus' earthly qualifications (born of the seed of David) and partly to speak of his office at the parousia (*Christos*, Son of God). *Kyrios* would be used to express the authority of Jesus' word and the church's submission to it, and also to invoke Jesus' coming again at the parousia. Jesus' earthly life would also be interpreted in terms of the Mosaic prophet-servant. Part of this tradition was merely preserved in a fossilized form, notably in the synoptic Son of man sayings.[1] Part of it was not only preserved, but actively continued. This was especially the case with the suffering and resurrection of Jesus as *Christos*,[2] but also to some extent with *kyrios* as applied to the authority of the word of the earthly Jesus[3] and to his coming again.[4]

However, it was impossible for the Greek speaking Jewish Christians simply to repeat the tradition or even merely to develop it along the lines laid down by the earliest Aramaic speaking Christians. Not that they were given to speculation, or to development for development's sake. But three tasks lay immediately before them. First, there was the kerygmatic task of announcing the Christian message to the Greek speaking Jews. Secondly, there was the need to instruct adherents to the message. Thirdly, there was the apologetic task of defending the gospel in face of its Hellenistic Jewish critics. These tasks were begun while the Greek speaking Jewish Christians were still in close touch with the original Aramaic speaking community (Acts 6:9). It was of course continued in the diaspora. It was still going on when the next important step, the mission to the gentiles, was inaugurated. And it continued alongside of the gentile mission, as we see particularly in the case of St. Paul.

The Greek speaking Christians naturally used the LXX as their Aramaic speaking predecessors had used the Hebrew OT. Here lies the main clue to the christological development in early Hellenistic Jewish Christianity. The use of the LXX led to important and far reaching developments which concern the following christological titles: *Kyrios*, *Christos*, Son of God, Son of David.

2. *The Exaltation*

(i) Κύριος *and* Χριστός *("Lord" and "Christ")*

It will be remembered that in his essay, "The most primitive Christology of all?"[5] J. A. T. Robinson drew a clear distinction between the Christology of Acts 3:20f. and that of Acts 2:36. Acts 3:20f., he suggested, was more primitive, and Acts 2:36 a later development. In Acts 3:20f. Jesus is the One who at his resurrection or ascension was predestined to appear as the *Christos* at the parousia. In Acts 2:36 he has already been appointed *Kyrios* and *Christos* at his exaltation. This is an important insight. But no further attempt was made in that essay to locate the two christological conceptions in the history of the tradition. Now we have seen that Acts 3:20f. tallies with the earliest Son of man Christology of the Palestinian community, except for the terminological shift from Son of man to *Christos*. Where, then, are we to locate the christological conception behind Acts 2:36? It is clear that a far reaching shift of perspective is involved. In the earlier conception, characteristic, as we have seen, of the earliest Palestinian community, Jesus was briefly assumed into heaven, there awaiting the parousia. Acts 2:36 however, asserts that from the moment of his ascension Jesus *becomes* Lord and Christ and is henceforth actively reigning.

E. Schweizer[6] has protested against the view that the earliest church regarded Jesus as inactive between the ascension and the parousia. On that ground he would assign the christological conception of Acts 2:36 to the earliest Palestinian community. Schweizer's protest is legitimate up to a point. For Jesus was certainly conceived in the earliest community as still active. However, this action was not yet expressed in terms of his reigning from heaven. Rather, it was continued in the church through the repetition of his earthly message of salvation and demand. This conception was expressed by making him speak as Son of man about his *earthly* activity, by circulating his earthly words as words of "the Lord", and by claiming that he would vindicate this continued offer of salvation at his parousia. But in the earliest Palestinian community no attempt was made to evaluate the present status, dignity and function of Jesus in heaven. He simply was waiting for the parousia. How, when and why was this far-reaching step taken?

First, how? The context of Acts 2:36 gives the answer. Verse 36 is the Christian application of Ps. 110:1:

> The Lord said to my Lord, Sit at my right hand
> till I make thy enemies a stool for thy feet.

Here *Kyrios* is predicated for Jesus at the moment of his ascension, not only for his earthly life and for his final parousia as in the Christology of the earliest Palestinian church. And this step is taken with the aid of and on the basis of Ps. 110:1, cited vv. 34f.

Second, when? As we have seen from Mark 14:62, the motif of the session at the right hand had already been taken up from Ps. 110:1 in the earliest community. But there are difficulties in the way of inferring from this that the earliest Palestinian church applied Ps. 110:1 *in toto* to Jesus' exaltation, as in Acts 2:36. The chief difficulty is linguistic. For the second occurrence of *Kyrios* in this quotation is, in the Hebrew, "(l)*adhonî*." Two circumstances militate against the application of this title to Jesus in the Aramaic speaking church. (i) By the first century A.D. the term "*'adhonai*" had become restricted to God.[7] Most commonly it was used as substitute in reading for the tetragrammaton. For that reason it did not become part of the vocabulary of Palestinian Jewish Messianology. (ii) The Palestinian church called Jesus "Lord" both in respect of his earthly word and work, and in respect of his second coming. But the term used was *maran(a)*, not *'adhonî*.[8] Too much should not be made of the fact that in Acts 2:34 the quotation is a verbatim transcription of LXX. There is always the possibility of secondary assimilation. But the application of the second *Kyrios* in the text to Jesus would seem to be possible only from the LXX, and not from the Hebrew text. Everything, therefore, points to the application of Ps. 110:1 to Jesus at his exaltation. And the consequent dating of his Lordship from that point was due to the creativity of the *Hellenistic* Jewish community. It was this community, seemingly, which took the revolutionary step of bringing forward the titles *Christos* and *Kyrios* from the parousia to the exaltation. It was this community which first conceived of Jesus as actively reigning in heaven.

Third, why? The answer must surely be, the delay in the parousia,[9] and the increasing experience of the Spirit's working in the church. It was satisfactory to conceive of Jesus' present working in the church in terms of the extension of his earthly word and work and of the ratification of it by the parousia, only so long as the parousia was expected very soon. But soon it became apparent that the interval between the ascension and the parousia was to last longer. It was then inevitable that the church should reflect upon that interval, and upon Jesus' relation to it, and that it should endeavour to work out a more satisfactory position.

The effects of this adoption of the *kyrios* title for the exalted Jesus are far-reaching. KYRIOS IESOUS becomes the proclamation of the Hellenistic Jewish missionaries.[10] Their converts believe and confess their faith in Jesus as Lord,[11] and are baptized in the name of the Lord Jesus.[12] Tentative beginnings are made in transferring to Jesus LXX passages referring to *YHWH-kyrios*, a procedure which would have been impossible in Aramaic speaking Christianity.[13] At this stage all that is involved is a transference of *functions* from God to the exalted Jesus. Or rather, it is precisely *through* the exalted Jesus that God carries out these functions. These transferences must be clearly distinguished from later extensions of the same tendency in the gentile mission. There the transference of the divine name to Jesus is stated quite consciously (Phil. 2:10f.) and with ontic implications. There too the transference of OT texts implies the later belief in the active pre-existence of the redeemer (Heb. 10:10ff.).[14]

Similar considerations apply to *Christos*. Once it had been adopted as a title for the exalted Jesus in the Hellenistic Jewish mission, it became a succinct summary of the Christian proclamation.[15] To prove from the LXX that Jesus *is* the *Christos* (not only that he had suffered as the Messiah, and would return as such) becomes the main burden of apologetic.[16] CHRISTOS IESOUS or IESOUS CHRISTOS becomes a confession of a faith.[17]

(ii) *Son of God*

It was argued in chapter VI that as a christological title Son of God was derived from Jewish Davidic Messianology, and that it first came into Christian usage in connection with the parousia. With the shift of emphasis from the parousia to the exaltation and present Lordship of Jesus in the Hellenistic Jewish Christian mission, it was only natural that the term Son of God, like *Kyrios* and *Christos*, should be transferred to the exaltation.

First, we note that certain Davidic texts, whose earliest application was to the parousia, are shifted to Jesus' enthronement after the resurrection.[18] In Acts 13:33, Ps. 2:7 is used as a proof for ἀνάστησας ("having raised"). Also, earlier in the same speech (v. 22), 1 Sam. 13:14 and Ps. 89:21 (which are closely connected with the royal title, Son of God) are applied to the inauguration of David's reign. The intention here is clearly typological. David's accession typifies the enthronement of Jesus after his resurrection. In Heb. 1:4f., after the statement about the exaltation in terms from Ps. 109 (110):1 in v. 3, Ps. 2:7 and 2 Sam. 7:14 are quoted (v. 5). In Heb. 5:5 the same psalm verse is again cited, this time in connection with Jesus' appointment as high priest at his exaltation. The author of Hebrews, as he makes plain in his exordium (Heb. 1:1f.), has himself a very different Christology of Jesus' Sonship. For him υἱός is a generalized designation covering the whole of the Redeemer's work from pre-existence through incarnate life and death to resurrection, exaltation and parousia. This proves that in the OT quotations we have been examining he is drawing upon much earlier exegetical tradition.

Secondly, the original Palestinian formula enshrined in Rom. 1:3f.[19] undergoes expansion in the Hellenistic Jewish stage:

> descended from David *in the sphere of the flesh*;
> appointed Son of God *in the sphere of holy Spirit*
>   from the time of his resurrection from the dead.

The christological perspective of the second half is now exactly that of Acts 2:36. Divine Sonship is the royal function to which Jesus is exalted after the resurrection.

There are several NT passages where the term Son applies specifically to the Exalted One. Cf. e.g. 1 Cor. 15:28, where it occurs in combination with ὑποταγήσεται ("will be subjected") from Ps. 8:7 (though here υἱός, "Son", looks to the parousia, thus indicating the context in which the shift occurred). Also, there is Col. 1:13. Note here the phrase *"kingdom* of his Son". This is the same conception as the "kingdom" of the exalted Christ in 1 Cor. 15:28. In Hebrews, in addition to the specific use of the OT passages mentioned above, υἱός is used as a title for the Exalted One in his capacity as the heavenly high priest (Heb. 4:14). Probably, however, this is not a survival of earlier usage, but an accidental coincidence between the author's generalized conception of the Son of God and the earlier usage.

3. *Jesus' Earthly Work*
(i) *Son of David*

In Hellenistic Jewish Christianity we can trace a significant re-shaping of the Davidic Christology. Perhaps the best starting point for an examination of this process is the Son of David question (Mark 12:35-37). This pericope already presumes the christological perspective of Acts 2:36, in which *Christos* and *Kyrios* are transferred to the Exalted One. By a verbalistic argument from the verse on which this Christology was based (Ps. 109 [110]:1) this pericope refutes the applicability of Son of David to the Exalted One. This blocks the way to accompanying *Kyrios* and *Christos* in the shift from the parousia to the exaltation.

Some commentators have supposed that the Son of David question represents an attempt to eliminate Son of David from Christology altogether.[20] Yet both the earlier Palestinian tradition (in the genealogies and birth at Bethlehem) and the later Hellenistic Jewish Christian tradition (in the birth narratives, blind Bartimaeus, and the triumphal entry) all apply the Davidic sonship to the earthly Jesus. This makes it hard to suppose that our pericope was intended to deny the relevance of the title Son of David to Jesus' earthly life.[21] We must therefore suppose that the Son of David question has simply taken over one of the positions of the earlier Palestinian tradition, while denying the other. The Davidic descent of Jesus is relevant in so far as it qualifies him for the Messianic office, now conceived to be entered upon at the exaltation. But it yields nothing for the understanding of that exalted office itself. No positive evaluation, however, is as yet accorded to the Son of David as a title for the earthly life. But the possibility is kept open.

This possibility is realized in the Hellenistic Jewish Christian revision of the formula in Rom. 1:3.[22] Here κατὰ σάρκα ("according to the flesh") is added to the earthly side of the antithesis, in contrast to κατὰ πνεῦμα ἁγιωσύνης ("according to the spirit of holiness") on the heavenly side. This means that the Davidic sonship is now not merely the qualification for the end-time Messianic office, but has a positive significance for the whole of Jesus' earthly history.

But what positive significance can it have? In the Marcan version of the healing of blind Bartimaeus the invocation "Son of David" has been combined (secondarily)[23] with the cry, "have mercy on me". Thus the Davidic sonship is used to express, not the royal descent or Messianic rule of Jesus, but his miraculous help for the sick and suffering. Now in the earlier tradition, this idea was associated with the Mosaic prophet-servant. Indeed (see above, p. 111), the blind Bartimaeus pericope, in its Palestinian stage, had probably been composed in terms of that Christology. What seems to have happened is that in at any rate some circles[24] of Hellenistic Jewish Christianity the term Son of David has taken over the functions of the Mosaic prophet-servant. It is interesting and perhaps significant that the later gospel of Matthew, which has preserved more fully the Son of David Christology (Matt. 9:27, 15:22), also quotes Isa. 53:4 (Matt. 8:17) in connection with the miracles. Matthew clearly associates Son of David with the Servant.

This is perhaps one of the most impressive achievements of Hellenistic Jewish Christology. Jesus is qualified for the Messianic office which he performs from the time of the resurrection not by mere physical descent, but by his sovereign sympathy and powerful treatment of the sick and suffering.

The infancy narratives in Matthew and Luke are largely built around the Son of David Christology. As we have seen, the factual tradition of Jesus' birth at Bethlehem may well, after some hesitation, have been accepted already in the Palestinian community. There it was connected with the Davidic descent as the qualification for the Messianic function upon which Jesus was to enter at the parousia. By contrast, the infancy narratives themselves express the more positive evaluation of the Davidic sonship in Jesus' earthly life. In Luke 2:1–20 the birth at Bethlehem is combined with the promise that Jesus is to be σωτήρ ("Saviour"). This term belongs to the Mosaic Prophet-servant Christology (Acts 5:31; cf. Acts 7:25; also, in combination with the Davidic sonship Christology, in Acts 13:23). This combination of Son of David and prophetic servant represents the same christological perspective as the blind Bartimaeus pericope. Jesus as Son of David is the one sent from God to *save* men (σώζειν, σωτήρ).[25]

The Lucan genealogy, as we have seen, was probably constructed in the Palestinian church to assert Jesus' Davidic descent. It does not appear to have undergone any change at the stage which we are considering. No attempt is made to reshape the Davidic sonship here. It is simply the qualification for Jesus' Messianic office. The later extension of the genealogy to Adam expresses not the reshaped Davidic Christology but the Adam/Christ typology, which belongs to a different christological conception.[26]

The Matthean genealogy was, like the Lucan, originally conceived by the Palestinian Church in terms of Jesus' qualification to the Messianic office at the parousia. But it has been extended back to Abraham, and includes the remarkable series of "doubtful women", Thamar, Rahab, Ruth, and Uriah's wife (Bathsheba). These developments belong to various later stages of the tradition. By tracing Jesus' descent back to the patriarchs the Davidic sonship is combined with the Hellenistic Jewish conception of the OT man of God. It thus witnesses to the shift of the Son of David from mere qualification to a positive evaluation of Jesus' earthly life. The doubtful women probably came in much later (perhaps from the Evangelist himself) in response to the Jewish slander of Jesus' illegitimacy, which in turn arose in reaction to the virginal conception.[27]

While the annunciation to Joseph in Matt. 1:18-25 has been constructed as an apology in face of this slander, it also enshrines the earlier tradition of Jesus' Davidic descent (v. 20). Hahn[27a] would assign the interpretation of the name of Jesus to the same pre-virginal-conception stratum. This suggests the same combination of the Davidic sonship with the σωτήρ ("Saviour") motif as in Luke 1:32, and therefore the same positive evaluation of the Davidic sonship for Jesus' earthly work.

The magi story, Matt. 2:1-12, refers to the birth at Bethlehem (vv. 1, 5, 6, 8), The titles ὁ Χριστός ("the Christ") (v. 4) and ὁ βασιλεὺς τῶν Ἰουδαίων ("the King of the Jews") seem to be here (uniquely) used as equivalents for the Davidic sonship, thus showing (cf. τεχθείς, "born") that Χριστός is here applied to Jesus' earthly life. In the Evangelist's perspective those terms cannot refer to earthly majesty but to the paradoxical lowliness and humanity which he associates with the Son of David.

(ii) *Christos*

The common view that Christology developed by pushing back the Messiahship of Jesus progressively from the exaltation to Jesus' earthly life is an oversimplification.[28] Indeed, as a term applied to Jesus in his earthly life *Christos* is surprisingly rare.

The Petrine confession is often taken as evidence for this backward shift. This explanation is especially favoured by those who, with Bultmann, think that it is a post-resurrection scene read back into Jesus' lifetime. It is accepted even by Hahn, who thinks that it enshrines a genuine biographical tradition in which Jesus repudiated the title. If, however, as we have argued, Jesus' rebuke in Mark 8:30a was part of the original story, it is difficult to see how *Christos* could have been used positively, except in connection with the passion prediction. Otherwise the rebuke remains unexplained. At this stage of the tradition, therefore, the title *Christos* is legitimate. But it must be reserved for Jesus until after the passion. This corresponds with the perspective of Acts 2:36.

In Matt. 11:2 (τὰ ἔργα τοῦ Χριστοῦ, "the works of the Christ"), however, we do have a clear application of *Christos* to Jesus' earthly life. This occurs in an editorial modification of Q. Now the idea of the Christ as a worker of miracles is completely foreign to Jewish and earliest Christian tradition. Here it is not a simple case of reading back the Messiahship into Jesus' earthly life, but an extension of the title ὁ Χριστός, "the Christ", long since established for the passion, resurrection and exalted state, to cover the earthly work of Jesus as the Mosaic prophet-servant. Since as such Jesus was "anointed" with the Holy Spirit (ἔχρισεν, Acts 10:38) the shift is not hard to explain. It is a shift in terminology, rather than the christologizing of a life previously interpreted unchristologically. *"Christos"* now does duty for all that the Mosaic prophet-servant had stood for in the Palestinian stage.

But once it had thus been transferred to the earthly life of Jesus, it continued to be used as a title, though in various senses. In Matt. 1:17; 16:20 it has no particular colour. In Matt. 2:4 it expresses the earthly Son of David Christology (see above pp. 189f.). In Matt. 23:10 it may be colourless, but it may equally have referred originally to the exalted Christ. Except when Luke is following Mark (Lk. 9:20), he seems to avoid it until he comes to the passion. There, however, it reflects the early and authentic tradition that Jesus was crucified as a Messianic pretender (Lk. 23:2, 35). It is not a reading back from the exaltation into the earthly life. Only in the Johannine gospel is it used for the earthly existence of Jesus with any frequency. Here it occurs once as an indirect self-designation (4:26), but more often in the questions and confessions of others (1:41; 4:29; 7:26; cf. 9:22; 10:24; 11:27). In the Johannine writings this application of *Christos* to the earthly life has a markedly anti-docetic twist when used as a confession of faith (John 20:31) and is especially prominent in the epistles (1 John 2:22; 5:1).

(iii) *Son of God*

Despite the future orientation of its faith toward the coming Son of man, the earliest Palestinian church had been deeply concerned with the earthly work of Jesus. It interpreted this work, first, in terms of the Son of man (but only in sayings ascribed to Jesus), and secondly in terms of the eschatological prophet-servant. That this early prophetic Christology lived on and was further developed in the Hellenistic Jewish mission may be seen from Stephen's speech in Acts 7. In the description of Moses, the speech, as is widely recognized, presumes a Moses-Christ typology. Features ascribed to Moses are also relevant to the underlying interpretation of Jesus' earthly ministry. In a manner typical of the modified Hellenistic Jewish conception of the divine man or man or God, Moses is described as "mighty in his words and deeds" (v. 22), and as a performer of "wonders and signs" (v. 36).

The same portrait of Jesus is given in Luke 24:19b and Acts 2:22. In Acts 10:38 the miracles of Jesus are associated with a permanent endowment of the Spirit. This again is in conformity with the Hellenistic Jewish modification of the pagan divine man, in which the more biblical concept of permanent charismatic endowment has replaced the pagan concept of substantial divinization. The idea is of course not altogether new. It echoes the language of Isa. 61:1, a passage which was used by Jesus himself in the answer to John, and which was directly employed by the earliest Palestinian church (Luke 4:16ff.) in connection with its view of Jesus as the Mosaic eschatological prophet. What is new is the emphasis on the permanent endowment with the Spirit. The same conception is found in Matthew's modification[29] of the Q saying about exorcisms, in which "by the Spirit" of God replaces the original "by the finger".

The term adopted for this modification of the prophet Christology was "Son of God". If the theory originating with Bousset is correct, this term has directly replaced παῖς ("servant": it can also mean "child") in the baptism and transfiguration narratives.[30] We need not deny the influence of Ps. 2:7 in this terminological shift. The fact that Jesus was already regarded as Son of God in his exalted state provided a springboard from which to read back the title into his earthly life. Ps. 2:7 contributes the notion of "adoption", i.e. appointment. But the content and meaning in the shift is controlled, not by Ps. 2:7, but by the Hellenistic Jewish concept of the Son of God as we find it, e.g. in the Book of Wisdom.[31] Jesus is now appointed at his baptism as the Son of God and endowed with a permanent charisma of the Holy Spirit. Here the use of "Son of God" evidenced by the Book of Wisdom may well have played an important part.

Two of the temptations in the Q version have perhaps[32] undergone the same terminological shift, παῖς ("servant") again being replaced by υἱὸς τοῦ θεοῦ ("Son of God"). It is precisely as the Son of God endowed with the permanent charisma of the Spirit that Jesus is tempted to misuse his miraculous powers.

In one of the Marcan exorcisms, the demon addresses Jesus as "Son of the Most High God" (Mark 5:7, cf. also the Marcan editorial summary, 3:11). In the earlier exorcism (Mark 1:24) the demon uses the Palestinian title, "Holy One of God", which is associated with the servant-prophet conconcept.[33] Here is another indication of how the concept of Jesus as the Son of God on earth grew out of the prophet-servant Christology of the earliest Palestinian church.

In this context we may also refer to the parable of the vineyard. In chapter VI it was suggested that if not authentic to Jesus this parable was first composed as an allegory on the history of salvation by the Aramaic speaking community in terms of its prophet-servant Christology. In conformity with the terminological shift in the baptism and temptation narratives, the term "Son" is now introduced into the allegory (υἱὸς ἀγαπητός, "beloved Son"). But here the christological conception goes beyond that of the baptism. For the first time the Son's pre-existence is broached: God "had" yet one, a beloved Son (Mark 12:6) even before he "sent" him. This type of pre-existence is to be distinguished from the type which postulates an activity of the pre-existent One, and his own initiative in the incarnation. The latter conception has quite a different origin in the Hellenistic Mission, as we shall seek to show later.

Thus, there is no reason to derive the motif of the "sending" of the Son of God into the world from the gnostic redeemer myth, or even to postulate for its origin the Hellenistic (gentile) community. It originates rather within Hellenistic Jewish Christianity as a development from the Palestinian prophetic-servant tradition through the Hellenistic Jewish modified conception of the divine man, or man of

God. This conception of inactive pre-existence and sending lies behind Gal. 4:4; Rom. 8:3; 8:32; John 3:16. All of these passages are traditional formulae.[34] Their intention is not to speculate about the Redeemer's pre-existence, but to assert that the historical mission of Jesus rests on the divine initiative.

A somewhat different development of this Christology, which represents Jesus as Son of God on earth, is found in the virginal conception as it occurs in the annunciations of Matthew and Luke (Matt. 1:18–25 and Luke 1:26–38). Now the rest of the infancy narratives are, as we have seen, built around the Son of David Christology, evaluated positively for Jesus' earthly life. Their creative milieu is early Hellenistic Judaism. This same Davidic Christology is also presumed in the annunciations (Matt. 1:20; Luke 1:27, 32).[35] But the virginal conception clashes headlong with this earlier Davidic-sonship Christology, for the latter depends on Jesus' *physical* descent from David through Joseph (ἐκ σπέρματος Δαυείδ, "from the seed of David"!). Both Evangelists leave the two concepts side by side, thus indicating their concern not with historical facts, but with christological affirmation.[36] This patent inconsistency indicates that the virginal conception represents a different Christology from the Davidic sonship. What is its *Sitz im Leben*? And what Christology does it express?

For those who, contrary to the obvious intention of the Evangelists, insist on treating the Virgin Birth as a straightforward historical fact, the question is of course pointless. If, however, we accept the traditio-historical approach, there are three possible candidates for the creative milieu: (1) Palestinian Aramaic Christianity;[37] (2) Hellenistic Jewish Christianity;[38] (3) Gentile Christianity, from pagan sources.[39]

Everything points to (2) as the correct solution. There are two dominant motifs in the annunciation stories: the virginity of Mary[40] and the pneumatic conception.[41] The former is the pre-supposition for the latter. Now the virginity of Mary is based foursquare in both narratives upon Isa. 7:14 LXX,[42] which reads παρθένος (virgin, against MT ʿalma, "young woman"). Thus the virginity of Mary is an idea which could only have arisen in the LXX sphere, i.e. in the Hellenistic Jewish stratum. Secondly, as Dibelius has shown, the idea of pneumatic conception with the elimination of an earthly father was already applied in Hellenistic Judaism to the great figures of the OT, particularly to Isaac.[43] That the narrator has the birth of Isaac in mind in the Lucan annunciation is clear from the allusion to Gen. 18:14 in Luke 1:37. This idea differs markedly from the pagan notion of the "sacred marriage", in which the deity comes down and has sexual intercourse with a human maid. Rather, it expresses the Hellenistic Jewish conception of the Spirit of God as a creative power, initiating by his own creative act the culminating event in the history of salvation. So much for the creative milieu of the virginal conception.

What, next, is its christological intention? This is indicated in part by its origin: in Isa. 7:14 LXX and in the midrash on the OT births of the holy men of God. It expresses the Hellenistic Jewish Christology of Jesus as the earthly Son of God in the sense of the modified Hellenistic Jewish concept of the divine man. This is clinched by the language of Luke 1:31, and by the allusion to the birth of Isaac in Luke 1:37.

The christological thrust of Matt. 1:18–25 is not essentially different, despite the absence of the term Son of God here. For the Evangelist selects for special emphasis the Emmanuel promise of Isa. 7:14, "God with us". Matthew obviously regards "Jesus" as equivalent in meaning (vv. 21, 25) to Emmanuel and expounds it to mean the one who will *save* ($\sigma\dot\omega\zeta\epsilon\iota\nu$—$\sigma\omega\tau\dot\eta\rho$) his people from their sins. Here we are back again at the Moses-Joshua prophet-servant typology.[44]

In short, we find in Hellenistic Jewish Christianity a far-reaching christological development of "Son of God" in application to Jesus' earthly work. It combined the early Palestinian Mosaic servant-prophet Christology with the eschatological Son of God Christology of Ps. 2:7 (which had already been shifted from the exaltation to the earthly life). It also enriched that combination with charismatic elements drawn from the Hellenistic Jewish OT divine man. In the sayings which speak of the "sending" of the Son, we are brought to the threshold of the fully fledged doctrine of incarnation. This may seem a far cry from the earliest church's identification of Jesus with the coming Son of man, and from Jesus' own self-understanding as the one whose word and work would be ratified by the coming Son of man. But it is not so really. For it is expressing in terms intelligible to the Hellenistic Jewish world that the whole history of Jesus is God's saving, eschatological act, "his presence and his very self".

4. Summary

The task of the Hellenistic Jewish missionaries was to convey the Christian message of the saving act of God in Jesus to Greek speaking Jews who, like themselves, were reared on the LXX. Its achievement was to transform the earliest Palestinian kerygma, with its two foci of Jesus' historical ministry of *exousia* and the parousia as its vindication, into a proclamation orientated chiefly upon the present work of the Exalted One. To this present, exalted work the historical ministry was a preliminary stage and the parousia the expected consummation. But the Hellenistic Jewish mission still thought in functional terms: it was not concerned with the nature of Jesus in his earthly life. And it had barely raised the question of the pre-existence of the Redeemer. And, while it could apply to Jesus in a functional sense OT texts originally referring to kyrios-YHWH, it had not yet raised the ontic question of the divinity of the exalted Lord. But it had laid the necessary foundations for these developments in the gentile mission.

NOTES ON CHAPTER VII

1. As we have seen in ch. VI, the synoptic Son of Man sayings reached the peak of their development in the Palestinian-Aramaic stratum. In the Hellenistic stage only a few additions from LXX and the παθεῖν (suffering) motif were added to the original stock. The Johannine tradition, however, witnesses to a unique development of Son of man sayings in the interest of the enthronement and katabasis Christologies. See below, pp. 229f.

2. See ch. VI, note 69.

3. See the Pauline references in ch. VI, note 45.

4. E.g. the parousia parables and the apocalyptic material in 1 Thess. 4:15–17.

5. See above, ch. VI, p. 158 and note 57.

6. E. Schweizer, *Lordship*, p. 57.

7. See the full discussion in Hahn, *Hoheitstitel*, pp. 114f.

8. Lindars, *NT Apologetic*, p. 46, sees no difficulty in assuming that the Palestinian church called Jesus אֲדֹנִי. But would it have accorded Jesus a title which by this time was reserved for the Deity? Lindars is right in assigning Mark 12:35–37 to a *Gemeindetheologie*, but on linguistic grounds the *Gemeinde* concerned must have been Greek speaking. He is also right (*contra* Hahn, *ibid.*, pp. 113–117) in placing Acts 2:34–36 prior to Mark 12:35–37, for the latter assumes the position of the former, and raises the difficulty about the Davidic sonship which arises from that position. Hence Mark 12:35–37 is here relegated to the section on the Son of David.

9. Hahn, *ibid.*, p. 113. Hahn propounds an important distinction between "assumption" (*Entrückung*) and exaltation (*Erhöhung*). Assumption is the view of the earliest community: Jesus was taken up to heaven (cf. Elijah, also Moses in later apocalyptic) and was waiting in a state of inactivity until his manifestation as χριστός at the parousia (Acts 3:20ff.). Hahn finds the same view in the ascension story (Acts 1:1–11) and in the answer to the high priest (Mark 14:62). "Exaltation" denotes enthronization as *Kyrios* and *Christos* at the ascension, followed by an active rule until the parousia.

10. E.g. Acts 11:20; 14:3; 16:31. Phil. 2:11 is a survival of this conception in the gentile mission, see below, ch. VIII, pp. 204ff.

11. Acts 11:17 (in combination with χριστόν); 16:31 (acc. to the best MSS: inferior MSS have χριστόν); 18:8. Cf. 15:11 and esp. Rom. 10:9, also Phil. 2:11 in combination with χριστός.

12. E.g., Acts 8:16; 19:5.

13. The commonest example is ἡ ἡμέρα τοῦ κυρίου (= יוֹם יהוה), "the day of the Lord"), e.g. 1 Thess. 5:2 and the phrase ἐπικαλεῖσθαι τὸ ὄνομα τοῦ κυριόυ "to call upon the name of the Lord", from Joel 3:5 LXX (יהוה שֵׁם), e.g. Rom. 10:13f. Cf. also the alteration of Mal. 1:3 (πρὸ πρόσωπου σου and ὁδὸν σου, "before thy face," and "thy way"), Mark 1:2, and the commentaries *ad loc.*

14. Cullmann, *Christology*, p. 234f., does not draw this distinction clearly enough. While Phil. 2:9–11 accurately reproduces the conception of Acts 2:36, it goes beyond it in the phrase, "gave him the name which is above every name". This implies not merely functional, but ontic identity. See E. Käsemann, *ZThK* 47 (1950), p. 347; G. Bornkamm, *Studien*, p. 183.

15. E.g. Acts 8:5; 24:24; the Aramaic church had proclaimed Jesus as the One who would return as χριστός, and a little later as the One who had suffered as such. But as a succinct summary, Jesus *is* (note the present tense, whether expressed or understood) χριστός. The title reflects the exaltation theology of the Hellenistic Jewish mission.

16. E.g. Acts 9:22; 17:3b; 18:28.

17. The direct evidence is surprisingly meagre: Peter's confession at

Caesarea Philippi, after its re-interpretation in a positive sense; also, as a late survival, 1 John 5:1. But it would seem that "Jesus Christ" and "Christ Jesus" were originally confessions of faith, not a proper name. It is perhaps significant also that the nickname χριστιανός ("Christian") arose in the Hellenistic Jewish mission (Acts 11:26) (so Hahn, p. 222).

18. On the original application of these texts to the parousia see ch. VI, p. 167.

19. For the history of the tradition see above, ch. VI, pp. 165f.

20. So e.g. J. Weiss, *Die Schriften des Neuen Testaments*, Göttingen: Vandenhoeck u. Ruprecht, 1907–8, p. 189.

21. So A. E. J. Rawlinson, *The Gospel according to St. Mark* (Westminster Commentaries), London: Methuen, 1949, pp. 173f., against Bousset and Weiss; Taylor, *Mark*, p. 491. Both these commentators are, however, concerned to defend the authenticity of the logion as well. A more satisfactory position is that of G. Bornkamm, *Jesus of Nazareth*, p. 228. While locating the saying in Hellenistic Jewish Christianity, Bornkamm recognizes that it does not deny Son of David as a title to Jesus, but implicitly restricts it to his earthly life: "the title 'Son of David', however, is no longer used in its typical Jewish sense as a title for the Messiah, but in its later Christian meaning, according to which his descent from David shows the Messiah in his humanity and lowliness, in contrast to his exaltation and dominion."

22. For the history of the tradition see above, ch. VI, pp. 165f.

23. Hahn characterizes this as a "two stage" Christology (*ibid.*, pp. 251–268, esp. 267f.), in which the Davidic sonship is a preliminary stage of majesty, succeeded by the full majesty of the exaltation. But to speak of "majesty" (*Hoheit*) in the earthly life is questionable, for it implies a highly paradoxical conception which one would not expect to meet until Paul or John.

24. Hahn (*ibid.*, pp. 264–267) also includes the triumphal entry among the earthly Davidic sonship passages. The Marcan version raises a number of difficulties. Jesus is not yet identified with the Son of David (contrast Matt. and, in a different terminology, Luke; see above, ch. V note 47). The acclamation of the crowds is still future-eschatological. On the other hand, it is very probable that vv. 2–7 are coloured by Zech. 9:9, despite the absence of specific quotation as in Matt. and John. This was contested by W. Bauer, *JBL* 12 (1953), pp. 220–229, in an article seeking to prove that πῶλος in Mark meant a colt, not an ass (!), but established by H. W. Kuhn, *ZNW* 50 (1959). Kuhn compares v. 2 with πῶλον νέον, Zech. 9:9, the acclamation v. 9f. with χαῖρε σφόδρα, θύγατερ Σίων, *ibid.*, and also calls particular attention to the repeated πῶλον δεδεμένον (vv. 2, 4), which he compares with Gen. 49:11 (so also Nestlé in margin), δεσμεύων τὸν πῶλον αὐτοῦ. This text was Messianically interpreted at Qumran (4 Q *Patr. Bless.* I; see J. M. Allegro in *JBL* 75 (1956), pp. 174–176). It seems clear, therefore, that Mark 11:1ff. is conceived in terms of an earthly Davidic Christology. But this is strange, since it is combined with a future Davidic eschatology, contrary to Mark 12:35–37. Thus the Marcan triumphal entry represents

the new, positive evaluation of Jesus' earthly life in terms of the Davidic Christology, as in the Hellenistic Jewish stratum. V. 10, on the other hand, retains the future Davidic eschatology of the earlier Aramaic tradition. Matt. and Luke have variously eliminated the latter and conformed the pericope entirely with the earthly Davidic Christology.

25. χριστὸν κύριον ("Christ the Lord") is perhaps best regarded with Dibelius (*Botschaft* I, pp. 62f. and Hahn *ibid.*, p. 272) as a Lucan redaction, disturbing the unitary Christology of the pre-Lucan tradition. This holds good whether or not we accept the emendation χριστὸν κύριου ("the Lord's Messiah").

26. For this see below, ch. VIII, Appendix pp. 233f.

27. So J. Schniewind, *Das Evangelium nach Matthäus* (*NTD* 2), Göttingen: Vandenhoeck u. Ruprecht, 1953, p. 11.

27a. *Hoheitstitel*, p. 275.

28. So even Lindars, *NT Apologetic*, p. 187. The situation is, however, somewhat different. In the Palestinian tradition χριστός covers first the parousia, then the passion. In the earliest Jewish Hellenistic stratum χριστός was extended to cover the exaltation, and only much later and sparingly to cover the earthly life. But from the very first there was always a high christological estimate of Jesus' earthly ministry. This high estimate, however, was in terms of not χριστός but of the Son of man and Mosaic prophet-servant.

29. For the priority of the Semitic ἐν δακτύλῳ ("by the finger") see *Mission and Achievement*, p. 37.

30. It is a moot point whether the shift to υἱός ("son") took place first at the baptism or at the transfiguration. Those who believe with Bultmann (*Tradition*, p. 259) that the transfiguration is a misplaced resurrection appearance will naturally postulate its priority over the baptism (so also, from a different starting point, Lindars, p. 144.). But if υἱός ("Son") in the baptismal voice represents an original παῖς ("servant") it is more likely that the change was made simultaneously in both pericopes.

31. See above, ch. III, pp. 70f., where it was suggested that "Son of God" had become current as a term for the Hellenistic Jewish modification of the pagan divine man, of which the righteous men of the OT were supreme examples.

32. If, as suggested above (ch. VI, p. 170), the two Son of God temptations reach back to the Aramaic stratum, where they were originally conceived in terms of the παῖς ("servant") this will hold good. If, however, they are assigned with Bultmann (*Tradition*, p. 257) to the Hellenistic stratum they must have been created *de novo* at the Hellenistic Jewish stage (so also Hahn, pp. 303, 401f., n. 5).

33. For ὁ ἅγιος τοῦ θεοῦ ("Holy One of God") as a Palestinian prophetological title, see above, ch. VI, p. 171.

34. Cf. Hahn, *ibid.*, pp. 315–317, who assigns all these formulae to the Hellenistic gentile tradition. But two strata are discernible here: (1) ἀπέστειλεν ὁ θεὸς τὸν υἱὸν αὐτοῦ ("God sent his Son") (Gal. 4:4) and ὁ θεὸς τὸν ἑαυτοῦ υἱὸν πεμψας ("God, having sent his Son") (Rom.

8:32). These represent the same perspective as Mark 12:6. There is no speculation about or activity assigned to the Son's pre-existence, nor does he take the initiative in the incarnation. Also ἑαυτοῦ υἱόν "his Son", (cf. ἰδίου υἱοῦ, "his own Son", Rom. 8:32) is equivalent to υἱὸς ἀγαπητός ("beloved Son") and expresses the servant-Son Christology (cf. also μονογενῆ, "only", John 3:16) and combines Isa. 42:1 with Gen. 22:16, (cf. O. Michel, Römerbrief, p. 184, n. 2). (2) γενόμενον ἐκ γυναικός, "born of a woman", (Gal. 4:4) and ἐν ὁμοιώματι σαρκός, "in the likeness of flesh" (Rom. 8:3) explicitly assert the incarnation and the Hellenistic idea of the sphere of the σάρξ under the thrall of the powers.

35. In the Lucan annunciation the Davidic sonship plays a more constitutive role. It forms the substance of the angelic promise, which enshrines very ancient material (see above, ch. VI, p. 162). This makes it possible that the annunciation was first conceived in terms of the Davidic (parousia) Christology at the Palestinian stage. Later, at the Hellenistic stage, it would have been transformed in the interests of the virginal conception.

36. Cf. G. Delling TWNT V, pp. 834f., s.v. παρθένος. The Virgin Birth is not a "verfügbares Ereignis", "a manageable event".

37. O. Michel and O. Betz in Judentum-Urchristentum-Kirche, Ed. W. Eltester, (J. Jeremias Festschrift) BZNW 26, 1960, pp. 3–23. They derive the concept of miraculous birth ultimately from the royal theology and find evidence at Qumran for the miraculous birth of the Messiah (1 Q Sa 2, 11). But there it is the adoption concept of Ps. 2:7 and nothing is said of the Holy Spirit.

38. Dibelius, ibid., pp. 18–34 esp. pp. 29f. In addition to the arguments mentioned in the text he proves the Hellenistic Jewish origin of ἐπέρχεσθαι ("to come upon"), ἐπισκιάζειν ("to overshadow"), δύναμις ὑψίστου ("power of the most high"), and of πνεῦμα ἅγιον ("holy spirit") as creative rather than as the source of inspiration. Cf. also J. M. Creed, The Gospel according to St. Luke, London: Macmillan, 1930, p. 20 against pagan derivation.

39. The earlier History of Religions school (Usener, Schmiedel et al.), also more recently, against Dibelius, H. Braun (ZThK 54 (1957), p. 354, n. 3) derive the virginal conception from the more refined pagan stories. Since however, the evidence Braun gives includes Philo, de Cherubim 40–45, immediate Hellenistic Jewish provenance is after all more probable, and, taken with the linguistic evidence adduced by Dibelius, is almost certain.

40. In Matt.: πρὶν ἤ συνελθεῖν αὐτούς ("before they came together") 1:18; Joseph's reaction in v. 19; οὐκ ἐγίνωσκεν αὐτὴν πρίν ("he knew her not until"), v. 25. In Luke: πρὸς παρθένον ("to a virgin") 1:27; πῶς ἔσται τοῦτο, ἐπεὶ ἄνδρα οὐ γινώσκω; ("how shall this be, since I know not a man?") v. 34. The virginity of Mary as such is not stressed, but only the elimination of the man.

41. In Matt.: ἐκ πνεύματος ἁγίου ("from holy Spirit"), 1:18; ἐκ πνεύματός ἐστιν ἁγίου ("is from holy spirit"), v. 20. In Luke: πνεῦμα ἅγιον ἐπελεύσεται ἐπὶ σέ καὶ δύναμις ὑψίστου ἐπισκιάσει σοι ("holy

spirit will come upon you, and the power of the Most High will over-shadow you") 1 :35.

42. Not only is Isa. 7:14 explicitly quoted by Matt. That text impreg-nates both the Matthean and Lucan annunciations (Matt. 1:21, 25; Luke 1:31).

43. *Ibid.*, pp. 25–34. The starting point of the midrash was Gen. 21:1, which asserts God's act in Isaac's birth. The Rabbinic midrash stressed the divine intervention but without eliminating the man. The Hellenistic Jewish development of the midrash eliminated the man. This development is not directly attested, but underlies Philo's allegorical treatment of the conceptions of Sarah, Leah, Rebecca and Zippora in *de Cherubim* 40–45 (note esp. 45: "God visited Sarah *in her solitude*") and also Paul's typological treatment of the birth of Isaac in Gal. 4:21–31. Here note esp. the statement that Isaac was born κατὰ πνεῦμα ("accord-ing to the Spirit"), v. 29, and the quotation of Isa. 54:1 in v. 27, indicating the elimination of the man (τῆς ἐρήμου "the desolate woman" contrasted with ἐχούσης τὸν ἄνδρα, "the married woman"). The Hellenistic Jewish development of the midrash may have been influenced by the refined pagan stories—this much we may concede to Braun (note 39). T. Boslooper, *The Virgin Birth*, Philadelphia: Westminster Press, 1962, rightly recognizes the Hellenistic Jewish provenance of the tradition. Unfortunately, however, he derives it directly from Philo's allegorizations, instead of seeing that these like Gal. 4:21–31, depend upon the *popular Hellenistic* Jewish midrash of the literal miraculous births of the OT heroes. This leads him in turn to misconstrue the christological thrust of the virginal conception. See my review in *JR* 43 (1963), p. 254.

44. For those who are concerned about the historicity of the "Virgin birth" ("virginal conception" is a more accurate term), let it be stated that to believe in the Virgin birth is not to accept the historicity of a biological parthenogenesis but to adhere to the christological intention of the narratives, which is to express the transcendental origin of Jesus' history. See the present writer's essay, "The Virgin Birth. Historical Fact or Kerygmatic Truth?", *BR* I (1956), pp. 1–8. In a letter to me, J. Jeremias proposes to substitute "*Glaubensaussage*" ("affirmation of faith") for "kerygmatic truth", on the ground that the Virgin birth was never actually a part of the kerygma as such. Accepting the correction, we may say that to believe in the Virgin birth is to adhere to the *faith* which the story expresses.

Chapter VIII

THE HELLENISTIC GENTILE MISSION:
THE THREE STAGE CHRISTOLOGY

1. Preliminary Considerations

THE title of this chapter is chosen advisedly. The crowning stratum of the NT tradition is often referred to as "Hellenistic".[1] It is often forgotten that it was predominantly Hellenistic *Jewish* missionaries who were engaged in this mission, as we see from Paul and his associates. There were others before him (e.g. the missionaries of the Stephen party from Jerusalem), alongside of him and after him (e.g. the author of Hebrews and the Johannine school), who were engaged in the same mission. It was not the converts who did the translating of the Jewish-Hellenistic kerygma into their own terms, but the missionaries themselves. Of course, the converts' own presuppositions must have coloured their own understanding of the kerygma they received, and have contributed to its future development. But it was not they who shaped the kerygma and Christology which Paul and the other missionaries to the gentiles use in their writings. We cannot suppose for instance that Phil 2:6–11 was composed by converts before it was taken up and used by Paul.

Side by side with more genuinely Hellenistic Jewish thinking controlled by the LXX, which is reflected in the Christology dealt with in chapter VII, there is also a more pronounced syncretistic tendency exemplified by Philo (see above, ch. III). It is this syncretistic tendency which is laid under contribution by the missionaries to the gentiles. The christological perspectives of the two preceding chapters continue, sometimes in a state of fossilized preservation, sometimes under active development. But there are also more pronouncedly syncretistic elements in the Christology of the missionaries to the gentiles, and it is with these that we are concerned in this chapter.

2. The Christological Hymns
(i) Philippians 2:6–11

The best starting point for a consideration of these developments is the christological hymn in Phil. 2:6–11. Since Lohmeyer's celebrated essay,[2] it has become generally accepted that this passage is a liturgical hymn. Lohmeyer's analysis of the hymn into two strophes, each consisting of three stanzas of three lines, is also widely, though not universally, accepted.[3] The poetic structure requires the elimination of v. 8b (θανάτον δὲ σταυροῦ) as a later addition to the original hymn: it is also typically Pauline in language and in theological emphasis. Lohmeyer argued that the hymn was not only pre-Pauline, but Aramaic in origin, and he interpreted its Christology in terms of the pre-existent apocalyptic Son of man who became incarnate as the Ebed Yahweh.[4] These further views have found far less general acceptance.

To begin with, we must decide upon the hymn's *Sitz im Leben* (though the decision is already indicated by our inclusion of the passage in this chapter). It has sometimes been suggested that, although a hymn, Phil. 2:6–11 is actually by St. Paul himself.[5] This conclusion is, however, ruled out both on linguistic and on theological grounds. First, the hymn contains a striking number of non-Pauline terms.[6] Second, Paul's own kerygma is focused on the cross and resurrection, rather than on the incarnation and exaltation. For Paul the cross has an intrinsic saving significance of its own and is not, as the hymn views it, merely the culmination of the incarnation. Finally, the threefold division "things in heaven, things on earth, and things under the earth", is not characteristic of Paul. Its non-Pauline origin may, therefore, be taken as assured.

But does this mean that it is of Aramaic origin, as Lohmeyer thought? The case for an Aramaic origin rests on four phrases: (i) "in the *form* of God" (v. 6), which is equated with *demuth* or *ṣelem* from Gen. 1:26; (ii) "emptied himself" (v. 7), which is equated with "poured out his soul" (Isa. 53:12c); (iii) "servant" (δοῦλος), which has often been equated with *'ebhedh* Isa. 53, etc.[7]; (iv) "as a man" which has been equated with $k^e\underline{bhar}\ ^en\ \check{s}$, (Dan. 7:13), one like a son of man. In no case, however, is an Aramaic origin compelling, and, as we shall see, the theory obscures the natural meaning of the passage. Also, in what we have have been able to discover in chapter VI, the motif of the Son of Man's pre-existence was never exploited in Aramaic Christianity. And if, as is by no means improbable, the pre-existent first man and the eschatological Son of man had a common mythological origin, they had in any case completely bifurcated in Judaism. The first man is found only in Hellenistic Judaism, the Son of man only in Palestinian. The one was related to the Beginning, the other to the End. This rules out arguments (i) and (iv).

(iii) is a more plausible argument for Aramaic origin, since the obedience of Jesus in his earthly life as $^e\underline{ebhedh}$ Υhwh is, as we have seen, part of the accepted stock of Aramaic Christianity. And yet there are difficulties. One minor difficulty is that everywhere else the Greek speaking Christian church used παῖς ("servant") to translate $^e\underline{ebhedh}$. A variant translation is not unthinkable, but it does warn us to consider carefully the possibility of a different source for δοῦλος here. In any case, the context in which doulos occurs in the hymn is not the earthly ministry or death of Jesus (which are not reached until v. 8) but the moment of the *incarnation*. In our investigation of the place of "paidology" in the Aramaic tradition we nowhere found the $^e\underline{ebhedh}$ concept linked with the moment of incarnation. Indeed the very idea of incarnation, with its corollary of pre-existence, was quite foreign to the Christology of the earliest church.[8] With the rejection of (iii) the rejection of (ii) follows. It is somewhat of a far cry from $he^eerah=$"poured out" to ἐκένωσεν ("he emptied"). And the latter statement is here made, not (as in Isa. 53:12) in connection with the death of the servant, but again in connection with the moment of the incarnation.[9] Finally, if the thesis of chapter VI is sustained, the exaltation Christology of the second strophe was probably quite foreign to Aramaic Christology. Rather its *Sitz im Leben* must be sought in Hellenistic *Jewish* Christianity.

But the christological hymn takes us even beyond the two stage Christology of chapter VII. It speaks not only of the humble history of Jesus, followed by his enthronization, but of an exalted origin in a pre-existent state, and of a full-blooded incarnation. This incarnation is undertaken upon the Redeemer's own pre-incarnate initiative. It is not just a historical "sending" of the Son into the world. Even the enthronization is differently portrayed. All the elements of "not-yetness" are thrown to the winds. There is nothing about the incompleteness of the victory *"until* all enemies are put in subjection." The enemies are all subjected from the moment of the enthronization. This Christology can only be assigned to a later stage than the early Hellenistic Jewish Christianity of chapter VII.

Now everything points to its origin within the gentile mission. As F. W. Beare has written: "The terminology is best interpreted within the framework of Hellenistic (syncretistic) religious thought. . . . The 'form of God' and the thought of 'equality with God' are hardly compatible with any late form of Judaism. The whole tone is peculiarly and distinctively Christian, and Christian against a Hellenistic, non-Jewish background."[10] Beare's conclusion as to the *Sitz im Leben* must be accepted in principle. The hymn can only be understood from a syncretistic background. But Beare's exclusion of Jewish connections depends upon the full-blown theory of the gnostic redeemer myth, which he accepts from Käsemann. As we saw in chapter IV, however, this theory in its commonly accepted form is based on insufficient evidence, and it is a question-begging term. As an alternative, we would propose that Phil. 2:6–11 is the product of Hellenistic Jewish Christian missionaries working in a mainly Hellenistic gentile environment. They were sensitive to its outlook and needs, and used materials provided by the sophia and anthropos myth already current in Hellenistic Judaism, by the Hellenistic world view, and by the earlier Hellenistic Jewish kerygma. There is no need to look further afield for the origin of this hymn.

The hymn is set out here in verse form, following Lohmeyer's arrangement:

I

Who, though he was in the form of God,
did not count equality with God
a thing to be grasped,

II

but emptied himself,
taking the form of a servant,
being born in the likeness of men.

III

And being found in human form,
he humbled himself,
and became obedient unto death.

IV

Therefore, God has highly exalted him,
and bestowed on him the name
which is above every name,

V

that at the name of Jesus
every knee should bow,
in heaven and on earth and under the earth,

VI

and every tongue confess
"Jesus Christ is Lord"
—to the glory of God the Father.

Presupposed throughout this hymn is the Hellenistic world view, with its three storied universe consisting of heaven, earth, and underworld (v. 10). The lower world is under the thrall of the "powers" and needs redemption. This redemption is brought through a revelation which comes from the world above and ascends to it again. This is the pattern of the sophia myth. Our hymn asserts that in the Christ event this redemptive revelation has occurred. Christ has descended to earth, entered the sphere of bondage, and reascended to heaven. Thus the Redeemer passes through five phases of existence: (*a*) pre-existence; (*b*) becoming incarnate; (*c*) incarnate life; (*d*) re-ascension; (*e*) exalted state. Of these, phases (*b*) and (*d*) are transitional. Each phase will be examined in turn.

(*a*) *Pre-existence.* ἐν μορφῇ θεοῦ, "in the form of God", (v. 6) is to be interpreted not from *d⁰mûth* ("image") or *ṣelem* ("likeness") in Gen. 1:26, but in the light of the parallel phrase in the immediate context, εἶναι ἴσα θεῷ, "to be equal with God". To be in the "form" of God, means to exist in a state of equality with God. The term μορφή had by now lost its classical sense of "underlying reality" in contrast to outward appearance,[11] and it means here "mode of existence".[12] The pre-existent One dwelt in an existence which was equal to that of God. This goes somewhat beyond the claims made for *sophia* in Hellenistic Judaism, where wisdom was a hypostatization of the being God, not an actual divine being. This accounts for Beare's seemingly bold conclusion: "It must be said that there is nothing specifically Jewish about this language. The 'form of God' and thought of 'equality with God' are hardly compatible with any late form of Judaism."

Yet we cannot set limits to what may have happened in a syncretistic environment. Even Hellenistic Jews may have "upgraded" their doctrine of wisdom through such influences. And it is unlikely that the Christian missionaries (who after all were Jews) to the gentiles should have taken over such an idea direct from their gentile converts. At all events, in other places they draw upon the established sophiological vocabulary of Hellenistic Judaism in statements about the Redeemer's pre-existence, Cf. e.g. Col. 1:15 (εἰκών, "image" πρωτότοκος, "firstborn") and Heb. 1:3 (ἀπαύγασμα, "reflection", and χαρακτήρ "stamp"). Consider also John 1:1. This also borrows from the sophia myth, but goes beyond it. Although the term λόγος had already been used by Philo as an equivalent for the divine wisdom, the assertion θεὸς ἦν ὁ λόγος ("the Logos was God") goes beyond what we know of the possibilities of the Hellenistic Jewish sophia myth in exactly the same way as Phil. 2:6.

In the light of this interpretation of μορφή, ("form"), ἁρπαγμός cannot mean "something to be snatched at" (*res rapienda*). This would introduce already into the pre-existence a contrast with Lucifer or Adam (so Cullmann and others). But what could be higher than existence ἐν μορφῇ θεοῦ, which means equality with God? It must therefore, mean "something to be held on to", more nearly[13] the *res rapta* of the Fathers. It is the exact opposite of ἐκένωσεν ἐαυτόν, "he emptied himself".

(*b*) *Becoming incarnate.* Unlike the incipient incarnational formulae which speak simply of God's historical "sending" of the Son (see above, pp. 194f.), the process of becoming incarnate is here a voluntary act of the Redeemer, as in the sophia myth. ἐκένωσεν ἐαυτόν [14] means surrendering the μορφή θεοῦ, equality with God as a mode of existence (cf. "he became poor", 2 Cor. 8:9).

The Redeemer exchanges[15] the μορφή θεοῦ, the divine mode of existence, for the μορφή δούλου, the slave's mode of existence. If δοῦλος, "slave", here were the equivalent of 'ebhedh, "servant", this phrase would not be asserting the fact of the incarnation (i.e. the Redeemer's sharing of our common human lot) but the uniqueness of the incarnate life. But that is not the thrust of this part of the hymn. Rather, in accordance with the Hellenistic world view, its intention is to assert the Redeemer's entry into the common human lot of man, his δουλεία, his thralldom to the powers of evil.[16] The same (Hellenistic) assessment of man's predicament is found in Gal. 4:3, 8f.; Rom. 8:21 (of the κτίσις, "creation"); Heb. 2:15. And redemption is depicted precisely as deliverance from this predicament of bondage in Gal. 4:5 and Col. 2:20. In every instance except the last, δουλεία, "bondage", the cognate of the word δοῦλος ("slave"), appears. Again the idea of the incarnation as the Redeemer's entry under the sphere of the powers is by no means unique to Phil. 2:7, but occurs also at Gal. 4:4 ("born of a woman, born under the law"). Here the first clause states the entrance into humanity (cf. the ensuing clause in our hymn, ἐν ὁμοιώματι ἀνθρώπων γενόμενος, "being born in the likeness of men"). The second clause is a distinctively Pauline version of the common Hellenistic notion of human bondage. Paul equates the power which holds man in thrall characteristically with the *law*. Similarly, Heb. 2:14 begins by affirming the incarnation. The Redeemer "partakes of flesh and blood". Then the ensuing phrase, "by means of death", goes on to suggest that *death* is the power which holds man in thrall.

Nor can it be objected that in none of those passages is man under the powers actually called a δοῦλος, "a slave". For Paul can speak of unredeemed man in his own distinctive existential reinterpretation of the powers precisely as the δοῦλος, "slave" of sin (Rom. 6:17, 20; cf. John 8:34), while in Gal. 4:7 he contrasts unredeemed man as δοῦλος with redeemed man as υἱός, "son" (cf. also the metaphor in 4:1). It may be taken as established, therefore, that the background of μορφὴν δούλου, "the form of a slave" in our hymn is not the *ebhedh* of Isa. 53, but the mythological conception of man under the thralldom of the powers. The term δοῦλος, "slave", is here not a christological assertion of the distinctive character of the Redeemer's incarnate life—which does not come into purview until v. 8[17]—but the mode of existence which by becoming incarnate he shares with all men.

The phrase ἐν ὁμοιώματι ἀνθρώπων γενόμενος ("born in the likeness of men") is thus not an entirely new point, but a summary of the previous clause in different terms. However, it does contain two new nuances. First, γενόμενος, "born" (cf. Gal. 4:4, Rom. 1:3, John 1:14) throws particular stress on the *birth* as the moment of the Redeemer's entry into the "form of a servant" ("being born into this world as all men are born", Beare). At the same time, by using the word ὁμοίωμα, "likeness", it keeps open the distinctiveness of *this* particular man from all other men,[18] thus preparing the way for v. 8.

The first stanza about the relation of the pre-existent Redeemer's relation to God is based on the sophia-anthropos myth. Can the same be said of the transition to the incarnate life? That the mythological first man descends into the world of matter, has already been noted (chap. III, p. 77). But this is at his creation, conceived as a fall. The first man does not descend as Redeemer. Rather it is the heavenly wisdom that descends in a revelatory and redemptive capacity to seek abode with men. But that the Redeemer should actually become *incarnate* is without precedent. Accordingly it must be pronounced a Christian adaptation of the myth to the concrete history of Jesus. Mythology has provided first the description of the divine mode of the Redeemer's pre-existence, and secondly the notion of the thralldom of this world under the powers. But the Redeemer's entry into that sphere by a historical incarnation is a specifically Christian adaptation of the myth to the history of Jesus of Nazareth. In the wisdom myth there was no specific incarnation.

(c) *The incarnate life* (vv. 7c, 8). The incarnation has already been stated in verse 7a, b. But in order to avert any possible docetic misunderstanding of ὁμοίωμα ("likeness") in the previous clause, the consequences of 7a, b are restated in summary fashion in the words σχήματι εὑρεθεὶς ὡς ἄνθρωπος ("being found in fashion as a man"). The Redeemer really was a man, and appeared on earth as such. Yet the carefully chosen expression leaves open the "thought of something more within the human frame" (Beare). Here is One who in his origin was the pre-Existent One, equal to God.

The incarnate life is now described as one of humiliation and obedience unto death (v. 8). Here we are on the firm rock of history. Yet v. 8 is not just straightforward historical description but an assessment of Jesus in terms of an earthly Christology based on the Adam/Christ typology.[19] It is important to notice that this is a different assessment of Jesus' history from that which later became current in the gentile mission. The latter view, as we shall see, interpreted the incarnate life as an *epiphany* of the divine glory, in terms of the more outspokenly Hellenistic conception of the divine man. Our hymn interpreted it as a kenosis. This circumstance incidentally suggests that our hymn was composed at a comparatively early stage of the gentile mission.

If we agree that the hymn is non-Pauline in origin, and that the Adam/Christ typology underlies v. 8, it follows that this typology is not a Pauline creation, but the common stock of the gentile mission. This conclusion may draw some support from another hymn, namely Col. 1:15–20 (v. 18b). Here again the Adam/Christ typology is used to describe the redemptive work of Christ. Its origin appears to lie in the anthropos part of the sophia-anthropos myth. In the myth the anthropos is fallen man, and thus the first man. But in the Christian adaptation of the myth the anthropos is equated with the incarnate Redeemer who reverses the fall of the first man. Whereas the first man disobeyed and fell, the

second, or last Man (1 Cor. 15:45, 47) obeys and is vindicated as the Redeemer. As a result (though this aspect is not
developed in Phil. 2:6–11) the last man, like the first,
becomes the inclusive head of an order of humanity. But
whereas the first Adam was the head of a fallen humanity,
the last Adam is the head of the redeemed humanity.

It is an oversimplification to derive this whole scheme
directly from the so-called gnostic redeemer myth. That
myth, as we have seen, falls into two parts, the sophia part
and the anthropos part. The sophia part is used by the
gentile mission to work out the pre-existence of the Redeemer, his relation to God in the pre-existent state, and his
descent as the revealer-Redeemer. The second or anthropos
part is divided between Adam and Christ. Adam is fallen
man who became the head of fallen humanity. Christ is his
antitype, the second or eschatological Man, who by his
obedience becomes the head of the redeemed humanity.[20]

(d) *The exaltation.* "Therefore God has highly exalted him"
(v. 9). The resurrection is not mentioned as it is in the normal
Pauline kerygma. This omission occurs in other passages
which draw on the same mythological scheme[21] of the descent
and ascent of sophia. In that scheme there is naturally no
place for a resurrection. The compound form $ὑπερ$—
$ύψωσεν$ ("highly exalted") has occasioned much discussion.
Cullmann, notably, interprets it to indicate exaltation to a
higher degree of glory than that of the pre-existent state: "he
did more than exalt him".[22] This interpretation is unlikely.
For surely there could be no higher dignity than the equality
with God which the pre-existent One had already enjoyed
before the incarnation. It is true that the Exalted One is now
endowed with the name Kyrios (v. 11). But this can hardly
be a higher status than was implied by $τὸ εἶναι ἴσα θεῷ$ ("to
be equal with God"). It must therefore mean the manifestation of a dignity heretofore hidden to and unacknowledged
by the powers.[23]

Now Beare accepts Käsemann's exclusion from $ὑπερύψωσεν$
any comparative force and his interpretation of it in a
superlative sense, with no idea of a comparison between the
pre-existent and exalted states. But he immediately proceeds
to re-introduce a comparison "between the earthly condition

of slavery . . . and the consequent exaltation".[24] Clearly, there is some confusion here. First, in order to refute Cullmann's interpretation, Beare rejects the idea of comparison, and then re-introduces it in a weaker form. The same confusion is evident in Käsemann and Bornkamm. It seems that we had better frankly admit, with Cullmann, the comparative force of *hyper-upsosen*. But with what is the exalted state compared? The clue lies within the same stanza. The very next line continues: "bestowed on him the name which is *above* (ὑπέρ) every name." As so often in this hymn, the same point is stated twice over in different language: "to exalt more highly" is precisely to confer the name above every name. The comparison is between the name of the exalted Redeemer, and the names of the powers which are now subjected to him. For the "names" of the powers cf. Eph. 1:21; Heb. 1:4, where the same point, viz. the exaltation of Christ above them, is made. So at his exaltation Christ is exalted triumphantly above all the other powers.

(*e*) *The exalted state.* In the last two strophes this hyper-exaltation is acknowledged by the cosmic powers themselves. In v. 10 the "things" are the powers in heaven, earth, and the underworld. The "things on earth" are not the human inhabitants of the earth, or the ecclesia, but the powers which had held the earth in thrall: "The proskynesis is objective, and cosmic; not subjective, human, ecclesiastical or cultic" (Käsemann). Here again, although the exaltation of Jesus was already part of the earlier Hellenistic Jewish Christology conceived on the basis of Ps. 110:1, the christological hymn goes further. There is no longer any eschatological reservation, nothing about "until all enemies are subjected". For they are already subjected, completely and entirely and without qualification. The use of Ps. 110 is similarly modified elsewhere in passages influenced by this myth, e.g. Eph. 1:22; 1 Pet. 3:22.

In the final stanza the name given to the exalted One is identified as KYRIOS, the LXX rendering of *Yhwh*. Here again, despite Lohmeyer, it is the *Hellenistic* Jewish Kyrios-Christology which is presupposed. Henceforth God exercises his Lordship through the incarnate and obedient One who has been exalted. This does not mean that God has abdicated.

Rather, he has asserted his Lordship effectively over the cosmos, where previously it had been denied by the powers who had held it in bondage. Again, this goes beyond the earlier Hellenistic Jewish identification of the Exalted One as Kyrios. For this is no unreflective transference to the Exalted One of a LXX text about *Yhwh*, but a conscious and deliberate transference of the "name". It is not just a *functional* identity between the exalted One and Yahweh, but an *ontic*, though not yet ontological, identity: "Name declares dignity and nature, radiates being and makes it manifest."[25] Yet it is the manifestation of the name which he had already possessed hiddenly before the incarnation.[26]

The same "Christ myth" underlies three other hymns in the epistolary literature, Col. 1:15–20; 1 Tim. 3:16, and 1 Pet. 3:18–22, as well as Heb. 1:1–4 and John 1:1–14. Each of these passages will be analysed in turn.

(ii) *Colossians 1:15–20*

Underlying this passage is a hymn[27] of three stanzas. The first describes creation, the second preservation and the third redemption.

I

Who is the image of the invisible God, the first born of all creation;
For in him were created all things in heaven and earth;
Through him and to him were all things created.

II

He is before all things,
And in him all things hold together,
And he is the head of the body.

III

Who is the beginning, the first-born from the dead;
For in him all the fullness of God was pleased to dwell;
And through him to reconcile all things to himself.[28]

Strophe I describes the pre-existent One in terms derived from the sophia myth. He is the εἰκών ("image")[29] of God. This is a more restrained description than Phil. 2:6, which, as we have seen, passes beyond the known precedents of Jewish thought. He is the πρωτότοκος ("first born").[30] Like sophia he is the agent of creation.[31] The expression τὰ πάντα ("all things"), as in other similar passages, has special reference to the powers. The interpolation "visible . . . authorities" is therefore a correct interpretation.

Strophe II begins by summing up the previous stanza, in a manner reminiscent of Phil. 2:6–11. It then proceeds to describe the pre-existent One as the upholder and sustainer of creation, a thought which is again derived from the sophia myth.[32] The phrase "head of the body" (v. 18) naturally suggests to us the church, even without the gloss. But in that sense it occurs too soon in the hymn, for this strophe is still concerned with creation, not with redemption. Hence it is perhaps better to take σῶμα ("body") to mean the cosmos, a familiar idea in Hellenism.[33] Philo calls the logos the *head* of the universe.[34] As in Philo the meaning of κεφάλη ("head") here will be that the pre-existent One is supreme over the universe and the source of its life. It thus interprets the previous line of the stanza.

Strophe III switches to the redemption. Here we leave the sophia myth for the Adam/Christ typology. It is true that nothing is said of the earthly life of the Redeemer as one of obedience. There is no implied contrast to the life of Adam, as in Phil. 2:8. Still, the effect of the redemptive work is described in terms derived from the Adam/first man myth. For that myth, the first man was also the "beginning"—but the beginning of the fallen order. Here Christ is the beginning, but the beginning of the new redeemed humanity.[35] The meaning of ἀρχή ("beginning") is then interpreted by the next phrase, "first-born from the dead". Not only was Jesus the first instance of a resurrection, he is the *constitutive* instance which determines the resurrection of the redeemed. For he is the life-giving spirit (1 Cor. 15:45) just as Adam was in his fall the constitutive and determinative for fallen humanity.

The meaning of πλήρωμα (v. 19) is much disputed.[36] The chief alternatives are: "the entirety of God's attributes", or, in a gnostic sense, the total hierarchy of aeons. Now in choosing between these two senses, it seems important to recall that in the corresponding section of the Philippians hymn (Phil. 2:11) it is stated that at the exaltation God gave the Exalted One his own name *Kyrios*. That, as we saw, denoted the "fullness" of his own divine Lordship. Henceforth God rules the powers through the exalted One. The meaning is very much the same here. Henceforth, from the resurrection onwards, God concentrates the plenitude of redemptive activity, his being-for-the-world, in the person of the risen One. As in the Philippians hymn, the powers (τὰ πάντα, "all things") are next dealt with. Whereas in the earlier hymn they are subjected, here they are reconciled. The Adam/ Christ typology is still evident. It was through Adam's fall that the universe was set at odds with itself (Rom. 5:12–21; 8:20), and it is through the last man that it is reconciled.

When we compare the form of the Christ myth in this hymn with that of our earlier hymn, we notice certain salient differences. The pre-existence of the Redeemer is explicated further. Not only his divine mode of existence, but his active participation in creation and preservation are described. His becoming incarnate and the incarnate life, on the other hand, are presumed rather than stated. Here the resurrection, not the exaltation, is the turning point in the redemptive scheme. But the exaltation is implied in the statement that it pleased God that the fullness of his divinity should henceforth dwell bodily in the Redeemer. Despite these differences, however, both hymns are an adaptation of the same mythological scheme, the sophia-anthropos myth. The sophia part provides the materials for a Christian doctrine of creation. The anthropos part is adapted so as to reverse Adam's history and to describe the redemption.

(iii) *1 Timothy 3:16*

        A Who was manifested in the flesh,
        B vindicated in the Spirit,
        B   seen by angels,
        A preached among the nations,
        A believed on in the world,
        B   taken up in glory.

The hymnic character of this passage is widely recognized, and even RSV prints it as a poem. Its structure has been analysed by E. Schweizer.[37] He demonstrates that it is constructed in a chiastic form, ABBAAB, in which A denotes an affirmation about an event in this world, B an event in the transcendent order. The phrases, "who was manifested in the flesh, . . . preached among the nations, [and] . . . believed on in the world" refer to earthly events, while "vindicated by angels, . . . preached among the nations, [and] taken up in glory" refer to events in the heavenly sphere. Because of its chiastic arrangement the hymn does not follow a chronological order. But despite its curious form the same mythological scheme underlies this hymn.

The pre-existence and becoming incarnate are not mentioned, but implied in the phrase "manifested in the flesh", which speaks of the incarnate life. One wonders whether the hymn has been decapitated. Did it originally begin with a pre-existence clause? The chiastic structure makes this unlikely. The incarnate life is interpreted very differently compared with Phil. 2:6ff. There, the incarnation is conceived in terms of a kenosis. The divine glory is not revealed, but hidden. The form of God is exchanged for the form of the slave. The process of becoming incarnate was described in terms which stress what is held in common between the Redeemer and all other men. The uniqueness of the incarnate life was expressed in terms of obedience. This kenosis Christology remained constitutive for St. Paul's own christological thinking. In 1 Tim. 3:16, on the contrary, only the uniqueness of the incarnate life is stressed, not the features it shared with all men. It is a manifestation of the divine glory. It is not a kenosis but an epiphany. This takes us beyond the Christ myth, and results from a combination of that myth with the concept of the Hellenistic divine man. The origins and development of the epiphany Christology in the gentile mission will be traced later in this chapter.

It was a defect of the Christ myth, with its kenosis view of the incarnation, that it allowed insufficient room for a positive evaluation of the historical life of Jesus. This evaluation had in the Palestinian stage been expressed in terms of the authority of the earthly Son of man, of the earthly kyrios and of the Mosaic prophet-servant. In the Hellenistic Jewish stage it had been expressed in terms of the Son of God. The epiphany interpretation of the incarnate life enabled the gentile mission to do justice to these earlier appreciations of the exousia of Jesus' history. Hence despite its dubious origin and the resistance of St. Paul, who deemed it incompatible with his cross-centred Christology, it eventually won acceptance in the gentile mission.

"Vindicated in the Spirit" refers to the exaltation in language reminiscent of the earlier Jewish Hellenistic Christology (Rom. 1:4). "Spirit" is here used in the same Hellenistic sense of the upper or heavenly sphere.

"Seen by angels" has the same mythological background as Phil. 2:10. The angels are the cosmic powers. The victorious Redeemer is presented to them in order to receive their homage. It is a kind of coronation ceremony.

"*Taken* up into glory" is a reverential passive denoting that God is the subject, as in Phil 2:9.

The significant contribution of this hymn is its positive evaluation of the incarnation: it is not just a concealing, but a revelation of the divine glory.

(iv) *1 Peter 3:18–22 (1:20)*

Here is another hymnic passage. Following Bultmann,[38] we may reconstruct it thus:

who suffered once for sins,
    that he might bring us to God,
being put to death in the flesh,
    but made alive in the spirit,
in which also he preached to the spirits in prison,
    and having gone into heaven sat down at the right hand of God,
angels and authorities and powers having been made subject to him.

In this hymn the Redeemer's pre-existence and his becoming incarnate are neither stated nor implied. However, if Bultmann is right, what we have here is only a fragment of the hymn, and it was preceded by another verse now found in 1:20,

who was destined before the foundation of the world,
but was made manifest at the end of the times.

Here the Reedemer's pre-existence is affirmed in terms

different from those of the other hymns, with an apparent suggestion of pre-destination. This seems to deny objective pre-existence, as though the Redeemer pre-existed only in the mind of God. However, $\pi\rho o\epsilon\gamma\nu\omega\sigma\mu\acute{\epsilon}\nu o\varsigma$ should probably be translated "known beforehand". God "knew" the Redeemer in a Johannine sense before the creation. The background is here again the sophia myth (cf. Prov. 8 and Ecclus. 24).

In the second line of v. 20 the incarnation is described not in terms of kenosis (Phil. 2:6ff.), but, as in 1 Tim. 3:16, as an epiphany of manifestation.

Returning to 1 Pet. 3:18–22, we find that, unlike the other hymns, our hymn has worked in the Palestinian-Pauline kerygma of the atoning death (v. 18). This was not part of the original mythical pattern, and it looks like a Paulinist insertion into the original hymn. In that case the hymn will originally have run from 1:20 to 3:18d, "being put to death in the flesh". Here we have the same contrast between the two spheres, "flesh" (the earthly sphere) and "spirit" (the heavenly sphere) as in Rom. 1:3f. and 1 Tim. 3:16. This solves the much debated problem about the meaning of "in the spirit". It does not mean "in spirit-form" (=the resurrection body) nor does it mean "raised *by* (instrumental $\epsilon\nu$) the Spirit", but denotes the cosmic sphere in which the resurrection took place. Note that, contrary to Phil. 2:6–11, but as in Col. 1:15–20, the resurrection rather than the exaltation is the turning point of the myth.

As its position in the hymn shows, v. 19 refers to what happened after the resurrection, not, as in the apostles' creed, to a *descensus ad inferos* between the death and resurrection. Also, the removal of vv. 20f. as a redactional comment by the author of 1 Peter clarifies the original meaning of the "spirits" in prison. They are not the dead,[39] but the cosmic powers. The thought is the same as in Phil. 2:10, 1 Tim. 3:16 ($\mathring{\omega}\phi\theta\eta$ $\mathring{\alpha}\gamma\gamma\acute{\epsilon}\lambda o\iota\varsigma$ "appeared to angels").[40]

"He went into heaven" parallels the similar statements about the exaltation in Phil. 2:10 and 1 Tim. 3:16. But here the ascension is the triumphant action of the Redeemer himself, not the act of God (cf. Heb. 1:3, which also echoes Ps. 110:1).

The final line of the hymn is a coda which, on our interpretation, resumes and clarifies the meaning of the reference to the spirits in the previous stanza.

The same mythological pattern underlies this hymn as the others. The Redeemer's pre-existence and incarnation are described in terms of the sophia myth. His redemptive work is described in terms of the Adam/Christ typology as a victory over the powers.

(v) *Hebrews 1:1–4*

This passage has never been treated as a hymn,[41] although there are features which invite its reconstruction as such. First, its content: it exhibits the same mythological pattern as the other hymns. Second, v. 3 begins characteristically with the relative ὅς ("who") (Phil. 2:6; Col. 1:15; 1 Tim. 3:16), and continues with a series of participles. Third, its vocabulary contains a number of *hapax legomena* to Hebrews.[42] On the other hand v. 1 expresses the concept of *Heilsgeschichte* which does not figure in any of these hymns, while the contrast between the prophets and the Son is reminiscent of the contrast between Moses and the Son in 3:1–6. Also, the latter part of v. 2 ("whom he appointed . . . the world") belongs to the same mythology as v. 4, and is rhythmical in character, but is out of position here. For the first phrase ("appointed heir of all things") apparently refers to the exaltation (cf. v. 4), while the second phrase about the pre-existent One as agent of creation would more logically follow the assertion of his divine being, as in Col. 1:15, 17.

At first sight, one is tempted to rearrange the hymn so as to bring each of these phrases into its logical position. This, however, is impossible for two reasons. First, it will disturb the structure of the hymn, which, as will be seen, contains two stanzas of three lines each. Second, the grammatical structure of these phrases is incompatible with the rest, for in them God is the subject, and in the rest the Redeemer. It will, therefore, be necessary to leave these phrases aside. Perhaps they are fragments of another hymn or kerygmatic formula in which God is the subject. In v. 4 τοσούτῳ . . . ὅσῳ ("so much . . . as") is characteristic of the author (cf. 4:7; 7:22; 10:25, 12:1). Note especially the structure τοσούτῳ . . .

ὅσῳ in 10:25, as is also the comparative διαφορώτερος ("more excellent") 8:6; cf. 9:10. With these necessary eliminations, a hymn of two three-line stanzas can be reconstructed:

I
Who reflects the glory of God
and bears the very stamp of his nature,
upholding the universe by his word of power;

II
Who, when he had made purification for sins,
sat down at the right hand of the majesty on high,
having become superior to the angels.

The first stanza is clearly based on the sophia myth. The word ἀπαύγασμα ("reflection") is used of sophia in Wisd. 7:26 and in Philo, while Philo also applies χαρακτήρ ("stamp") to the Logos.[43] The hymn begins by describing the divine mode of being enjoyed by the pre-existent One, exactly as in Phil. 2:6; Col. 1:15 and 1 Pet. 1:20a. Unlike the Colossian hymn, however, this hymn jumps at once to the sustaining functions of the pre-existent Redeemer (cf. Col. 1:17a) without any prior reference to his agency in creation. Apparently the author of Hebrews spotted the omission, and amended it by prefacing the hymn with a fragment from another formula (v. 2c). The sustaining functions are a further feature of the sophia myth (see above pp. 73f.).

The incarnation is passed over, and there is no direct mention of the Redeemer's death. Both however are implied in the next stanza, which speaks of the purification of sins (implying the death) and the exaltation (implying a previous descent). The heavenly session is described in the language of Ps. 110:1, as in 1 Pet. 3:22 (cf. also Eph. 1:20). The last line ("having become superior to the angels") is a reference to the triumph over the powers, as in Phil. 2:10; Col. 1:20a; 1 Tim. 3:16 (ὤφθη ἀγγέλοις, "appeared to angels") and 1 Pet. 3:19, 22b. This conception stems from the Christian adaptation and reversal of the anthropos myth. Thus, Heb. 1:3f. appears to be yet another example of the Christ myth, with its pattern of pre-existence, incarnation and exaltation.

(vi) *John 1:1–14*

The Johannine prologue differs from the other hymns in that it presents only the first part of the Christ myth, covering the pre-existence of the Redeemer and his incarnation. But so far as it goes, it reflects the same mythological pattern as the hymns already discussed.

That it is a hymn is a thesis which commands fairly wide, though by no means universal, assent. In the mind of the present writer, however, the hymnic origin is beyond all question, and for the following reasons. First, the prologue is marked off from the rest of the gospel by the use of the term Logos. Although the underlying myth of katabasis-anabasis penetrates the whole of the gospel, the term Logos appears only here. Second, apart from certain verses which appear to be prose interpolations, the prologue falls clearly into verse form.[44] Third, the thought and language of the interpolations are characteristic of the Evangelist himself.

It was contended by Burney—and in this he has been followed, perhaps rather surprisingly, by Bultmann—that the hymn was originally composed in Aramaic. Whether this is so or not will depend not a little on our view as to the provenance of the Logos concept. But it may be stated with confidence that there is nothing in the Prologue to *compel* the hypothesis of an Aramaic original—e.g. no obvious mistranslation or obscurity which can be corrected or elucidated by reference back to a hypothetical Aramaic original.

As regards the origin of the Logos concept, on which so much depends both for the source of the Prologue and for its interpretation, Bultmann has successfully eliminated four of the popular candidates.

1. It is not derived from the OT *d^ebhar 'Elohîm*.[45] Although the opening words, "In the beginning", are clearly an allusion to Gen. 1:1, and although the Word of God in the OT has a creative as well as revelatory function (Ps. 33:6, 147:18 and Deutero-Isaiah) the *d^ebhar 'Elohîm* is quite a different concept from the Johannine Logos. For the *d^ebhar 'Elohîm* is not a hypostasis or divine being. Rather it denotes God in the act of speaking in the concrete moment—whether it be in his primal word, "Let there be light", or in his ethical demand,

"Thou shalt", or in the message of the prophets who report, "Thus saith the Lord". In the Prologue, however, the Logos is "with God" prior to the utterance of his very first word, "Let there be light". Also, and corroboratively, *dabhar* in the sense of *d^ebhar 'Elohîm* never occurs as an absolute like Logos in the prologue, but always with a possessive genitive.

2. It is not the *memra de YHWH* of the Targums.[46] The *memra* is not a divine being distinguishable from God, but a reverential periphrasis for God himself present and acting in history. Also, and corroboratively, *memra*, like *dabhar*, is never used absolutely.

3. A stronger case might be made for the Torah[47] as the source of the Johannine Logos. In Rabbinic Judaism, Torah had largely taken the place of *hokhma*, and had assumed its functions as the pre-existent agent of creation and of continuing revelation. However, in the Rabbinic tradition this revelation was narrowly confined to Israel, whereas in the Prologue the revelatory activity of the Logos is universal in scope.

4. It is not derived from the Greek philosophical tradition. The Logos of Heraclitus and the Stoics was the immanent principle of law and order in the universe, whereas the Logos of the prologue is a transcendent being, who comes into this world from outside.

5. Less convincing, however, is Bultmann's attempt to eliminate the wisdom tradition of OT-Hellenistic Judaism as a possible candidate. He does not deny the affinity between wisdom and the Johannine Logos. For, like the Logos, *hokhma-sophia* was also of mythological origin. It too was pre-existent. It sought an abode among men, but being rejected, ascended back into heaven. Bultmann's rejection of it as a source for the Johannine Logos is based on two grounds. First, the difference in terminology—sophia in Hellenistic Judaism, Logos in the Prologue. Second, the wisdom myth as such was no longer a living force in Judaism. This is indeed astonishing. For, as Bultmann himself coolly recognizes,[49] Logos appears in synonymous parallelism with sophia in Wisd. 9:1f., while Philo shows a marked tendency to replace sophia by Logos. As for the second alleged difficulty, the sophia tradition was surely very much alive, not

indeed in Palestinian, but certainly in Hellenistic Judaism, as both the Book of Wisdom and Philo show. Of course, if it has been decided in advance (though on grounds which appear to be inadequate) that John 1:1–14 is of Aramaic provenance, this is enough to discount a Hellenistic Jewish origin, but not otherwise.

Instead, Bultmann then argues that sophia and the Logos are independent variants of the same oriental revelation myth. Is there any reason for deriving the Johannine prologue *directly* from this myth? Only if there are elements in the Prologue which are inexplicable from the Hellenistic Jewish sophia tradition. Now there is one difficulty, though Bultmann does not mention it in this connection. In the Book of Wisdom and in Philo sophia-logos appears only as an hypostasis of God himself, whereas in the prologue the Logos is a divine being (John 1:1). This is the same obstacle we encountered with $\mu o \rho \phi \dot{\eta}$ $\theta \epsilon o \hat{v}$ ("form of God") and $\tau \grave{o}$ $\epsilon \hat{\iota} v a \iota$ $\check{\iota} \sigma a$ $\theta \epsilon \hat{\omega}$ ("to be equal with God") at Phil. 2:6. There we suggested it was hazardous to set limits to the process of syncretism which was going on in Hellenistic Judaism.[50] The same explanation will serve here. Accordingly, we see no reason to derive the prologue *directly* from the oriental myth, but only indirectly, *via* the growing syncretism within Hellenistic Judaism. This avoids the difficulty of Bultmann's alternative theory. For all the evidence he quotes for the gnostic redeemer myth is later than John and under obvious Christian influence.[51]

We conclude therefore that the Logos hymn of the prologue is a pre-Johannine hymn which contains material derived ultimately from the growing Logos speculation within Hellenistic Judaism. But it is a Christian adaptation of that myth. For the statement in John 1:14, "the Logos became flesh", is only possible within Christianity, and as a result of the history of Jesus of Nazareth.[52]

Following Bultmann, we may reconstruct the hymn thus:

> In the beginning was the Logos,
>   and the Logos was with God,
> And the Logos was God.
> He was in the beginning with God.

All things were made through him,
and without him nothing was made.
That which was made, in him was life,
and the life was the light of man.

And the light shines in the darkness,
and the darkness has not overcome it.
He was the true light,
which lightens every (man) coming into the world.

The world was made through him,
yet the world knew him not.
He came to his own,
and his own received him not.

But as many as received him,
he gave to them the power to become the children of God.[53]

And the Logos became flesh,
and dwelt among us,
And we beheld his glory,
glory as of the only begotten of the Father,
Full of grace and truth.

And from his fullness we have all received:
grace upon grace.

Like the hymn of Phil. 2:6–11, the Prologue begins by describing the divine mode of being of the pre-existent One (v. 1). The Logos was sharing the godness of God, (cf. μορφὴ θεοῦ, "form of God" and τὸ εἶναι ἴσα θεῷ "to be equal with God"). But he was also distinct from God, for he was πρὸς τὸν θεόν, turned "towards God" in a relationship to him. This ontic state he enjoyed ἐν ἀρχῇ ("in the beginning"), an assertion which goes beyond Phil. 2:6. There the divine mode of existence preceded only the incarnation, and nothing was said of its priority to creation. But the priority of the Logos is paralleled in Col. 1:15 (προτότοκος πάσης κτίσεως, "first-born of all creation") and in the sophia tradition.[54]

The second stanza describes the Logos as the agent of creation in language almost identical with the last phrase of Col. 1:16, except that ἐγένετο ("was made") replaces ἔκτισται ("has been created"). The last line of this stanza however (v. 4) introduces an aspect of the sophia myth which was not taken up in any of our earlier hymns, viz. the Logos as the agent of general revelation.[55] As in the earlier hymns the unredeemed world is under the thralldom of the powers, so here it is under the dominion of darkness (v. 5). Most men reject the revelation. The World refused to know the Logos (v. 10), although the Logos was the agent of its creation, and he was only coming to his own (τὰ ἴδια, "his own", in v. 11 refers not specifically to Israel, but to the cosmos as the creation of the Logos). However, as in the sophia myth, there were a few who accepted the Logos. To them was given the privilege of becoming children of God (v. 12). This feature recalls Wisd. 7:27, "in every generation she passes into human souls and makes them friends of God and prophets".

Down to v. 13 there is nothing which could not have been derived from the sophia-logos myth. In v. 14 the hymn passes beyond the possibilities of the sophia myth with the distinctively Christian affirmation that the Logos became flesh. Flesh, σάρξ, means man, specifically man under the dominion of darkness (cf. Phil. 2:7; Rom. 8:3). But there is also a difference here. As in 1 Tim. 3:16 the incarnate life is portrayed not as a kenosis, but as a manifestation of the divine glory, and thus in terms of the Hellenistic concept of the divine man.

The incarnate Logos is the μονογενής, "only begotten," of the Father. At first sight, this would appear to parallel John 3:16. There, μονογενής ("only begotten") is synonymous with ἀγαπητός ("beloved"), ἴδιος ("his own") and ἑαυτοῦ, ("his"), which occur in similar passages in the NT which speak of the "sending" of the Son into the world.[56] This, as we have seen, is the early Hellenistic Jewish Christology of Jesus in his earthly life as the Son of God, which replaced the Palestinian prophet-servant conception. But μονογενής ("only begotten") is also part of the sophiological vocabulary. In Wisd. 7:22 it is stated that in sophia there is a "spirit", which is described in a whole series of adjectives, one of which is μονογενής ("only begotten"). Philo, it is true, never uses it, though as we have seen he does speak of the Logos as πρωτόγονος ("first-born"). The meaning of μονογενής in John 1:14 would appear to be similar.[57] This is a significant advance on the Christology of the earlier hymns, an advance which corresponds to the abandonment[58] of the kenosis conception. In the earlier forms of the Christ myth, the wisdom Christology was employed only for the pre-existent state. Here it continues to describe the incarnate life.

So, too, the Incarnate One is *"full* of grace and truth". Grace and truth describe the being of God (Bultmann). What Col. 1:19 could only say.of the Exalted One (*pleroma!*), the Prologue can already assert of the Incarnate.

It is surprising at first sight to find that the Prologue does not go on to speak of the subsequent *anabasis* or ascent of the Redeemer. Only the first half of the Christ myth appears here. But for the christological conception of the Prologue this is not really necessary, for the *anabasis* is concentrated as it were into the incarnate life. The powers are already overcome, and the Redeemer already possesses the name which is above every name. At the same time, however, all this is affirmed of the Incarnate One only in the light of his resurrection. The anabasis is presumed.

3. *The Hellenistic Divine Man*

In two of the christological hymns, 1 Tim. 3:16 and John 1:1–14, there occurs, as we have seen, a new conception of the incarnate life as an epiphany. It was suggested that this new conception was influenced by the Hellenistic conception of the divine man.[59] The history of this epiphany christology must now be investigated.

If the thesis of D. Georgi is correct,[60] the wandering evangelists Paul is opposing in 2 Cor. 10–13, the purveyors of "another Jesus" (11:4), were interpreting Jesus in his earthly life as a Hellenistic "divine man". As such, Jesus proved his divinity by a miraculous display of power. Paul vigorously repudiated this conception. Not only did it cut right across his own kenotic Christology and his cross-centred preaching, but it undermined the whole conception of his apostolate. So he refused to have any truck with such a "Christ according to the flesh" (2 Cor. 5:16). But Paul's resistance to the idea persisted, and has left traces in the Hellenistic (gentile) modification of the miracle stories, as we find them in Mark.[61] Some of the marginal traits in these stories suggest the Hellenistic wonder worker.[68] This is particularly evident in the healing of the woman with the haemorrhage. Here Jesus' healing power is portrayed as a *dunamis*, a king of physical mana which flows out of him and is conveyed at touch apart from his own volition. In his analysis of the pre-Marcan tradition Dibelius[63] has discovered in many other pericopes the popular Hellenistic understanding of Jesus' ministry as a divine "epiphany". By his device of the Messianic secret[64] and by using the pericopes as a preface to the passion narrative Mark himself has sought to tone down the epiphany motif in the interest of his own kerygma of the cross and resurrection.

Matthew and Luke retain the Messianic secret, but by prefacing their gospels with the Virgin Birth they offer an explanation of the origin of Jesus' divine sonship, understood as ontically divine in a Hellenistic sense. Jesus is the Son of God because he is conceived by the Holy Spirit. This (see ch. VI) was not the original intention of the virginal conception, but a later development.

John uses a miracle tradition which has been impregnated even more strongly with the divine man conception.[65] Unlike Mark, however, he does not try to tone it down, but puts it to positive use. This he does by prefacing his gospel with the prologue. Jesus is the divine epiphany, because in him the pre-existent Word is made flesh. Secondly, John uses the miracles as springboards for revelation discourses. This means that he shifts the emphasis away from the miracles as displays of divine power and reinterprets them as signs of the revelation which the pre-existent is bringing into the world. The incarnate life is an epiphany not of a pagan wonder worker, but of the light and life and truth of God himself.

This eventual victory of the divine man conception, albeit in a profound transformation, is not an "acute Hellenization" of Christology. The kenotic Christology of Phil. 2:6–11 had a great devotional profundity, which has inspired many of our Christmas hymns. It also had a high theological value as a bulwark of the true humanity of Jesus. But it was inadequate to express another element in the church's assessment of

Jesus which was present right from the start, namely his exousia and his conveyance of a direct confrontation with the revelatory presence and saving action of God himself. The divine man concept was able to do just this for the Hellenistic milieu of the gentile mission.

4. *The Christological Titles in the Gentile Mission*

It now remains to examine the effect of this pre-existence incarnation Christology upon the christological titles.

(i) *Son of Man*

As we have seen, in the Hellenistic Jewish stage of the tradition the synoptic Son of man sayings received only slight embellishments. The title itself sank to the level of a mysterious self-designation of Jesus devoid of any specifically christological colour (cf. Matt. 16:13). Thus it was on its way to become, as in the post-NT writers, a designation for Jesus' humanity, contrasted with "Son of God" as a designation for his divinity. Any idea that it was originally a title of majesty is completely lost. In the gentile mission it played little part outside the sayings of Jesus.[66] For in Greek ὁ υἱὸς τοῦ ἀνθρώπου (literally "the son of the man") conveyed no obviously titular meaning, any more than it does in English.

The fourth gospel, however, contains a unique development of the Son of Man sayings in terms of the *katabasis-anabasis* Christology:

> No one has ascended into heaven,
>> but he who has descended from heaven,
> the Son of man.
>> (John 3:13)

> What if you were to see the Son of man
>> ascending where he was before?
>> (John 6:62)

These sayings must be distinguished from those Johannine Son of man sayings which speak only of his exaltation and which arose from pushing back to the exaltation or enthronement the original associations of the parousia.[67] For John 3:13 and 6:62 speak not only of the exaltation but also of the pre-existence, descent (explicitly in 3:13, implicitly in 6:62) and subsequent ascent. This is the pattern of the Christ myth. Note that in these two sayings there is no transfer of the parousia associations (judgment, etc.) to the ascension. This shows their diverse origin.

(ii) *Christos*

As is widely recognized, Χριστός ("Christ") lost its distinctive titular force, and sank to the level of a proper name, both when standing alone, and also in combination with "Jesus". This is often (though not always)[68] the case in Paul. Having lost its titular force it was often combined with other titles, especially in the familiar phrase, "Jesus Christ our Lord".

(iii) *Kyrios*

This title is prominent in the christological hymn, Phil. 2:6–11. With the explicit statement that Yahweh has transferred his own *name* (ὄνομα) to the Exalted One we seem to be passing beyond the bounds of Hellenistic Jewish Christology proper to a less purely functional, and a more ontic, if not ontological, type of thought. The Exalted One shares the divine "nature" of God himself.[69] This is underlined in v. 10, which speaks of the divine *worship* accorded to the Exalted One by the subjected powers.[70] Indeed, it is possible that the Exalted One is conceived here as resuming the divine mode of existence which was already his before he stripped himself of it in the incarnation. The name granted to him at the exaltation was perhaps the name he had already possessed in his pre-existent state of equality with God. The difference is that it is *Jesus* who now has this name. God's Lordship is now effectively asserted in Jesus' history, and made manifest to the powers so that they acknowledge it. If this be so, then the pre-existent was already *Kyrios*.[71] *Kyrios*, Lord, in the gentile mission, has come to denote not merely functional lordship, but divine nature ontically conceived.

That the gentile converts should have read into the title *Kyrios* the associations of the mystery religions[72] was only natural. There are hints of this in 1 Corinthians. St. Paul did not, of course, derive his own understanding of κύριος from the mystery religions, but from the Christ myth enshrined in Phil. 2:6–11, which in its turn was rooted in the Christology of the earlier Hellenistic Jewish Christianity. It is on the ground of this Christology that Paul polemically asserts the exclusive right of Jesus to the title *Kyrios* over against the many cult deities of the pagan world (1 Cor. 8:4–6). His predilection for the *Kyrios* title in connection with the Lord's Supper (1 Cor. 10:21; 11:27), while not *derived* from the mystery usage, may well be *occasioned* by the presuppositions of his Corinthian converts.[73] Over against these Paul is concerned to assert the right understanding of Jesus as *Kyrios* and a right understanding of the Supper. It is not an automatic conferral of divinization, but a participation in the death of Jesus, with its ethical and eschatological implications.

Finally, as we have seen,[74] the *Kyrios* title was coming into increasingly frequent use at this period in connection with the imperial cultus. In no case can we *derive* the Kyrios Christology from this source.[75] But it was sometimes *asserted* polemically against the imperial cultus. This is clear from such passages as 1 Pet. 3:15 and Rev. 17:14; 19:16, which emanate from a time when emperor worship was being imposed upon Christians with resultant persecution. Their polemical use of the title indicates that the later NT writers understood κύριος ("Lord") in the Hellenistic sense as a divine title.

(iv) *Son of God*

Together with the *Kyrios* title, this designation was very popular in the Gentile mission. Derived ultimately from the prophetology which spoke of Jesus' historical sending, it became in combination with the incarnation concept the title *par excellence* for the Redeemer's pre-existence (Gal. 4:4f., Rom. 1:3; 8:3; John 3:16).[76] In the Pauline literature, however, the title "Son of God" is never evaluated positively for the pre-existent One's work in creation, but only in connection with his historical sending. The title "Son of God" for instance is absent, not only from Phil. 2:6–11 (which, as we have seen, probably thinks of the Redeemer as the pre-existent Kyrios), but also from those passages which speak of the pre-existent One's active role in creation (1 Cor. 8:6;

Col. 1:15f.). Only in Heb. 1:2 and, if the reading of the majority of MSS be correct, in John 1:18[77], is the title "Son" directly used for the pre-existent One as the agent of creation. The NT does not speculate about the origin of the Son from the Father in eternity, though the terms μονογενής, "only begotten", (John 1:14, 18)[78], πρωτότοκος (Col. 1:15, 18; Heb. 1:6) and εἰκών[79] posed ontological problems for the later church.[80]

5. Summary

The Gentile mission did not take its Christology from the thought of its converts. But it did adopt certain features of the more syncretistic types of Hellenistic Judaism in the diaspora. With these elements it produced a threefold christological pattern of pre-existence, incarnation and exaltation to replace the twofold pattern of earthly life-exaltation. The parousia was frequently, though not invariably, discarded. Where it survived, it did so only as an appendage, leaving open the consummation of that which had already been in principle effected (e.g. the later Pauline and Deutero-Pauline writings and the Johannine literature).[81]

More controversial was the acceptance of the θεῖος ἀνήρ epiphany Christology, which even in Philo had been taken over only in a form considerably modified by the OT tradition. Paul resisted it. Mark exploited it, but modified it with his device of the Messianic secret. John, however, eventually adopted it and combined it with the categories of pre-existence and revelation.

Thus a full-blown doctrine of incarnation was evolved. The redeemer was a divine being who became incarnate, manifested the Deity in his flesh, and was subsequently exalted to heaven. This seems a far cry from the "adoptionist" two stage Christology of the earlier Hellenistic Jewish Christianity and still more from the two foci Christology of the earliest Palestinian community, to say nothing of Jesus' own self-understanding. But it is not so really. Jesus had understood his work as the proleptic presence of the coming salvation. From the very first the post-Easter church had proclaimed his victory as the eschatological act of God. Thus the quintessence of the Christian message is variously interpreted to the succeeding environments of the Christian mission. But it was essentially the same message throughout, the message of the divine salvation in Jesus of Nazareth.

Appendix: THE ADAM/CHRIST TYPOLOGY AND THE SON OF MAN

J. Weiss (*Earliest Christianity*[1] I, 485f.) and W. Bousset (*Kyrios Christos*[2], pp. 140ff., 203) appear to have originated the thesis that St. Paul derived his designation of Jesus as ἄνθρωπος ("man") from the title υἱὸς τοῦ ἀνθρώπου, *bar naša* ("son of man"). This view has found widespread acceptance (e.g. Rawlinson, *NT Doctrine*, pp. 130f.; Jeremias, *TWNT* I, pp. 142f., s.v. Ἀδάμ; Cullmann, *Christology*, pp. 166–174; C. Colpe in the Jeremias *Festschrift* [see chap. VII, note 37], pp. 182f.). Usually this thesis has been combined with the view that in 1 Cor. 15:45ff. Paul was polemizing against the Philonic or Hellenistic Jewish identification of the first man with the heavenly man, though this is not invariably the case (e.g. notably, Rawlinson). Other commentators appear to accept Paul's polemical intention in 1 Cor. 15:45ff. but ignore the theory of the derivation of ἄνθρωπος ("man") from υἱὸς τοῦ ἀνθρώπου, ("Son of man") (e.g. Lietzmann, *I Kor.* HBT 1949[4], pp. 85f.), W. D. Davies, *Paul and Rabbinic Judaism* (London: S.P.C.K., 1948, pp. 41ff.). Most recently, Hahn (*Hoheitstitel*, p. 21) has called in question the theory that the Adam/Christ typology is directly derived from the Son of man, but without giving any particular grounds for his scepticism. A re-examination of the thesis seems due.

Two arguments are usually adduced in support of the theory. (1) ἄνθρωπος ("man") is an idiomatic rendering of the impossible Greek, but Semitic idiom, ὁ υἱὸς τοῦ ἀνθρώπου ("the son of the man"); (2) In 1 Cor. 15:27, Ps. 8:6 is quoted. This implies Ps. 8:4, where "son of man" occurs. Hence, it is argued, Paul has the "Son of man" in mind in 1 Cor. 15.

Let us examine the arguments in reverse order. (1) In view of the atomistic exegesis current at the time (cf. only Isa. 53!) it is a hazardous *argumentum e silentio* to infer that Ps. 8:4 was in Paul's mind when he quoted Ps. 8:6. Indeed Ps. 8:4 plays no role in the Palestinian Son of man tradition or anywhere else prior to Paul. Nor is it quoted until Heb. 2:6. This is well on in the Hellenistic period, when the eschatological origin of the term Son of man had been largely forgotten. However, Ps. 110:1 had been widely used before Paul, both in the Palestinian and in the Hellenistic Jewish tradition (see above, pp. 145f. and 185). Now in both Ps. 100:1 and 8:6 the idea of the subjection of the enemies occurs, and in the LXX the same verb ὑποτάσσειν ("to subject") is used. But there is a difference between the two Psalm texts. Whereas in Ps. 110 the enemies are awaiting subjection in Ps. 8:6 "all things" are said already to be subjected. Here we see the shift of perspective in the Hellenistic church consequent upon the exaltation Christology (see above, pp. 184ff.). It would seem, therefore, that Ps. 110:1 led directly to Ps. 8:6. In the process Ps. 8:4 was completely by-passed.

(2) Ps. 8:4 lends itself naturally to the *katabasis-anabasis* christological pattern. That pattern is completely foreign to the Palestinian Son of man tradition (cf. the three categories of Son of man sayings in the synoptics). In fact, it does not penetrate the Son of man Christology until after Paul (Heb. 2:6, etc. and John 3:13; 6:62). In our opinion these are the latest of all the types of Son of man sayings (see above). Paul, of course shared the *katabasis-anabasis* Christology (Phil. 2:6–11). But, as we have argued, this pattern is a Christian adaptation of the sophia-anthropos myth. And although this myth may be derived from the same ultimate (Iranian) myth of the first man as was the Son of man, the original connection had by this time been completely forgotten. Accordingly, the case for Paul's derivation of ἄνθρωπος ("man") from υἱὸς τοῦ ἀνθρώπου ("Son of man") is much weaker than is generally supposed. It has therefore seemed advisable to look elsewhere for its origin, in some other pattern current in Hellenistic Judaism.

NOTES ON CHAPTER VIII

1. The term "Hellenistic" has been current since Bousset. Hahn introduces the qualification "Hellenistic *Gentile*" in order to distinguish it from his category of "Hellenistic Jewish". But "Hellenistic Gentile" is not altogether satisfactory for reasons given in the text.

2. Lohmeyer, *Kyrios Jesus, eine Untersuchung zu Phil. 2:5–11, SHA,*

Phil.-hist. Kl. 4, (1927–1928). This has not been accessible to me, but his treatment there is followed in his comm. *Der Brief an die Philipper*, K–KENT 1930[8], 1953[9], pp. 90–99. It is summarized and discussed by Käsemann, *Exegetische Versuche und Besinnungen* I, Göttingen: Vandenhoeck u. Ruprecht, 1961, pp. 51–95, (originally published in *ZThK* 47 (1950), pp. 313–360). See also in English F. W. Beare, *A Commentary on the Epistle to the Philippians* (Black's Commentary), London, 1959, pp. 73–88.

3. Lohmeyer's arrangement is followed by Beare (pp. 73f.). M. Dibelius (*HNT* 11, 1925[2], etc.), pp. 61–63 and J. Jeremias in *Studia Paulina*, pp. 152–154 propose different arrangements which have not met with wide acceptance. Jeremias arranges it in three strophes, referring to the pre-existent, incarnate and exalted One respectively. But by a curious inconsistency he interprets the third line of his Strophe I (ἑαυτὸν ἐκένωσεν, v. 8) as the "surrender of his life, not the kenosis of the incarnation".

4. Cf. also J. Jeremias, *ibid.*, p. 154, n. 3; O. Cullmann, *Christology*, pp. 174–181. The latter, following J. Héring, has extended Lohmeyer's argument by equating μορφή in v. 6 with דְּמוּת (Gen. 1:26), thus also equating the pre-existent One with the first man, and by interpreting οὐχ ἁρπαγμὸν ἡγήσατο τὸ εἶναι ἴσα θεῷ as the reversal of Adam's temptation ("eritis sicut Deus"). If this interpretation were correct it would mean that the Christology of the Palestinian earliest church already contained pre-existence and incarnation. But this is most unlikely.

5. So, according to Beare, E. F. Scott. British commentators frequently recognize its hymnic character, but hesitate to pronounce it pre-Pauline, so that the only alternative would be to take it as a Pauline composition. Paradoxically, it is the near-fundamentalist interpreters who seem to favour a pre-Pauline Palestinian origin for the hymn. So R. P. Martin, *An Early Christian Confession*, London: Tyndale Press, 1960; G. R. Beasley-Murray in Peake, p. 986.

6. μορφὴ θεοῦ, ἴσα εἶναι θεῷ, δοῦλος (in a christological sense), κενοῦν, ὑπερύψωσεν. See G. Bornkamm, *Studien zu Antike*, p. 178, n. 1a; P. Bonnard, *L'Épître aux Philippiens* (*CNT* 10) 1950, pp. 42–49. It is difficult to see why Bornkamm should include ἐχαρίσατο in the list, since it occurs quite frequently in Paul (e.g. Rom. 8:32, etc.).

7. By L. S. Thornton, *The Dominion of Christ*, London: Dacre, 1952, pp. 91, 95, n. 1; J. Jeremias, *Servant*, p. 97 and n. 455, where he quotes in support H. Wheeler Robinson, *The Cross in the Old Testament*, London: S.C.M. Press, 1955, pp. 57, 104f., also in *Stud. Paulina*, p. 154, n. 3.

8. Some will be troubled by this statement, suggesting as it does that the incarnation is a later accretion to the Christian faith. This is not so: the incarnation formula is an explicit assertion in ontic terms of what the earliest church already believed, namely, that Jesus and his history was the eschatological act of God. See also below, pp. 254f.

9. The attempts which have been made to eliminate pre-existence entirely from this passage (e.g. L. S. Thornton, *op. cit.*) must be pronounced a failure, though if accepted it would make an Aramaic origin

more plausible. The interpretations of Lohmeyer, Jeremias and Cullmann at least do more justice to the background of the hymn in the history of religions.

10. F. W. Beare, *op. cit.*, p. 77. Beare protests against calling the hymn "pre-Pauline" if by that is meant "prior to Paul". Accordingly, he proposes that the hymn should be regarded as "first composed by a gifted writer within his [*sc.* Paul's] own circle as an elaboration of 1 Cor. 15:47 and 2 Cor. 8:9". But "pre-Pauline" is not a chronological statement, only a material one, in the sense that it is not Paul's own composition. That it emanates from his own circle is speculative, and questionable in view of the fact that the same mythological scheme is found in non-Pauline writings (Heb. 1:1–4; 1 Pet. 3:18–22; John 1:1–14). The pre-existence-incarnation Christology is so widespread that it can hardly be specifically Pauline (cf. H. Braun, *ZThK* 54 (1957), p. 361, n. 3). We therefore prefer to assign the hymn less specifically to the "gentile Mission", leaving open the possibility that it was from the Pauline circle.

11. *Contra* Beare, pp. 79f.

12. Following Käsemann, Bornkamm interprets, *"göttliche Daseinsweise"*.

13. But not quite, according to Käsemann (*"etwas für sich ausnützen"*) and Bornkamm (*"etwas für sich ausbeuten"*). According to them ἁρπαγμός had in vulgar speaking lost its precise force and had come to mean "to exploit for oneself" or "to take advantage of".

14. In Gal. 4:4, Rom. 8:3 the original "sending" formula is combined with the incarnation formula derived from the mythological pattern; see above, p. 195. There the sending by God takes the place of the voluntary decision of the pre-existent One.

15. If the ontic interpretation of μορφή be accepted ("mode of existence") this occasions no difficulty. Only if, with the later dogmatics, μορφή is interpreted ontologically do we run into dogmatic difficulties.

16. C. A. Anderson Scott, *Christianity according to St. Paul*, Cambridge: University Press, 1932[2], p. 35, had already interpreted in this sense, as Beare points out.

17. For the same reason, E. Schweizer's interpretation of δοῦλος as the suffering righteous man of the psalms (*Lordship*, p. 63) is to be rejected. Cf. Bornkamm, *op. cit.*, pp. 181f.

18. So Käsemann, pp. 74–76, also followed by Beare.

19. So Beare, following L. Bouyer, who notes that wherever Christ is designated *anthropos* (here and Rom. 5:12–17; 1 Cor. 15:20–49) a contrast with Adam is intended. This point (which seems valid) is missed by Käsemann and Bornkamm. We see here how the Christology of the gentile mission took the sophia-anthropos myth and split it into two parts, using the sophia part for the pre-existence descent and ascent, and the anthropos part (by a reversal of Adam) for the incarnate life and its soteriological consequences.

20. On the connection of the Adam typology with the Son of man concept see Appendix to this chapter.

21. 1 Tim. 3:16; Heb. 1:3, 2:9, 10:12, 12:2 (in Heb. always with

the much more primitive conception of the session at the right hand); 1 Pet. 3:18; and perhaps also the Johannine passages which speak of the "lifting up" of the Son of man (though these are more likely due to a shift backward from the parousia to the exaltation). On John 3:13 and 6:62, see below p. 229. The Hellenistic origin of the pattern incarnation-exaltation disposes of G. Bertram's theory that the most primitive pattern was of an ascension direct from the cross with no intervening resurrection (*Festgabe für A. Deissmann*, Tübingen: J. C. B. Mohr (P. Siebeck), 1927, pp. 187–217). The resurrection was a constitutive part of the earliest kerygma. Cf. Hahn, *Hoheitstitel*, p. 130, n. 4. This does not of course invalidate the now commonly accepted view that the primitive church barely distinguished the resurrection and ascension, that the resurrection appearances were regarded as visions of the already Ascended One, and that the Lucan scheme of resurrection, forty days appearances and ascension is a later schematization. See e.g. A. M. Ramsey, *The Resurrection of Christ*, London: Bles, 1946[2], pp. 121–123; J. G. Davies, *He Ascended into Heaven*, London: Lutterworth, 1958, pp. 168–184.

22. *Christology*, pp. 180f., following Héring.

23. Bornkamm, *ibid.*, p. 183, following Käsemann.

24. Beare, *op. cit.*, p. 85.

25. Käsemann, *ibid.*, p. 83, quoted by Bornkamm.

26. The precise *Sitz im Leben* of the hymn is uncertain. Lohmeyer proposed the Lord's Supper. Käsemann favours the baptismal liturgy (p. 95), as he does also for Col. 1:15–20.

27. E. Norden, *Agnostos Theos*, Leipzig: Teubner, 1912[1], 1929[2], first provided the criteria for isolating this as a hymn, as also for all the hymns in the epistles. Käsemann proposed a somewhat different reconstruction (*op. cit.*, pp. 34–51, reprinted from *Festschrift für R. Bultmann*, Stuttgart: Kohlhammer, 1949). For a more radical rearrangement see J. M. Robinson, *JBL* 76 (1957), pp. 270–292; cf. also E. Schweizer, *ThLZ* 86 (1961), cols. 241–246.

The arguments for a hymnic origin are: (1) the poetic structure; (2) the basic subject matter: the Christ event interpreted according to a mythological pattern; (3) the initial ὅς; (4) the non-Pauline vocabulary and grammar. The last point, generally advanced by the Germans, is complicated by their habitual tendency to regard Col. as Deutero-Pauline.

The hymnic origin is questioned by C. F. D. Moule, *The Epistle of Paul to the Colossians*, Cambridge: Univ. Press, 1957, pp. 60–63, though what he appears to reject is the view (cf. Holtzmann *et al.*) that the hymn is a *subsequent* interpolation into the epistle (cf. p. 62). This is not the modern view, e.g. of Käsemann, to whose essay Moule does not refer. The view adopted here is the same as for Phil. 2:6–11, viz. that it is a hymn of the gentile mission adapted by St. Paul himself.

28. All of the reconstructions (Lohmeyer, Käsemann, Masson, J. M. Robinson and Schweizer) agree about these, however much they vary otherwise between themselves. Here Schweizer's arrangement is followed. Three phrases are omitted as disturbing the poetic parallelism,

viz. 16b, "visible . . . authorities", which has reference to the specific issue in Col.; 18a "the church", an interpretive gloss (and re-interpretation) of "his body"; 18c ("that in everything he might be pre-eminent"); 20c "making peace by the blood of his cross" = Pauline theology like θανάτου δὲ σταυροῦ in Phil. 2:8.

29. Wisd. 7:26, Philo, *Leg. All.* 1:43. Philo also uses the Logos, see above, chapter III, pp. 75f.

30. The sense is as in Prov. 8:22; Ecclus. 1:4; 24:9; Wisd. 9:9. Philo calls the Logos πρωτόγονος υἱός, *de Agricultura* 51; *de Conf. Ling.* 146. The Armenian text (Greek not extant) of *Quaest. in Gen.* calls Wisdom the "first born (?πρωτόγονος) of all things". Col. may have preferred πρωτότοκος here because it had already established itself in connection with Christ as the first and constitutive instance of resurrection (Rom. 8:29). According to our theory, this resurrection use will have been derived from the Christian reversal of the anthropos part of the myth.

31. Prov. 3:19, Wisd. 7:22a, Philo, *de Fuga* 109. See above, pp. 73ff.

32. Schweizer, *ibid.*, cites Ecclus. 24:5f.; Wisd. 8:16, where sophia binds together heaven, earth and the underworld.

33. Schweizer, *ibid.*, col. 244: he provides full documentation in his article on σῶμα in *TWNT* VII, pp. 1035–1039. Cf. also W. L. Knox, *JTS* 39 (1938), pp. 243–246: *idem, St. Paul and the Church of the Gentiles*, Cambridge: University Press, 1939[1], 1962[2], pp. 160–162, who also thinks that the Pauline doctrine of the church as the body of Christ originates in a cosmic use, but from Stoicism. Is the Stoic use derived from the same mythological origin?

34. In a text of Philo's commentary on Exodus quoted by H. Schlier, *TWNT* III, s.v. κεφαλή, p. 676: "verbum est sempiternum sempiterni dei caput universorum". The passage continues with an exegesis of "caput" as indicating supremacy over the creation ("sub quo pedum . . . subiectus iacet universus mundus") and as the source of its life ("sicut et animantia opus habent capitis, sine quo vivere non possunt").

35. ἀρχή is applicable to both the sophia (Prov. 8:22) and anthropos aspects of the myth. Here it is transferred from the anthropos aspect to the eschatological man. There is thus both a parallel with Strophe I and an implied contrast with Adam.

36. See Moule, *Colossians*, pp. 164–169.

37. *Spirit*, p. 57; cf. *Lordship*, p. 65, n. 1.

38. Bultmann in *Coniectanea Neotestamentica* XI (*Festschrift* Fridrichsen), Lund: Gleerup, and Copenhagen: Muncksgaard, 1947, pp. 1–14. That it was a hymn had already been suggested by H. Windisch, *Die katholischen Briefe, HNT,* 1930[2], though no grounds or reconstruction were given. E. G. Selwyn, *The First Epistle of St. Peter*, London: Macmillan, 1946, rejected Windisch's suggestion on the ground that the passage was not easily recognizable in verse form nor easily detachable from its context. Bultmann's subsequent analysis has rendered the theory of hymnic origin much more plausible. He argues that (1) only v. 18a is relevant to the context of paraenesis: the rest of the hymn is quoted along with the immediately relevant part; (2) like Phil. 2:6–11 and Col. 1:15–20 it

contains glosses which disturb the poetic structure: δίκαιος ὑπὲρ ἀδίκων (an adaptation to the paraenesis of vv. 14, 16: πορευθείς (v. 19) modelled on v. 22: vv. 20f., a prose elucidation of v. 19, followed by a typological interpretation of ὕδωρ.

39. So even Bultmann. But in view of the strict chronological sequence of this hymn (unlike 1 Tim. 3:16) mention of victory over the powers should come here.

40. So rightly Selwyn, who, following Gunkel, Bousset, etc., thinks that the primary reference is to the fallen angels. He points out that πνεύματα is never used *absolutely* of the departed, not even in Heb. 12:23, which Bultmann still quotes in favour of his own interpretation. Selwyn's view is even more probable if vv. 20f. are the author's gloss on the original hymn.

41. Cf., however, Norden, *op. cit.*, p. 386, who sets it out in rhythmic form.

42. In vv. 2–4 (which for reasons given below is all we shall include in the hymn), ἀπαύγασμα, χαρακτήρ, φέρων (here only in the sense uphold, sustain). It is noteworthy that all of the *hapax legomena* occur in the first, creation part of the hymn. Key words from the redemption half are taken up and recur later in the epistle: καθαρισμὸς τῶν ἁμαρτιῶν cf. Heb. 9:14; 10:2; ἐκάθισεν ἐν δεξίᾳ τῆς μεγαλωσύνης cf. 8:1. This subsequent use of the same terminology appears to be derived precisely from the hymn.

43. Philo.

44. For details see Bultmann, *Johannes*, p. 2.

45. So G. Kittel *et al.*, *TWNT* IV, pp. 69–110; *SB* II, p. 333.

46. Very few interpreters have adopted Memra as the exclusive source, but it is often considered as one among others. E.g. by G. H. C. Macgregor (Moffatt Comm.). After a long excursus on Memra (pp. 302–333), *SB* conclude that it is never an hypostasis and therefore cannot be the source of the Joh. logos. It ought to be dropped from all future discussion. Cf. R. H. Strachan, *The Fourth Gospel*, London: S.C.M. Press, 1941, pp. 93f., n. 2.

47. So, above all, K. Bornhäuser; also W. F. Howard, *Christianity according to St. John*, London: Duckworth, 1943[1], 1953[2], pp. 49–52.

48. So many of the older English commentators reared in the classical tradition.

49. *Ibid.*, p. 9, n. 1.

50. See above, p. 208.

51. Bultmann's chief evidence is the *Odes of Solomon*, a collection which at best is contemporary with John, and hardly pre-John. J. R. Harris dates 1st century A.D.; J. H. Bernard, *Texts and Studies VIII*, Cambridge: University Press, 1912, dates 2nd century A.D. But in neither case is direct Christian influence on the *Odes* excluded, rather than vice-versa. The Hermetic literature, on which see C. H. Dodd, *Interpretation of the Fourth Gospel*, pp. 10–53, can however be more safely used as evidence for a simultaneous syncretistic process in pagan thought.

52. Cf. Augustine's famous remark in *Conf.* VII, 9. On the ground of

the Evangelist's polemical insertions in vv. 6–8, 15 and the general polemical tendency against too high an estimate of the Baptist in the earlier chapters of John. Bultmann concludes that the prologue was originally a baptist hymn. But it could hardly have included v. 14!

53. Is this last couplet the conclusion of the pre-Christian hymn? The couplet form seems to change after this point.

54. Cf. Prov. 8:22; Philo, *Leg. All.* I, 43.

55. In Wisd. 10ff. the examples of acceptance of sophia are *de facto* confined to Israel. In Ecclus., which is more strongly Palestinian, the examples are confined on principle to Israel.

56. In LXX יָחִיד is rendered by μονογενής at Judg. 11:34 and by ἀγαπητός at Gen. 22:2.

57. Cf. Arndt and Gingrich s.v.; W. Bauer, *Das Johannes-Evangelium, HNT* 6, 1925², *ad loc.* where Wisd. 7:22 is cited. Bultmann, *Johannes*, pp. 47, n. 2, gives many parallels from the history of religion for its use of a divine being. The hymnic origin of John 1:1–14 justifies our giving μονογενής an entirely different meaning, so far as the original hymn is concerned, from that in John 3:16, a formula of quite a different origin. The Evangelist himself would have interpreted both occurrences in the same sense.

58. This is perhaps put a little too strongly. For the glory of the incarnate One is even in John hidden beneath the veil of the flesh and perceptible only to faith, awaiting full manifestation in the resurrection to the disciples and at the parousia to the world.

59. For the divine man, see above, pp. 97f.

60. *Die Gegner des Paulus im 2. Korintherbrief*, Neukirchen, 1964.

61. Bultmann's contention (*Tradition*, p. 240) that the miracle stories proper (as opposed to the apophthegms) were *created* in this milieu, is already disproved by the prophet-servant (i.e. early Palestinian) Christology which characterizes the primary stratum of these stories, and by the Son of God Christology (in the modified Hellenistic Jewish sense) which qualifies the second stratum. But that they were *modified* in this milieu is plausible.

62. See *Interpreting the Miracles*, pp. 48–63.

63. Dibelius, *From Tradition to Gospel* (see above, ch. VI, note 24), pp. 100–102; cf. also H. Braun, *art. cit.*, p. 353.

64. W. Wrede, *Messiasgeheimnis*, first established the Messianic secret as a Marcan device. The phenomenon has often since been recognized, but its Marcan origin denied in favour of its historical authenticity. But this argument breaks down because the secret occurs in the redaction, not the tradition. Wrede, however, wrongly conceived it as an attempt to impose a Christology upon a non-christological tradition. For the tradition was already thoroughly impregnated with Christology (cf. H. Conzelmann, *ZThK* 54 (1957), pp. 293–295; art. *"Jesus Christus"*, *RGG*³). The purpose of the Messianic secret is rather to tone down the epiphany Christology in the tradition. Jesus' epiphanies are reduced to secret epiphanies; those who pierce their secret are enjoined not to

publish the secret until after the cross and resurrection. A careful study of the passages where the secret is employed (Mark 1:25, 34, 44; 3:12; 5:43; 8:26; also 4:10–12; 8:17–21, 30; 9:9) will show precisely what pericopes had been construed as θεῖος ἀνήρ epiphanies in the pre-Marcan Hellenistic stage.

For a consistent interpretation of Marcan Christology (which lies outside the scope of this book) see J. Schreiber, *ZThK* 58 (1961), pp. 154–183. I cannot, however, agree with the latter part of this article, where the author resuscitates the Tübingen theory that Paul's opponents were the Jewish Christians led by Peter, and that the issue between them was precisely christological, their Christology being that of Q, and Paul's the kenosis and cross Christology. Paul's opponents, as Munck, Schmithals, and others have recently shown, were "gnostics", not Jewish Christians from Jerusalem. And Mark is directed against the θεῖος ἀνήρ (Hellenistic) Christology, not against the Palestinian Christology of Q.

65. See *Interpreting the Miracles*, pp. 88–96.

66. See appendix to this chapter on the Adam/Christ typology and the Son of man.

67. E.g. 3:14; 12:23; 13:31.

68. The exceptions are the "suffering" formulae, where χριστός, whether used alone, or in combination with Ἰησοῦς, and usually preceding it, is still to be understood in a titular sense. See above, pp. 161f.

69. Käsemann. Cf. Bornkamm, quoted above, p. 208 and n. 12. It would be better to speak not of "nature" (which is ontological) but of "mode of being", which is ontic.

70. Cf. Hahn, *op. cit.*, p. 121.

71. This is the element of truth in Cullmann's interpretation of ὑπερύψωσεν (see above, p. 212).

72. On the mystery religions, see above, pp. 89ff.

73. On the eucharistic disorders at Corinth see Bornkamm, *Studien*, pp. 138–146, 175f.

74. On the imperial cultus, see above, pp. 87ff.

75. A. Deissmann, (see above, ch. IV, note 8) exaggerated the influence of the imperial cultus on the Christian use. While there are influences of a polemical motive in that use, those influences are not constitutive.

76. While the use of υἱὸς θεοῦ was not *derived* from the sophia-anthropos myth, it was certainly *used* there, for Philo e.g. calls the Logos the Son of God (*Agr.* 12, 51, etc.). This may account for its continued use in the Hellenistic mission for the pre-existent One.

77. Bultmann, *Johannes*, prefers this reading against θεός (א BC*) on intrinsic grounds, despite its inferior attestation. Hoskyns also strongly inclines to it (*The Fourth Gospel*, London: Faber, 1940¹, I, pp. 151f.).

78. For μονογενής in John 3:16 see above, note 57.

79. Paul applies εἰκών to the Redeemer in two different contexts: to the pre-existent One as agent of creation (2 Cor. 4:4 and Col. 1:15) and to the incarnate and exalted One in a soteriological context (Rom. 8:9; 1 Cor. 15:49; 2 Cor. 3:18; cf. Col. 3:20). In the former case it appears to

be derived from the sophia part of the myth, and in the latter case from the anthropos part *via* the Adam/Christ typology.

80. Matt. 11:25–27 par.; 28:19 and the fourth gospel use υἱός for the Incarnate One in his relation to the Father. This usage has historical roots in Jesus' use of Abba (see above, p. 106) but in the setting of the pre-existence-incarnation Christology it acquires ontic connotations.

81. The futuristic eschatology of the fourth gospel is not the result of interpolation by an "ecclesiastical redactor" (Bultmann) but the survival of earlier unassimilated tradition. See S. Schulz, *Untersuchungen*, pp. 109f.

Chapter IX

BUILDING ON THE FOUNDATIONS

1. *The Three Patterns*

IN the foundations of NT Christology we have discovered three strata, which we have designated "Earliest Palestinian", "Hellenistic Jewish", and "Gentile Mission" respectively.

As we look back upon them we can discern three different christological patterns, The first pattern, that of the Palestinian church, had two foci: the historical word and work of Jesus, and his parousia. But although Jesus' present status was not yet a matter for reflection, both foci were related to the present life of the church. Jesus' historical word had present authority for the church; his historical work had present soteriological significance. Jesus' return (*Maranatha!*) as Son of man was the matter for earnest prayer precisely because when he came he would validate his own earthly word and work which were still present in the church. This christological pattern may perhaps be pictured graphically thus:

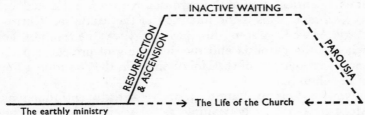

Among the works of the earthly Jesus was his death. At first, this was understood simply as the crime of the Jews, the culmination of their rejection of God's offer and demand

243

throughout their history. The resurrection on the other hand was God's yes to all that Jesus had stood for: that he was vindicated as the One who would return as Son of man to consummate his own word and work. Very soon, and within the earliest Palestinian stratum, the death of Jesus acquired a more positive significance—which was, however, implicit from the start. Since his death was both the culmination of his own soteriological ministry, as it was also the culmination of the Jews' rejection of it, the soteriological significance was extended to cover the death as well as the earlier ministry.

Here is a table indicating the titles used in the earliest Palestinian phase:

Earthly life	*Death-Resurrection*	*Parousia*
(1) *Maran(a)*	(1) Messiah-designate	(1) *Bar naša**
(2) *Bar naša**	(2) *Bar naša**	(2) *Marana*
(3) *'Ebhedh*	(3) (*'Ebhedh*)	(3) *Mašiaḥ*
(4) (Son of David)		

* In dominical sayings only.
[Parentheses denote that the actual title is not used, but only associated language.]

A major shift of emphasis took place in the second, or Hellenistic Jewish stratum. Hitherto the continuing work of Jesus had been thought of as an extension of the earthly work or as an anticipation of the parousia. Now it is evaluated for its own sake. This is the intention of the exaltation Christology. As we have seen, this Christology was the result of the delay in the parousia and the deepening of present experience—particularly of the Holy Spirit—in the continuing life of the church.

Now, at his exaltation, Jesus is already enthroned as Messiah, not merely waiting as Messiah designate. The pattern of this Christology may be represented thus:

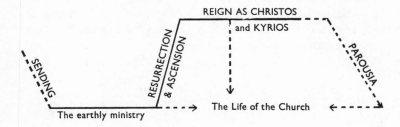

Increasingly, too, in this type of Christology, the earthly life of Jesus is given a positive assessment, so that it becomes a preliminary stage in his Messiahship. The Messianic titles are pushed back into the earthly life, though without losing the sense that there was a "plus" conveyed by the exaltation.

HELLENISTIC JEWISH TITLES

Earthly life	Death-Resurrection	Exaltation to parousia
(1) κύριος	(1) Χριστός	(1) υἱὸς τοῦ ἀνθρώπου
(2) (υἱὸς τοῦ ἀνθρώπου)*	(2) (παῖς)	(2) κύριος
(3) παῖς†		(3) Χριστός
(4) υἱὸς Δαυίδ		(4) υἱὸς τοῦ θεοῦ
(5) Χριστός		

* In dominical sayings only (except Acts 7:56), and in continuation of Palestinian tradition.
† Continued only in liturgical formulae.
[Parentheses denote that the title is not used, but the theological associations of the title appear.]

The search for redemption in the gentile world was centred not upon a hope of national restoration like that of Israel, but on deliverance from the powers which held man in thrall—fate and death. If the gospel was to be relevant it must offer redemption from this plight. Hence, the missionaries to the gentiles took another major step in affirming the Redeemer's pre-existence and incarnation. They developed a christological pattern in which the pre-existent One descended into the realm of our human plight at the incarnation, defeated the powers on their own ground, and reascended. In so doing he became the head of a new order of humanity and reversed the fall of Adam. The pattern may be represented graphically thus:

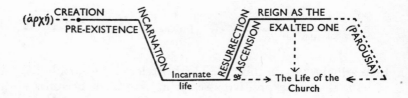

When the pattern first appears (Phil. 2:6–11) nothing is said about any activity of the pre-existent One. However this was probably implied, since we find the idea already in 1 Cor. 8:6. Also, its widespread appearance (Heb., John and perhaps implied in 1 Pet. 1:20) suggests that pre-existence was not a Pauline innovation, but a common feature of the Christology of the gentile mission.

At first, the incarnate life is conceived as a kenosis. But eventually, despite the resistance of St. Paul, and despite the efforts of Mark to tone it down with his Messianic secret, the conception of the incarnate life as an epiphany prevails (1 Tim. 3:16 and John). Pre-existence, agency of creation, descent in the incarnation, incarnate life as epiphany, atoning death, resurrection and exaltation, victory over the powers, continued reign in heaven until the parousia, final consummation at the parousia—this represents the fullest pattern of the Christology in the gentile mission, though it never appears *in toto*.

This pattern completes the foundations of NT Christology. The theologians of the NT (Paul and the Pauline school, the Evangelists, and the other sub-apostolic NT writings), all erect their theological superstructures upon the foundations, not indeed invariably upon the full pattern, but always upon parts of it. It is this pattern which lies behind the process of christological formulation which culminates at Chalcedon, and of which more will be said later.

Here are the titles of the Gentile Mission:

Pre-existence	Incarnation	Exaltation
(1) [κύριος]*	(1) ἄνθρωπος	(1) κύριος*
(wisdom)	δεύτερος or ἔσχατος	
(2) [wisdom]	(2) υἱὸς τοῦ θεοῦ*	(2) υἱὸς (τοῦ θεοῦ)
	and υἱός	
(3) υἱὸς (τοῦ θεοῦ)	(3) σωτήρ	(3) σωτήρ
(4) Logos	(4) θεός	(4) θεός
(5) θεός		

* In an ontic sense.

[Parentheses denote that the title is not used, but the theological associations of the title appear.]

2. Functional versus Ontological Christology

One can hardly say with Cullmann[1] that the Christology of the NT is purely functional. Much of it certainly is, especially in the purely Jewish phases. Yet even the Palestinian kerygma does not confine itself to statements of what God has done in Jesus. It also applies to Jesus' christological *titles*: Son of man, Lord, Messiah, servant. These christological titles are, however, almost without exception used in sentences which speak of action, sometimes it is the action of God in or through Jesus (e.g. "that he may send the Christ appointed for you" (Acts 3:20); "Christ . . . *was raised* [reverential passive, equivalent to God raised him] from the dead" (1 Cor. 15:4); "the Son of man came *eating and drinking* (Matt. 11:19 par.)). Sometimes it is the suffering of the Christ: "the Son of man *will be delivered* into the hands of men" (Mark 9:31); "you *will see* the Son of man . . . coming on the clouds of heaven" (Mark 14:62); "Christ *died* for our sins" (1 Cor. 15:3). Occasionally a christological affirmation can occur as the predicate of the verb "to be", e.g.: Peter's confession, "you *are* the Christ" (Mark 8:29); "the Son of man *is* Lord of the sabbath" (Mark 2:28); and, in Jesus' answer to the high priest's question, "*Are* you the Christ!"— "I *am*." But these statements are really functional in character, not affirmations about the "nature" or being of Jesus. They affirm what he is doing or what he will do. He will function as Israel's eschatological ruler; he decides over the sabbath question in the church, etc.

The same holds good of the early Hellenistic Jewish stratum. "God *made* him Lord and Christ" (Acts 2:36); "*appointed* Son of God" (Rom. 1:4). Again, there are in this stratum other christological statements in which a title is the predicate of the verb "to be", such as: "Thou art my beloved Son" (Mark 1:11).[2] But again, these statements are—at this stage—functional in intention. They assert what the Christ has done, is doing, or will do; not what he is, ontically. The same is true of the confessions of faith, "Jesus is Lord" or "Jesus is the Christ". Originally, these were confessions of what he had done, what he is doing or what he will do, or of what God had done, is doing or will do in him.

The gentile mission advanced beyond this to make ontic statements about the Redeemer. In his pre-existent state he *is* ($\dot{v}\pi\acute{a}\rho\chi\omega\nu$) in the *form* ($\mu o\rho\phi\acute{\eta}$, denoting not merely function, but mode of existence) of God. He *is* ($\epsilon\hat{\iota}\nu a\iota$) equal with God (Phil. 2:6). He takes the *form* ($\mu o\rho\phi\acute{\eta}$, mode of existence) of a slave, and is born in the *likeness* ($\dot{o}\mu o\acute{\iota}\omega\mu a$) of men, and is found in human *form* ($\sigma\chi\hat{\eta}\mu a$). These are ontic, not functional words. He does not merely function as a man, but he *is* man, ontically so, prior to his functional activity. At his exaltation he not merely functions as *Kyrios*, but is given the name ($\check{o}\nu o\mu a$, denoting the being) of God himself. In the Prologue of the fourth gospel, prior to his activity in creation, the Logos *was* ($\hat{\eta}\nu$) God and with God. Of his incarnation it is asserted that the Logos *became* ($\dot{\epsilon}\gamma\acute{\epsilon}\nu\epsilon\tau o$) flesh, which means not merely that he functioned as $\sigma\acute{a}\rho\xi$ ("flesh"), but that $\sigma\acute{a}\rho\xi$ was the mode of his earthly being. His whole incarnate life is an epiphany of the being of God: "He who has seen me has seen the Father." "I am the way, the truth and the life." Encounter with Jesus is encounter not only with God in revelatory-redemptive action, but encounter with his being.

It may, of course, be argued that this ontic language is merely the translation into Greek terms (and mythological terms at that) of what the earlier functional Christologies were affirming. This is true, but it is not the whole truth. For it is not just a quirk of the Greek mind, but a universal human apperception, that action implies prior being—even if, as is also true, being is only apprehended in action. Such ontic reflection about Yahweh is found even in the OT, e.g. "I AM" (Exodus and Deutero-Isaiah).

3. The Necessity of Ontology

Ontic affirmation raises ontological problems. If the pre-existent One is equal in being to God himself (as in the ontic statements of Phil. 2:6 and John 1:1), how can they share the same being, and yet be distinguishable? If Jesus is the presence of the divine Being in a human life (as in the epiphany theology of the fourth gospel), *how* can he be God and man at the same time? If the Exalted One shares the *Kyrios*-name with God, how can he be one with God, and yet distinguishable from God as the One who was on earth the incarnate Revealer of God in heaven and who is now exalted at his right hand?

These are the ontological questions which are posed by the ontic Christology of the gentile mission. If the church was to preserve and to proclaim the gospel in the Graeco-Roman world, it had to answer them in terms of an ontology which was intelligible to that world. Its answer to these questions was the doctrines of the Trinity and the Incarnation. These doctrines took the ontic language of the NT, $\theta\epsilon\delta s$, $\pi\alpha\tau\eta\rho$, $\mu\nu\nu\gamma\epsilon\nu\eta s$, $\nu\iota\delta s$, $\sigma\alpha\rho\xi$ and $\alpha\nu\theta\rho\omega\pi\sigma s$, (God, Father, only begotten, Son, flesh, and man), and explained them in ontological language derived from the Greek philosophical tradition ($o\dot{\upsilon}\sigma\iota\alpha$, $\dot{o}\mu\nu\nu\dot{o}\sigma\iota\sigma s$, $\phi\dot{\upsilon}\sigma\iota s$, $\dot{\upsilon}\pi\dot{o}\sigma\tau\alpha\sigma\iota s$), or in Latin dress, *substantia, consubstantialis, natura* and *persona*. With these tools it defined the pre-existent as "begotten of the Father" and as "of one substance with him", and the Incarnate One as "one person", uniting in himself the "two natures" of God and man. Perhaps, as is often said, these answers were not really answers at all, but only sign-posts indicating the direction in which the answers were to be found or boundary marks beyond which all answers would distort the ontic affirmations of the NT. At least they were valid attempts within a given intellectual framework. And so far as they went they have on the whole prevented serious distortions of the gospel.[3]

We must recognize the validity of this achievement of the church of the first five centuries within the terms in which it operated. It is sheer biblicism to maintain that the church should merely repeat "what the Bible says"—about Christology as about everything else. The church has to proclaim the gospel *into* the contemporary situation. And that is precisely what the Nicene Creed and the Chalcedonian formula were trying to do. "The Definition of Chalcedon was the only way in which the fifth-century fathers, in their day, and with their conceptual apparatus, could have faithfully credalized the New Testament witness to Christ."[4]

4. *Christology for Today*

This is the task of the proclaiming church, and, in a specialized sense, of systematic theology in each succeeding age. It cannot simply go on repeating either the New Testament kerygma (which is couched in terms of obsolete mythologies) or the orthodox formulae (which are couched in terms of an obsolete metaphysic). Here, it is difficult to assent without qualification to H. W. Montefiore's statement that "any attempt to formulate a Christology will properly *start* with the Chalcedonian definition."[5] Such an attempt must surely *start* where the fathers started, namely with the NT witness to Christ. This does not mean that we can bypass the definitions. For the fathers mapped out the territory and pointed up the problems, and in their answers defined the boundaries with notices saying "Trespassers will be prosecuted". It must be added that even their map was incomplete, for they concentrated almost exclusively on two parts of the complex NT christological pattern, viz. upon the eternal relation of the pre-existent Son to the Father and upon the incarnation. The ontological implications of the Son's work in creation, in general revelation, in Israel's salvation history, of his incarnate work, and of his work as the Exalted One (to say nothing of his parousia!)—all of which are included in the NT pattern and are covered by its christological titles—are almost entirely neglected. Here the Church Fathers were content simply to repeat the NT language. This is not to blame them for their omissions. But it is a reminder which the NT scholar must pass on to the systematic theologian who wrestles today with the ontological problems of Christology. That is another reason why the contemporary theologian cannot *start* with the Christology of Chalcedon.

It is not the NT scholar's task to work out an ontological Christology for today. That is the task of the systematic theologian. In view of the contemporary lack of any agreed metaphysic (and at least one influential school which denies the possibility of metaphysics in principle) his task is notoriously difficult, and we can only wish him luck. But it is the task of the NT scholar to interpret the documents before him, and to elucidate the intention of the NT writers and the intention of the tradition behind them at its various levels. In this, of course, he is a mere hewer of wood and drawer of water for the systematic theologian. Often—and this is especially the case among English theologians (one thinks for example of Professors Lampe and Richardson)—the two functions of NT scholar and systematic theologian are combined. But the two tasks must be distinguished. It is with the former of these tasks—that of the New Testament scholar proper—that this chapter is concerned. The remainder of it will endeavour to penetrate the underlying intention of the NT Christology. The mythological christological titles and patterns of the NT must be translated into propositional form. These propositional statements will then be available for the systematic theologian. His task will be to work out the ontological implications of these statements in a systematic theology which will speak the gospel relevantly to contemporary thought.

At all the levels of the tradition the one constant feature is the earthly work of Jesus. This would seem to suggest at first sight that his earthly work is the sole and primary datum of Christology, and that therefore the mythological affirmations which are made about Jesus are statements about the significance of his earthly history alone. This is the apparent assumption of Bultmann in his famous essay on demythologizing. Thus he treats the resurrection as merely a mythological way of expressing the significance for faith of the fact of the cross. This, however, would be a false impression.

The christological affirmations of the NT have as their point of reference not only the work of Jesus or the work of

God through Jesus in his earthly life, but also God's continuing work through Jesus in the life of the church. This is so even at the Palestinian stage. In the Q material, for instance, the words and works of the earthly Jesus are transmitted not merely for historical information, but precisely because his demand and offer are directly addressed to the continuing church. This becomes crystal clear with the present Son of man sayings in Q. They posit the authority of Jesus not only in his earthly life, but also in the church. Also the christological statement that "God raised Jesus from the dead" and that God had taken him up into heaven, where he waits as the one who will appear as the Messiah at the parousia, is an affirmation, not merely about the significance of Jesus' earthly life, but also of his significance in the continuing life of the church. Again, the ethical demand and soteriological offer which God made in the history of Jesus of Nazareth are still being made in the church. Salvation is not merely a past fact, but a present reality.

Similarly, the affirmation that God will send Jesus as Messiah at the End is statement about the present offer of salvation in the church. It affirms that this salvation is characterized by a "not yet", that is is only a partial anticipation of the salvation which will finally be disclosed. It asserts, too, that this salvation, which appears to be such a hole and corner affair, accepted only by a handful of insignificant men, is in fact the salvation which will be the culmination of the whole of human history and of the whole cosmic process. For the apocalyptic eschatology has corporate and cosmic as well as personal and existential dimensions. To reduce it to the latter is not to interpret the NT mythology, but to eliminate significant areas of it.

Similarly, the Christology of the Hellenistic Jewish community makes affirmations—indeed, stronger affirmations— about the continuing work of the God through the history of Jesus in the church. To say that "God has made Jesus Lord and Christ" is to say that God has erected the kerygma of Jesus as a figure not only of the past, but also of the contemporary present—as his act of salvation in the continuing church.

The salvation offered in Jesus, through his history and in

the kerygma, is not the first of God's acts. The whole history of God's dealings with Israel, which preceded the earthly history of Jesus and its proclamation in the kerygma, is part and parcel of the same activity. Indeed, the Christ event is the culmination and fulfilment of those saving acts. Thus the whole apparatus of typological and prophetic fulfilment, together with the narrations of Israel's *Heilsgeschichte* with Jesus at the apex (as in the parable of the vineyard), take us back behind the Christ event to the whole series of God's mighty acts in the past. The history of Jesus has significance for the salvation history behind it. It is part of, and the completion of, the series of God's preceding acts in Israel's history —the exodus, the monarchy, the prophets, the exile and the restoration. Christology is concerned with B.C. as well as with A.D.

The Hellenistic Jewish community was led to make even stronger affirmations about the continuing work of Jesus in his church. At the resurrection God had "exalted Jesus and made him Lord and Christ". This involves a deepening appreciation of the salvation which is already made available in the church on the ground of the history of Jesus. It is not merely a brief anticipation of the final salvation, but the reality of that salvation itself, only awaiting consummation at the end. So real is it that many of the Hellenistic Jewish formulae can even drop all reference to the parousia, as in Acts 2 and Rom. 1:3ff. Yet the parousia continues to be featured even down to the Johannine writings[6] and must always be presumed, even where it is not specifically mentioned.

The Hellenistic Jewish community also made ostensibly stronger affirmations about Jesus' earthly life. It too is interpreted messianically. The earthly Jesus is "Son of God" and "Son of David", and occasionally "Christos". In the last analysis, these are no higher affirmations than the earliest Palestinian claim that Jesus in his earthly ministry was already proleptically acting as Son of man. For as Hahn has characterized it, the Hellenistic Jewish Christology is a "two stage" Christology. The salvation effected in the history of Jesus of Nazareth is only preliminary to the salvation which is known in the church.

The backward-looking perspective from the history of Jesus back to Israel's history is still maintained by the Hellenistic Jewish Christology. The OT is still interpreted christologically, providing prophecies and types which find their fulfilments in the history of Jesus. The typological narrations of Israel's history become longer and more detailed. (Compare, e.g. Stephen's speech with the parable of the vineyard.) When the Hellenistic Jewish Christians speak of God's "sending" his Son into the world, or when they adapt the stories of the miraculous births of the patriarchs in the story of Jesus' virginal conception, they are not really saying anything new about Jesus. They are rather emphasizing that his history does not merely emerge out of the ongoing history of men, but is the direct, invasive act of God from outside all human possibilities. Yet these affirmations about the prior background of Jesus' history (Israel's *Heilsgeschichte*, the sending of the Son and the virginal conception) only make explicit what the Son of man Christology of the earliest community had already affirmed, namely that Jesus' history was the eschatological saving act of Israel's God.

The christological pattern of the gentile mission, derived as it was and adapted from the sophia-anthropos myth, affirms outright the pre-existence of the Redeemer, and his ontic identity-in-distinction with the being of God himself. At first sight this looks like a tremendous advance on the more primitive Christologies. But really it was implicit all along. For the act of God in Jesus' history and in the kerygma was never viewed in isolation from the previous acts of Israel's God, but always as their culmination. The same God who acted in Jesus' history and continues to act in the ongoing life of the church was already at work in history prior to the incarnation. There is indeed a shift of accent. Previously, the backward orientation had been confined to Israel's history. Now God's action is conceived in universal terms. He created the universe—and that after all was an OT-Jewish concept, presupposed in every affirmation about Israel's God and therefore always presupposed in the earlier forms of the kerygma. More than that, he was the source not only of the special revelation in Israel but of the general revelation to every man who comes into the world, even if men at large reject that revelation. All these earlier acts of God are of a piece with the incarnation, and all are bracketed together in the mythological assertion that the Redeemer was the pre-existent Son or Logos, the agent of creation and of general revelation as well as of the specific revelation to Israel. It was precisely he who became incarnate in the history of Jesus. To speak of the "Son of God" is to speak of a mythological divine being. But behind the mythology there is the proposition that the God disclosed in creation, general and specific revelation, in Jesus' history and in the kerygma, is a *God who acts*, who goes out of his being-in-himself to being-in-action; a God who communicates himself, who is essentially a self-communicating God. That is what is meant by "Son" or Logos.

Here, by the way, we might drop a hint to the systematic theologian. He might find the Logos concept, speaking as it does of God-in-self-communication, more satisfactory and less mythological in its overtones than the Son-concept, suggesting, as that inevitably does, paternity.[7] God-in-action is ontically distinguishable from God-in-himself, but not separable. For God-in-his-own-being is essentially a God who is ever ready to go out in action and communication, while God-going-out-of-himself-in-action is always God-in-his-own-being. All this is meant in the statement that the pre-existent One was in the μορφή (form) of God and equal to God, that he was θεός, God, and yet πρὸς τὸν θεόν, in a relation to God.

The NT language about the incarnation is irretrievably "katabatic". That is to say, it speaks in terms of a "descent" into the world. This is of course mythological language. As the Bishop of Woolwich has powerfully reminded us, we no longer think—and should no longer think—of a God "up there", or even of a God "out there". Yet the mythological language of descent stands for something. Even in ordinary speech we often use "up" and "down" to connote other than spatial movement. A man may "go up" in his firm, without necessarily shifting his office from the first floor to the second. Indeed, on promotion, he may actually move his books and papers to a lower floor! "Up" and "down" signify qualitative distinctions. The eschatological salvation "came down" from

255

heaven in the sense that in Jesus Christ an event occurred which transcended all human possibilities. The transcendent salvation became completely immanent in him. It appears in the lowly, time-conditioned form and with all the temporal and spatial limitations of a first century Aramaic speaking Palestinian Jew. We must *interpret* the katabasis myth in order to understand it, but we cannot jettison it as obsolete baggage in order to take on board some hypothesis of emergent evolution.[8] And we shall, it is to be hoped, continually return to the ontic mythology when we sing in our Christmas carols:

> Sacred infant, all divine,
> What a tender love was thine,
> Thus to come from highest bliss
> Down to such a world as this.

And we shall continue to mark with reverence the words of the Nicene Creed, "And was incarnate by the Holy Ghost of the Virgin Mary, and was made man." For although both carol and creed are couched in mythological language, they are the very life-blood of Christian faith and truth, which asserts that Jesus Christ is the saving act of God.

The fathers have well mapped out for us the problems involved in the unity of deity and humanity in the one person of Jesus. The Chalcedonian formula has set the bounds within which a solution compatible with the witness of the NT must be found. The NT scholar cannot suggest to the contemporary systematic theologian that he by-pass the whole ontological problem in favour of a purely functional Christology. But he must insist that the functional affirmations of the earliest Jewish Christology inevitably lead to the ontic affirmations of the gentile mission, and that these in turn raise pressing ontological questions. Here much valuable pioneer work has been done in recent years, especially by Anglicans,[9] towards a restatement of the traditional doctrine of the incarnation in terms of a more up-to-date ontology.

As we have seen, the orthodox christological formulae stopped short at the incarnation. They had nothing to say about the cross, though this has received the constant attention of the theologians throughout the subsequent history of dogmatics.[10] Nor did they have anything to say about the resurrection. To say that "God raised Jesus from the dead", is to make a mythological statement which needs interpreting. I have tried elsewhere[11] to offer an interpretation, suggesting that it means that God took Jesus out of the past into his own eternal contemporaneity. Traditional dogmatics has rightly insisted that Christ's human nature is thus exalted. For God continues to deal with us precisely in and through the historical work of the man Jesus. God has no further saving offer or revelation distinct from or additional to Jesus. It was the Epistle to the Hebrews which reared upon the *katabasis-anabasis* foundation a superstructure for this part of Christology in its doctrine of Christ's heavenly high priesthood.[12] The parousia, which completes the pattern of the NT Christology, has already been discussed. It, too, is mythological and needs interpreting. And the parousia again will have far-reaching ontological implications, both for the ontology of God and of the ontology of man and the cosmos.[13]

Thus the foundations of NT Christology are the foundations not only for the NT theologians themselves and for the christological formulations of the fathers, they are also the foundations for Christology today.

NOTES ON CHAPTER IX

1. Professor Cullmann seems to imply this when he writes "When it is asked in the New Testament, 'What is Christ?' the question never remains exclusively, or even primarily, 'What is his nature?' but first of all, 'What is his function?'" (*Christology*, pp. 3f.). With the qualifications, "never exclusively or even primarily" and "first of all" we agree. But it should be clearly recognized that the latest stratum does go on precisely to make ontic statements which raise ontological questions. Professor Cullmann's obvious preference for functional over ontological Christology comes out clearly in his lack of appreciation for the patristic achievement (*ibid.*). The same attitude is expressed, with fewer reservations, by H. W. Montefiore in *Soundings*, ed. A. R. Vidler, Cambridge: University Press, 1962, pp. 149–172. While Montefiore shows a greater respect for the Chalcedonian formula (as would be expected in an Anglican), he nevertheless construes the NT Christology too exclusively as functional. See pp. 157, 159.

2. It is, of course, arguable that the classical formulations of the Trinity

and the Incarnation have in practice proved insufficient barriers against tritheism and docetism, ever present dangers in popular orthodoxy. But these are due to distortions of the very careful statements of the orthodox formulae themselves.

3. This does not preclude the fact that in the gentile mission and in Mark himself the term "Son of God" in the baptism and transfiguration narratives was understood as an assertion of the divine "nature" of Jesus. This becomes particularly clear in the Hellenistic stratum or the transfiguration ($\mu\epsilon\tau\epsilon\mu\rho\rho\phi\omega\theta\eta$, "transfigured", Mark 9:2).

4. H. W. Montefiore, op. cit., p. 160.

5. Op. cit., p. 151, italics mine. Later, Mr. Montefiore does, however, go back behind the Chalcedonian formula to the NT, though, as we have seen, he conceives the NT Christology too exclusively in functional terms, without allowing for the difference between the earlier Jewish Christologies and that of the gentile mission.

6. See above, chapter VI, note 79.

7. It is to be regretted that after the abortive effects of the second century apologists the fathers settled upon the title "Son" for the Pre-existent One. For a contemporary attempt at christological restatement in terms of the Logos see W. N. Pittenger, *The Word Incarnate*, London: Nisbet, 1959, pp. 146–175 (see note below).

8. Some of the efforts to restate NT Christology in terms of emergent evolution or process philosophy fail to do justice to this katabatic element. This is notably the case with G. V. Jones, *Christology and Myth in the New Testament*, London: Allen and Unwin, 1956. This author eliminates the "katagogic" (to use his own terminology) entirely in favour of the "anagogic". More cautious is the attempt of W. N. Pittenger (op. cit.) to combine a restated Logos Christology with the insights of process philosophy. He rightly protests against an exclusively katabatic Christology as suggesting that God is an absentee landlord in the universe he created: "It is the same logos who is present in behind all phenomena and in deciding man's history who is incarnated in Jesus." Yet even here one feels at times that the incarnation is reduced to the supreme instance of what is imperfectly true of all men. Cf. pp. 167f.:

"But Christ is divine not by being utterly different from all other men in whom God dwells and through whom the divine activity works; rather he is divine in that he actualizes in human nature that transcendental divine principle which is at the root of man's being, but which through other men is only potentially or at best very partially expressed."

Behind the katabatic pattern of the Christology of the gentile mission lies the eschatological proclamation of the earliest church, which expresses the total newness of the Christ event. This somehow must be brought to expression without denying the prior presence and activity in the universe God created.

9. We might mention here particularly—despite the reservations of the previous note—W. N. Pittenger, op. cit. (see note 7, above) also, W. R. Matthews, *The Problem of Christ in the Twentieth Century*, Oxford: University Press, 1950, commended by Montefiore, op. cit., p. 162.

10. There are many modern treatments in English of the doctrine of the atonement. Most promising are those which approach it from the Pauline doctrine of Justification. This doctrine is really a demythologization of the primitive kerygma, "Christ died for our sins according to the scriptures", and of the gentile mission Christology of Jesus' entry into the sphere of the powers and his defeat of them. Paul demythologizes the powers by equating them with sin and the law. The Pauline doctrine of ἐν Χριστῷ and of the Body of Christ is in turn built upon the foundation of the Adam/Christ typology of the gentile mission.

11. See *The New Testament in Current Study*, p. 23.

12. The high priest Christology of Hebrews is built upon the foundation of the primitive christological use of Ps. 110:1 applied to Jesus' exalted work. As such it belongs to the superstructure rather than the foundation and therefore is beyond the scope of this book. Ps. 110:1 leads to Ps. 110:4, and the doctrine of Christ's high priesthood is elaborated with the help of certain aspects of the Logos-sophia myth (in Philo the high priest is the Logos). Käsemann would derive it from the gnostic redeemer myth (*Das wandernde Gottesvolk*, see above, chapter III, note 58).

It is doubtful whether the high priest Christology emerged prior to Hebrews. It is not derived from the Messiah high priest of Qumran, who invariably appears in conjunction with the Davidic Messiah. Cf. Hahn, *Hoheitstitel*, pp. 231–241, and above, pp. 32f.

Cullmann is surely mistaken in including the high priest Christology in his *Christology*, Part I, among the titles describing Jesus' earthly work. It should have been dealt with in Part III, among the titles for Christ's exalted work. Cf. Käsemann, *op. cit.*

13. For an attempt see *The Book of the Acts of God*, p. 261.

INDEX OF SCRIPTURE REFERENCES

260

INDEX OF ANCIENT AUTHORS

INDEX OF MODERN AUTHORS

266